'My Mother was the Earth.
My Father was the Sky.'

Nadia Majid

'My Mother was the Earth.
My Father was the Sky.'

Myth and Memory in Maori Novels in English

PETER LANG

Oxford · Bern · Berlin · Bruxelles · Frankfurt am Main · New York · Wien

Bibliographic information published by Die Deutsche Nationalbibliothek
Die Deutsche Nationalbibliothek lists this publication in the Deutsche Nationalbibliografie;
detailed bibliographic data is available on the Internet at http://dnb.d-nb.de.

A catalogue record for this book is available from the British Library.

Library of Congress Cataloging-in-Publication Data:

Majid, Nadia, 1978-
   'My mother was the earth, my father was the sky' : myth and memory in
Maori novels in English / Nadia Majid.
      p. cm.
   Includes bibliographical references and index.
   ISBN 978-3-0343-0224-1 (alk. paper)
   1. New Zealand fiction--Maori authors--History and criticism. 2.
Identity (Psychology) in literature. 3. Maori fiction--History and
criticism. 4. Myth in literature. 5. Memory in literature. 6. Maori
(New Zealand people) in literature. 7. Ihimaera, Witi Tame,
1944---Criticism and interpretation. 8. Grace, Patricia,
1937---Criticism and interpretation. I. Title.
   PR9625.5.I34M35 2010
   823'.91409899442--dc22
                    2010030328

ISBN 978-3-0343-0224-1

Cover photograph © Louise Docker

© Peter Lang AG, International Academic Publishers, Bern 2010
Hochfeldstrasse 32, CH-3012 Bern, Switzerland
info@peterlang.com, www.peterlang.com, www.peterlang.net

Printed in Germany

Contents

Acknowledgements

This book is based on my doctoral thesis by the same title, which was defended in the *Fachbereich 05: Sprache, Literatur, Kultur* at the Justus-Liebig-Universität Giessen, Germany, in February 2009. For publication, a significant part of the very long original had to be removed. As a result, only the work of two writers is used here to illustrate the findings. I would like to thank Witi Ihimaera for his inspirational powerful writing, his graciousness and the kind permission to reproduce his poem "Tangi".

The completion of this book would have been impossible without the advice of a number of people who have accompanied me during my research, either professionally or in private.

First and foremost, I would like to thank Raimund Borgmeier for supporting and advising me throughout the years as his student. My thanks also go to my second advisor, Wolfgang Hallet, who followed my progress throughout the three years in the International PhD Programme (IPP). His suggestions for improvement contributed greatly to the successful completion of this study and often gave the impulse for new ideas during in-class discussions.

My acknowledgements would be incomplete without mentioning Marc Colavincenzo, whose own example and enthusiasm for literature directed me towards my chosen career path. Most, if not all I learned about literature, I have learned from him in his inspirational classes. Last, but not least I learned that if you have the courage to let your love of literature shine through in your teaching, you cannot go far wrong. In the end, I suppose we have both become what neither of us ever wanted – the dreadful word "professional" comes to mind.

There have also been many outside my academic field whose encouragement and help was essential. I must thank Jude Camville and librarian Callista Kelly for being so generous and sending journal articles all the way from Canada. Matthew Moorcroft deserves my gratitude for the many useful and surprising suggestions, proofreading, and criticising better than many a literary scholar I have met. For lively, at first condescending and gradually brilliant discussions, I am grateful to William Mozal III, the man of many names, who struggles to write in the darkest of places. My heartfelt thanks go to Marie-Noëlle Biemer, who has been the best and most reliable friend and proofreader since our Middle-earthian days in Giessen.

And, now, my sincerest thanks remain with Mark Coxwell – for his support in so many ways, his invincible optimism, love, and faith in me when I needed them more than anything.

CHAPTER ONE

He Kupu Whakataki: Introduction

Looking in from the outside, New Zealand has a distinct identity not least because of the Maori people, their art, literature, and their continuing struggle for recognition and justice. Yet the indigenous people are still a minority in this land of immigrants. Maori resistance finds expression not only in political involvement on the streets, in courts or in government: indeed, Maori writers see literature as another useful tool that may help regain a secure place in New Zealand society and draw attention to Maori issues in a way that is both creative and real. Real, in this case, suggests that the fiction presents the Maori situation in fictional settings that do not detract from the reality of the indigenous people's actual circumstances.

From the inside, there is the sense of a loss of identity. The predominance of *Pakeha* notions of culture, knowledge, and identity ultimately inhibit the existence of other ethnic identities within the same community. As a result, the question of identity – first, its distillation and construction, and subsequently its preservation – comes to the fore in reality as well as in fiction. In this context, this study brings together three areas of interest that are able to shed light on Maori experience from the point of view of writers of Maori descent: myth and memory as influential factors in the construction of identity.

The majority of Maori writers incorporate myths that hark back to the distant or recent past, thereby creating and recreating memories, drawing attention to lost details of their culture or maintaining the most commonly held beliefs in their fiction. Thus proving their validity today as guides for the future, myths and legends are key features underlying Maori literature in all genres as significant parts of memory. Therefore, myth and memory are two primary aspects of Maori identity in particular and New Zealand identity in general.

The question of identity is ever changing and complex, a necessary construct evolving from the interaction of past, present, and expectations for the future. The state of the search for a national identity suggests the importance of a literary quest for Maori identity in particular and New Zealand identity in general. Therefore it is necessary to understand the continual interaction of past, present and future as perceived by Maori to form an underlying notion of identity as a flexible construct. Places such as the New Zealand National Museum Te Papa Tongarewa are aware of this and present a variety of perspectives to the public in changing exhibitions. Te Papa does not try to present a definitive view of history. Instead, its exhibitions are chosen and arranged in such a way that they "challenge our audience to explore, celebrate and question different viewpoints of New Zealand's past" (*MoNZTPT* 1993: 6). The exhibitions

> [...] were not designed to identify or suggest to the public any *single* distinct version or idea of New Zealand's identity – another illustration of changing museological practice, as museums no longer attempt to spell out definitive stories or historical interpretation. Put in another way, they no longer tell their visitors what is right or what to believe. Instead, museums often now encourage people to debate and explore different interpretations of history and to come to their own conclusions. [...] In other words, the history exhibitions were created to help people question the notions of national identity. (Gore 2007: 8)

The number of ethnic groups shaping the face of the country enhances the complexity. New Zealand is not only the land of *Pakeha* and Maori; instead, it consists of immigrants from all over the world, especially the Pacific Islands and Asia. Thus, finding a single definitive national identity is bound to be problematic. In this context, Jock Phillips, former Chief Historian and Conceptual Leader in History at Te Papa, observes that "identity is the sum of immigrant cultures, identity comes from interaction with a distinct environment, identity is a construct of the mind" (Phillips 2001: 149). In his 2003 presentation *Kiwi Myths and New Identities*, Phillips further illustrates that national identity is necessary for three reasons. Firstly, every nation requires common values and symbols that join its people; secondly, in the face of globalisation New Zealand needs to be more prominent as a country with a distinct identity; and thirdly, a national identity will be yet another step of decolonisation (Phillips 2003: slide 3). In the course of his paper, he identifies the paradox that even though there is a greater demand for a national identity, there is also greater disagreement as to what this identity might be and how to define it. Due to the country's diversity, coming to a satisfactory, all-encompassing definition is a challenging task, which leads him to the conclusion that a national identity – however necessary – is impossible since it eliminates diversity (*ibid.* slide 23–4). The rigid notion of a national self-image should be replaced by common themes deriving from the people's origin as "boat people" who came to the country and contributed to its diversity (*ibid.* slide 24), and from New Zealand as an immigrant nation as he already suggested in 2001, as Belich also notes:

> Four centuries after the death of Jesus Christ, two migrant ships pushed through dangerous seas. Strong men and women tended oars and sails; children crouched amidst livestock and household goods. Each crew valued kin above all, walked with live gods – Tu and Thor, Woden and Tane – and lived and died for weregild and utu. Each crew headed for a place of which little was known, and a great deal hoped. Too much can be made of their similarities, but they did have one thing in common: both were forebears of the New Zealanders. (Belich 1996: 13)

Still, the relationship between Maori and *Pakeha* is an issue, as Charles Royal's paper, delivered to the symposium Concepts of Nationhood in 2007, confirms. Like Phillips, Royal suggests moving away from rigid concepts of identity and focusing on the inappropriateness of the term *Pakeha* that carries with it certain colonial connotations. Royal (2007) has suggested that new ways of constructing and articulating identity must be found that will be better suited to represent Maori diversity today. His main criticism that the old but well-known Maori/*Pakeha* paradigm no longer reasonably reflects current developments is justified as it gives a restricted view of identity in both cases. In fact, the paradigm is another of those binaries that postcolonial literature tries to resist and undo: it is an artificial classification, something that was created out of necessity in the nineteenth century, but which no longer applies to the complexities of cultural identity in a multicultural society today.

Maori literature is one way to contribute to native culture by bringing some of its key elements to the readership. Texts set in an indigenous
context convey beliefs and customs which may encourage knowledge and
confidence in one's heritage. What is more, there is a strong sense of urgency
in Maori literature that expresses the active part Maori people play in the
nation's development in all areas. "Maori people," Royal succinctly summarises this point,

> want to contribute to New Zealand and to the world in ways that are meaningful
> to us. We want to be independent and decrease our reliance upon Government and
> other external agencies. We particularly seek to overcome perceptions that power,
> real power, exists outside of ourselves and hence, we want to increase our experi-
> ences of creative *mana motuhake* [separate identity, or autonomy]. We want to build
> sustainable cultural enterprises of mana that our nation can be proud of and we seek
> peace and understanding with our fellow New Zealanders by being Maori (or its
> successor) and New Zealanders at the same time. (*ibid.* 7)

The way to make this happen, he says, is by being creative. In fact, he
emphasises the importance of creativity in all enterprises as the best way to
contribute significantly to New Zealand and the world. Creativity is ideal
because it allows for innovative developments that do not restrict Maori
in any way. Being able to contribute, Maori people can use their originality
not only to uphold their identity as a complex cultural group, but also to
encourage progress in all aspects of national and global development.

Free to express themselves in any way that Maori *tikanga* (customs and
practices) allow, writers are able to become important contributors to the
Maori and New Zealand future. Their fiction captures their cultural past
in the form of expressed belief systems, each work portraying an image of
Maori identity in its time, be it the angry, violent, but powerless Maori in
Alan Duff's *Once Were Warriors*, the self-reliant, but isolated Kerewin of
Keri Hulme's *the bone people*, or the passionate young activist of Ihimaera's
The Uncle's Story (*US*). The novels reflect Royal's claim that there is great
diversity within the Maori community, supporting his demand for a move
away from binaries such as Maori/*Pakeha*. Though ethnicity cannot be
ignored, it is not the end all and be all: the diversity within cultural groups

belies generalisation, and this is what Maori writers express in their work and find reflected in their personal experiences.

The writers featured here create innovative constructions and reconstructions of identity. Memory is crucial: without a memory of the past, identity can never be whole. Like Keri Hulme's mysterious Simon in *the bone people*, the person without a past is broken and incomplete. At the same time, this image of brokenness is symbolic of the many Maori who struggle in a non-space between cultures, or, as Homi Bhabha (1994) has termed it, the third space. They seize this third space and make it their own, and it is not merely an amalgamation of cultures. It is in this third space that a new culture develops from the known two, a culture that has its roots in the Maori and the *Pakeha* world, but which grows into something of its own.

In this study, I intend to demonstrate that Maori fiction has become a third space in its own right. The novels suggest that identity can only be found by combining the knowledge of Maori history and spirituality with certain aspects of *Pakeha* society. Choosing just one of the two cultures leads to a loss of self and even to physical and mental illness, as depicted in Patricia Grace's *Mutuwhenua* (*M*). If Maori fiction is the site where writers practice the creation of something new, it would follow that the revival of memory, the re-education of the readership, and a relocation to the third space are major concerns in the featured novels.

Inevitably, dealing with the present and trying to create the future requires an evaluation of the past. In the novels, this can be seen in the many references to myths and legends, the importance of genealogy, and Maori values that have persisted through the years. Given that Maori culture was primarily oral, the importance of memory should not be underestimated. Memory in fiction is twofold, however: on the one hand, the stories often hark back to tales of the past that are mythic in nature, recounting events that are already known. On the other, the novels take an active part in the shaping of memory by selecting those tales, events or objects worth remembering for a specific reason. Thus, identities are created, deriving from a particular collage of memories that may have been reinterpreted to suit a purpose. Ann Rigney (2005) closely examines the link between

memory and literature, offering a first approach to the subject. Like Astrid
Erll (2005), she comments on the selectivity of memory that is reflected
in fiction and corresponds with the way in which the chosen novels use a
number of existing tales to create a new story or reinterpret the past for a
new future. This book will attempt to verify the links between novel, myth,
and memory with the help of existing research in these areas and try to
assess their importance for the construction of identity.

For the purposes of this analysis, I have distinguished three phases
of Maori writing in English which showcase the problems of each period
and how these novels serve as representations of their time and offer solutions to a frustrating and disruptive Maori experience. The novels are the
literature of cross-cultural contact, written about the problems arising from
the clash of cultures. From this point of view, even when the writing is not
intended to be political, as Patricia Grace says of her fiction, "whether you
do it deliberately or not, the writing is political" (Calleja 2003: 113).

Exemplarily, Ihimaera and Grace are the focus here, as their work is
represented in all three phases and in a number of genres, allowing for a
better observation of change throughout the years. They are prominent
writers whose work is part of the New Zealand literary landscape and
"ha[ve] gone on to take [their] place in the annals of national literature:
considered required reading in order to be conversant in the New Zealand canon" (Thornley 2004: 62). Their powerful work has managed to
breach the dominance of *Pakeha* literature in New Zealand and succeeded
in establishing itself as a significant part of the country's literature that
cannot be ignored. Furthermore, the writers' high standing in New Zealand derives from their determination to tackle those problems that have
seemed unsolvable for many years, and still persist to this day. Following
Ihimaera's writing from the early days till today, it is possible to see how
New Zealand society has changed since the 1970s when the motivation for
a Maori renaissance was at its highest. Most of Grace's work is not overtly
political, but skilfully subversive nonetheless. *Potiki* (*P*), published in 1986,
is the most obviously political, but even in this novel the mythic and the
indigenous way of life override politics.

To allow for in-depth analysis, the study focuses on these two writers
to showcase the development of the Maori novel. It is not my intention to

ignore the literary contribution of further Maori writers who have worked at the same time as those featured here. However, the scope of this book requires selectivity. Ihimaera and Grace lend themselves conveniently to our purpose due to their continuing contributions, world-wide recognition and the high standard of their work in a number of genres.

1.1 Maori Writing in Contemporary Discourse

By choosing Maori novels written in English, one ignores the tradition of writing in the native tongue which has existed since the colonial days in the form of diaries, private and public correspondence, creative writing and the like. Fiction in *te reo Maori* existed since the first publications in Maori magazines, and yet it is the literature in English that is accessible to most readers simply because the English language is more widely spread. Unfortunately, this often leads to the false belief that there is no Maori literature, particularly in the native tongue. Having been a British colony, Aotearoa New Zealand is far more familiar with writing in English than in its own indigenous language that steadily neared extinction.

Much attention has been devoted to the early Maori novels in English, but it should not be forgotten that the novelists have inevitably progressed and expanded their subject matter as well as their literary skill in the last three decades. "While constantly focussing on starting points and early moments is important," writes Alice Te Punga Somerville, "a limitation of this approach is that Maori literary studies can tend to be framed as a recent, tenuous and emerging phenomenon. It is surely time to think about the literature as something more established than recent, more substantial than tenuous, more nuanced than emerging" (Somerville 2007: 87).

Nonetheless, given the importance of the early novels for Maori identity, they must be included here. They are, however, not the sole focus of the analysis and serve as a starting point to illustrate how the novels have since changed. Equal attention should be awarded to new fiction that is proof of social and political changes. Since Ihimaera and Grace have been

active since the early years of indigenous fiction, their work is best suited
to mark changes from the 1970s until today and to prove that Maori literature is indeed established. These three decades of the Maori novel should
supply ample proof of Somerville's claim that native New Zealand literature
is more substantial and richer than often believed.

Despite – or perhaps because of – the supposed newness of native
New Zealand literature, Maori writers writing against *Pakeha* traditions
have been criticised for their seeming inability or reluctance to escape the
European framework and its literary traditions entirely (cf. C. K. Stead
[Stead 1985; Fee 1989], Judith Dale [1985] and Mark Williams [1995b]).
It appears that these critics believe complete detachment from European
literary traditions and content is actually possible and desirable. This forms
the foundation of much criticism that ultimately classifies the Maori novel
as a failed attempt of decolonisation. I would like to suggest, however, that
it is impossible to detach oneself fully without losing the broad readership that needs to be reached in order to affect the desired change. What
is more, the novelists introduced here have no intention of casting aside
everything foreign to their culture. Their work portrays the necessity of
interaction and mutual understanding as well as the desire to strengthen
one's weakened cultural traditions and the need for political involvement. Theirs is a more tolerant stance than their early critics especially
seem capable of.

As a consequence, the novels have a double frame: a European and
a Maori one deriving from the bicultural influence on the writers. Being
subject to these two influences enables authors to approach their work
from other angles, using familiar means for new purposes. In 1993, the
Samoan writer Albert Wendt pointed out why writer and critic approach
literature differently – the same problem applies to Maori literature that is
still mainly realist, but has a specific aim. "Some of these critics now dismiss
our literature as being old-fashioned," Wendt specifies,

> because they are still in the realist tradition. They fail to realize that we have a differ-
> ent purpose for our literature – a desire to explain to ourselves what has happened
> to us in the colonial process, and to argue for political change. We still see the novel
> as a weapon for social change. (Hereniko 1993: 57)

The notion of the novel as a weapon is evident in the work of all three chosen writers, but it must be remembered that political change does not necessarily mean complete separation from the dominant culture.

Considering these points, it is evident that questions of identity must be the primary feature of any study concerned with Maori writing. Nevertheless, identity may be approached from a number of different angles of which the use of myth and memory are but two. In this particular study, the choice of myth derives from the fiction's pervasion with Maori myths and the importance of traditional oral storytelling[1] that differentiate indigenous literature from most *Pakeha* fiction. In her essay on Grace's *Cousins* (*C*), Judith Dell Panny (2006)[2] laments the neglect of Maori literature and the lack of critical analysis devoted to the significance of myth in fiction. It is true that, generally, there is a bulk of research devoted to the study of myth and it is surprising, therefore, how little particularly Maori myths have sparked interest in literary studies. To some extent this may be explained by the focus on New Zealand as a former colony, the *Pakeha*/Maori dichotomy, and the loss of indigenous culture in general. It is high time, as Somerville and Panny would agree, that Maori literature is analysed with regard to the specific literary and cultural characteristics that prove it to be an established and powerful national literature.

In Panny's opinion, existing criticism of Maori literature by non-Maori critics is not as thorough as it ought to be due to a lack of insight into the

---

1   Often, orality is pitted against modern writing. In the context of Maori literature, however, this is not the case due to the use of oral storytelling strategies in fiction, as we shall see. This development demonstrates a balance between oral and written texts as described by Ashcroft *et al.*: "Recent studies have stressed the fact that oral and literary cultures in colonial and post-colonial societies existed within unified social situations and were *mutually* interactive. Rather than being restricted to the past and therefore inferior to the written, oral forms in African societies, for instance, have a continuing and *equal* relationship with the written. This therefore challenges the simplistic and culture specific assumption of post-stucturalist critics such as Derrida that the written has precedence over the oral (logo-centrism)" (2002: 166–7).

2   References without pagination from Panny (2006) stem from unpaginated sources such as publications made available online and are therefore cited by name and year of publication only.

Maori belief system. "When indigenous literature is written in English,"
Panny says,

> the assumption has often been made that any English speaking critic would be able
> to appraise the work. This is not necessarily the case. To appreciate the subtleties of
> a work by Māori from "the inside out", readers need an in-depth knowledge of Māori
> culture. The following aspects, vital to Māori literature, have to date received little
> attention from critics: mythology and its influence on Māori thought; symbolism
> derived from ancient oral traditions; spiritual and metaphysical beliefs; protocols,
> cultural values, obligations; and history as perceived by Māori, predating and fol-
> lowing colonisation. (Panny 2006)

It is undeniable that these aspects form the featured novels so that they
must be addressed if an understanding and appreciation of their significance should be gained. The novels will be discussed by placing them
within their respective cultural and historical contexts, which requires
an extensive analysis of myth and memory.[3]

Due to these lacunae in indigenous literary criticism, Panny suggests
a new historicist approach, especially with respect to cultural references
that remain hidden within metaphors, terms, and structure (cf. Greenblatt
1988). This would allow a more appropriate, Maori-centred discussion that
takes into account those aspects of their belief-system that also pervade
fiction. The advantage of such an approach, as she points out, is that it
presupposes two things:

> 1. that the text cannot be viewed apart from its social, cultural, and
> historical context – all of which greatly characterise Maori fiction –,
>
> and

---

3   I must point out here that as someone not of Maori descent there will be areas of
     the indigenous culture that remain inaccessible to me. It is not my intention to be
     insensitive about Maori customs and traditions and I deeply apologise should my
     efforts offend at any point. I shall work towards a critical analysis that considers the
     components of Maori literature that have been neglected thus far, but I can make no
     claim for completeness, which is beyond most European critics since we all "carry
     our own subconscious filters" (Ka'ai 2005: 3).

2. that the text's language contains "social energy" that supplies it with a vitality intensely involving the (native) reader.

Thus,

> [m]ythological beliefs, religious protocols and traditional symbolism can create intense reader involvement. Energy-bearing images, metaphors, allusions and signifiers need to be identified, if readers are to perceive how power can be invested in and released through the language. So-called "thick description" (Kaes, 1990: 62) advocated by new historicism, penetrates significant terms or expressions. Such an approach could surely be applied to disclose the cultural subtleties of motivation and causation that non-Māori readers may fail to notice, limiting appreciation of works such as *Potiki* or *Cousins.* (Panny 2006)

The suggested approach requires the examination of Maori *tikanga* (customs and values) as well as some of the recurring images and beliefs the reader encounters in Maori fiction as part of indigenous culture.

I agree with Achebe's opinion that "[w]e must apply to these African [or, in this case, Maori] writers the same stringent standards of literary criticism with which we judge other writers" (Achebe 1975d: 47). The origin of these standards does not render them ineffectual for the study of ethnic literature. If we refused Maori literature the chance to be studied in view of these standards, we would either take the very colonial stance of regarding this literature as inferior to the vast majority of Western fiction that is not suited to be analysed with the same tools, or it would suppose that Maori literature is so vastly different from any other that it is utterly impossible to interpret it with the knowledge we have (cf. *ibid.*). Neither is the case. Since even the distinct quality of Maori fiction does not separate it entirely from other fiction, the same tools may be used for its study. The hope for new standards of evaluation has yielded no satisfactory results as yet, and for now we are left with the familiar tools, but also with an awareness of cultural difference that may change interpretation. The study of Maori novels may prove to be as complex and hybrid as the fiction itself.

The study will therefore introduce and combine existing definitions of myth, which will then be expanded on with current influences such as hybridity, continuity, variation, identity, and memory. Thus demonstrating an interrelationship between separate areas of study, the groundwork has been laid for a new approach to the analysis of Maori literature. Furthermore, the critical attention devoted to memory, identity, and narrative has been prominent in literary and cultural discourse since the 1990s (see particularly Jan and Aleida Assmann's contributions since 1992). Building upon research in psychology, literature, linguistics, and cultural studies, the connections between memory, identity, and narrative are being laid open and applied to fiction. Consequently, conclusions drawn from the relationship among these three topics underlie and enhance the analysis of Maori novels in English so as to present an expansive understanding not only of their literary quality, but also of their significance as a Maori literature of survival, identification, and empowerment.

CHAPTER TWO

Myth and Memory: Functions and Methods

2.1 Myth and the Emergence of Maori Identity

New Zealand myths have existed all throughout its history, before and after it became a modern nation state in 1840. It is a land of immigrants who brought their own mythologies with them, myths that were already established in their home countries, but the new life brought with it peculiarities based on New Zealand's location, its landscape, and the demands of living at the other end of the world. New myths developed especially at the time of colonisation to further the image of a homogenous country. Myths are generated and live on if they have a purpose. This was the case with Polynesian waves of settlement and subsequent European settlement for reasons such as the preservation of origins or the construction of a national identity.

The past is reconstructed to justify the present for whatever purposes one may have. Some of these myths originally propagated by *Pakeha*, such as the Great Fleet Theory, were so successful that they are still believed today despite scientific evidence against their accuracy. Generally, we are confronted with two different types of myth in the study of Maori novels: one type is a result of circumstance and recent history, which I shall term colonial or political myths due to their importance for the creation of a nation. The most common type of myth found in the featured novels, nonetheless, goes back to the very origins of Maori life. Both share a common purpose: they serve to unify and to propagate a certain (national or tribal) image at the time of their emergence.

Many theories in the context of colonisation deal with the status of the Maori people, which varied according to European settlers' aims. Despite the Maori King Movement that led to the election of the first Maori king in 1859, it was only in the twentieth century that Maori actively sought to establish their own identity as a people. This is not to indicate that Maori were passive in the past: the amount of correspondence in newspapers and letters to individuals is ample evidence for their interest in the goings on right from the beginning (cf. McRae 1997). While the King Movement of the mid-nineteenth century was a means by which to be noticed as a group with a certain measure of authority, the ambition to be accepted as a culture with a unique identity, its own purposes and specific needs culminated at the time of the Maori renaissance a century later. In 1985, in response to the amount of Maori activism, the historian Michael King observed that "[s]ome Pakeha have the impression now that all Maori are opposed to Pakeha participation in Maori activities, that a mood of separatism is evolving that will eventually lead to Maori and Pakeha living in their own enclaves" (King 1985: 170). At the time, led by determined leaders of their own community, the indigenous people of New Zealand became stronger than at any other point in history.

This will have been in no small part also due to the remembrance of Maori myths which, as Rawiri Taonui concludes in his encyclopedia entry on Maori canoe traditions, "[...] merge poetry and politics, history and myth, fact and legend" (Taonui 2006). This is how Maori myths and tribal traditions should be viewed here: not as either factual historical accounts or complete inventions, but as an amalgam of many influences. These myths differ from colonial myths in that they are of an entirely native origin, as far as we can tell, and deal with cosmogony and important aspects of Maori life, tradition and spirituality. They are the stories that explain origins rather than future aims. In other words, Maori myths look back while colonial myths look forward.

Maori literature incorporates many indigenous myths. Among the most popular ones are those of the separation of earth and sky, the trickster hero Maui, and stories that explain natural phenomena in mythical terms. Often, both scientific explanation and myth exist side by side in Maori consciousness and in fiction. So it comes as no surprise that both views appear in fiction, though a preference for one or the other is expressed according to the novels' arrangement.

The separation of earth and sky is a central myth that appears in several novels such as Ihimaera's *Tangi* (1973). It is not the creation of the world itself that is significant here, but the connection between earth and sky and their children that determines the relationship between Maori and the land. The myth forms the basis of customs and traditions such as the burial of the placenta in the earth or farming rituals which emphasise the connection between people, Mother Earth and Father Sky. To take an example, Panny explains in an article on Grace's novel *Cousins* (1992) that, "[w]hen the whenua is buried in the earth, a contract is established. The earth will protect and succour the child and the child will take responsibility for the earth. The land adjacent to the burial place of the whenua is forever 'home' to the child" (Panny 2006). Furthermore, referring back to this first and central myth connects the Maori characters to the very origin of the world, defining Maoriness and granting an authority that can only be established by being able to draw one's lineage back to the very first parents.

Also known as the story of Rangi and Papa, the myth tells of the primordial parents Earth and Sky. They hold each other in an embrace so tight their children have to live in the darkness between them. The number of their children varies between tribes, but among them are Tawhirimatea god of the winds, Tangaroa god of seas, Tane god of forests, Rongo god of cultivated foods and peace, Haumia god of uncultivated foods and Tumatauenga or Tu god of war. Clearly, the children are gods representing important aspects of nature and life. Tired from living in the cramped space and the darkness, the children decide to separate their parents in order to live in the light with Rangi above them and Papa below them. The children push against the sky in an attempt to separate their parents, but they fail because their parents' embrace is too strong. Eventually, Tane takes his turn and, lying on his back, he pushes with his legs and the embrace is finally broken.

The separation, though brutal, gives the chance for more life and it strengthens the Maori connection to the land by stressing the importance of living off and with the land. A separation of people and land would be unnatural and cruel, and would mean the loss of a source of nourishment. In Grace's *Cousins*, the importance of land is illustrated when one of the characters suggests a marriage that will not only secure the genealogy, but which will also ensure land. No land equals no future: "We know your family. It's a very good family, from a strong line, a family strong in the customs, but, Polly, they've got no land. Through no fault of theirs, they've got no land" (*C* 102). Obviously, the land is needed to allow a place to live and grow food, but also to add to a family's *mana*, their prestige.

The Maori Land Wars (1845–1872) and the consequences as seen at the Waitangi Tribunal since 1975 prove the importance of land to Maori tribes. Without it, an essential part of Maori livelihood and cultural heritage is taken from them and destroyed. The stories and memories associated with it are lost as well, and without stories there is no identity because the land is not only a home: it is the origin of life and the place of rest in death, and it is alive with myth.

Aside from the creation myth, a number of stories exist about Maui, the trickster hero of Maori mythology. One of the best known is that of Maui's fish, again a story related to land. New Zealand consists of the North Island, the South Island, and Stewart Island, also known as the fish, the canoe of Maui and its anchor stone, respectively. One day, Maui and his brothers set off to fish in their canoe, the South Island, also known as Te Waka-a-Maui (Maui's canoe). Reaching the deepest part of the sea, Maui drops the fishhook made of his grandmother's jawbone, his blood as bait, into the sea. It sinks and is caught on the house of Tonganui, grandson of Tangaroa, god the sea. Maui, stands at the peninsula at Kaikoura and pulls until the land that is now the North Island, also known as Te Ika-a-Maui, the fish of Maui, comes to the surface: "Then his fish came to the surface. [...] That fish continues to lie here as land. It is still inhabited by Māui, his elder brothers and their children. This is the origin of the presence of the Māori ancestors in this island" (Reedy 1993: 123).

Once again, this is a myth of origin and creation as well as a hero myth. The new home of the Maori emerges from the sea, created by the hero's labours, and it accounts for the location and existence of Aotearoa. The myth goes even further and offers a reason for the land's shaping. It is said that Maui and his brothers are responsible for the North Island's form:

> Māui left his brothers and returned home. He said to his older brothers, "After I leave, please do not partake of the fish. [...] Do not cut up our fish. [...]" However, [after he

left] they did not do what he said. They began to cut it up and eat it [...]. When he returned Māui became enraged. [...] He was greatly distressed as they cut the head, the tail, the gills and the fins. [...] This is why this land lies unevenly – there are mountains, plains, valleys and cliffs. If they had not fought over the fish, then the land would have retained its fish shape. (George Grey, 1971. Quoted in Royal 2006)

Like many Maori myths, the story of Maui's brothers is used to give reasons for natural features.

Another similar and recurrent myth is found in Grace's fiction. The story of Rona appears in her work more than once and Grace explains Rona's plight in *Mutuwhenua*'s glossary as follows:

One night at full moon a woman called Rona was going to the spring to fill her calabashes when the moon was suddenly obscured by a passing cloud. Rona tripped and hurt herself, so she cursed the moon for having withdrawn its light. The moon heard her, came down and snatched her up, and began to carry her away. Rona caught at the branch of a ngaio tree and clung to it, but the tree got torn out by its roots and, with Rona, taken up to the sky and placed on the moon's surface. At full moon Rona can be seen, clutching the tree and her calabashes. (*M* 154–5)

Rona's presence on the moon is a mythical explanation of the moon's surface as seen from earth and is a part of the group of myths that give reasons for what is seen in the world without scientific explanations. At the same time, it is a useful metaphor in fiction to picture the alienation of Maori within New Zealand Society who have been transplanted into a *Pakeha* world, though this is by no means an exhaustive interpretation of Rona.

What these and other myths accomplish within Maori novels is that they lead the characters in a cathartic journey from alienation to purification and on to redemption (cf. Elizabeth Fiorenza in Coupe, *Myth*, 79: Fiorenza distinguished these three steps as parts of myths and rituals in general). This is a feature commonly found in many myths and rituals, but it is also a characteristic of Ihimaera's and Grace's novels. In this sense, their fictions incorporate myths following this succession on the one hand, and the narratives follow a mythic pattern themselves on the other. This does not necessarily make the texts myths in themselves, but it adds to the mythic quality evident in many of the novels since the 1970s. Though they may feel like and contain elements of myth in content and form, the novels can only imitate but not be myths at this stage. What fiction lacks is the age-old tradition that gives myth its multiple layers, ancient references, anonymity and the subsequent depth. Nonetheless, fiction contains the potential to become myth since the prerequisites are there: the authors have created texts of great significance for their culture and all of New Zealand by following mythic patterns and adapting the English language to suit their type of fiction and choice of topic. They stay true to Maori storytelling traditions.[1] The fact that the novels have a political purpose and demand social change is the greatest barrier between the texts as myths and the texts as pure fiction. Myths lose their power and do not work if they are anchored in time and allow us to pinpoint their moment of creation.

Awareness of a First Maori Identity
Myths of origin not only bonded, but also resulted in an overall Maori identity that did not exist prior to the coming of the *Pakeha*, making it a fairly recent phenomenon. In that sense, the Maori have only comparatively recently become a unified group, something that is reflected in a common language as opposed to the many dialects that existed before European settlement due to the relative independence from one another in which the tribes lived. The Maori language was "[f]ormerly fragmented into a number of regional dialects, some of which diverged quite radically from what has become the standard dialect" (Gordon 2005). Today, some dialects remain, but it is the standard dialect that is taught and spoken all over the country. Keeping this in mind, Maori culture is one which has been born out of and been formed by interaction with the *Pakeha* and the awareness of difference. It can therefore be seen as an unexpectedly modern culture, albeit one which draws on historical ethnic roots.

---

1   Maori understanding of *story* may be more expansive than commonly recognised: "Grace thus uses the word 'story' to cover many forms of discourse, from myth and legend through chronicle and history to fiction and orature" (Skinner 1998: 123). What all these have in common is the traditionally oral context in which these stories were/are passed on. As will be demonstrated, the oral tradition contributes to the style of Maori writing as well.

Maori identity gradually developed in opposition to *Pakeha* identity as a means of furthering and strengthening indigenous culture. As a result, it is a culture of survival, a term Otto Heim (1998) employs in his book on violence and ethnicity in Maori literature. In *Writing Along Broken Lines*, Heim refers to Maori fiction as narratives of survival that are a result of a Maori culture of survival. The texts he analyses express different kinds of violence, some more overtly than others. In his opinion, this violence is the means used to free oneself from colonial legacy so as to achieve the survival of the indigenous culture. All of Ihimaera's and Grace's selected novels are also narratives of survival and represent a culture of survival whose work is not yet completed. This culture's aim is to find ways to resist extinction by working with or against the *Pakeha* to further Maori interests.

The new settlers had their own identity crisis and tried to establish themselves as better Britons in the Britain of the South, a common nineteenth century name for New Zealand also used in the *New Zealand Examiner*, March 19, 1861. The country was praised as superior to Britain, where there was "progress without the price, paradise without the serpent, and Britain without the Irish" (Belich 1996: ch. xii). Meanwhile, the Maori began to see themselves as a large, unified group for the first time – a sameness that was based on their shared "unEuropean-ness" (Belich 1997: 15). Gareth Griffiths puts this down to the colonial policy of assimilation that aimed at homogenisation and the suppression of difference that succeeded in marginalising native cultures (cf. Griffiths 1994), but it is also born out of necessity. In order to effect any change and to oppose colonial authority, there must be a united force so it will be perceived as powerful. Even the native name is a result of contact with the new settlers and a means of differentiation on the one hand and unification on the other: "Now known as Māori, these tribes did not identify themselves by a collective name until the arrival of Europeans when, to mark their distinction the name Māori, meaning 'ordinary', came into use" (Wilson 2007). The Maori saw themselves as the ordinary, original inhabitants of Aotearoa while the settlers were the strangers.

A common slogan of the nineteenth century was that New Zealand was "98% British" (Belich 1997: 14) with which the ties to Britain could be maintained while New Zealand would at the same time remain distinctly different and potentially superior to the old country. The myth of a better stock of British citizens emerged to reinforce the settlers' identity and to avoid racial degeneracy, which might have had a negative influence on connections with Britain. Consequently, there was little space for a distinct and powerful Maori community at the time.

In the settlers' eyes, Maori weakness signalled their extinction, but this did not happen quite as expected. Still, the superior Maori were politically useful in establishing the Britain of the South as better than other English colonies. This term of superiority is related to European racial stereotypes: Maori were divided into three groups – White or Whitening, Grey and Black Savages. They were, respectively, the convertible, the dying and the permanently inferior of whom only the superior White Savage (the Noble Savage) was willing and able to embrace Europe (cf. Belich 1997: 10–11). In the twentieth century, however, more organised indigenous attempts at creating a clear Maori identity to enable autonomy took place. The goal was to influence "Pakeha opinion to a more kindly attitude and respect towards the Maori" (Sorensen 1986: I 178–80) and make them see the value of Maori culture. This was achieved through things as simple as sports matches or as complicated and dangerous as joint participation in war, and, not least, with myths of origin and writing.

2.1.1 Writing a New Maori Identity

In the mid-twentieth century Maori writers began to make use of European literary genres, writing in English to portray Maori life. Literacy among Maori people in their own language developed in the 1800s, as Jane McRae explains in her article "From Maori Oral Traditions to Print":

> Letters dated from the 1830s offer outstanding material for enquiry into Māori use of writing and print. The popularity of letter-writing is noted in all the studies of literacy cited above. Pleasure in conversation with those at a distance led to letters being delivered on paper, slate, leaves. As personal, individual examples of writing they provide evidence of use of the orthography, representation of dialect, development of a writing style—letters often follow the formalities of oratory (as heard in speeches on the marae), beginning with traditional greetings, closing with a song.

> The topics of letters are also instructive. They were a means of expressing personal feelings, of making requests (often for pens, paper, ink, books), and especially of discussing political matters. Formal and informal letters in Māori can be found in great number in the papers of officials of church and government [...]. Opinion was also put in written and printed petitions [...], and in letters to newspapers and journals. The sense of an audience in this public readership brought rhetorical strategies to pen; argument, challenge and provocation typical to oral performance were transferred to a written forum. [...] Another way in which Māori used writing was to record domestic matters. There are diaries and personal records of monies, family celebrations, meetings, problems. (McRae 1997)

This is ample evidence for the active place Maori took in society by making use of the written word. They did not accept change passively but took interest in politics and opinion from the beginning, taking influence in the new development wherever possible. Writing was primarily functional as a means to influence developments and put forth opinion, not as literature.

In the late 1800s it became more important to be able to communicate in written English so that the native tongue was mainly confined to oral traditions of speechmaking and the communication of traditional (tribal) knowledge. Thanks to the Maori renaissance since the 1970s, there is a strong sense of purpose and readership at the end of the twentieth century with publications of various kinds in Maori and English. Among these are books for schools, records, and translations that make use of the native tongue in a predominantly English context.

It was often said that there is no Maori literature, but McRae traces this opinion back to the serial publications in which Maori writing appeared. *Te Ao Mārama* (1992–1996), a five-volume collection of Maori writing in English, contains examples of how the indigenous people have used both native and *Pakeha* oral and literary conventions to create their own brand of creative writing:

> The writing exemplifies how Māori use both oral and literary genres. In English there are short stories, novels, poetry, plays. These styles are known and emulated by Māori writers from their unavoidable experience of English literature at school. In Māori there are songs, mythological accounts, stories of tribal tradition, a little creative writing. But there is also movement between genres; writing in English often pays homage to the oral traditions by quotations and allusions. [...] Literature helped Māori cross the divide between the oral traditions and English. (McRae 1997)

These influences can be observed in the novels chosen for this study, no matter the topic or time of publication.

The first Maori novels were published in English in the 1970s, but even though they were a way of making the Maori perspective accessible to a greater readership, they were not confrontational or violent yet, lacking an anger that was still developing in fiction. Writing was a way in which Maori could create an image of themselves that would be visible outside of their own community at last. However, their writing presented the harmonious life in the country, the importance of old customs and myths, but little of their strife. Text, a medium of great authority in the Western world, could now further a Maori cause as it had done before in letters and journals.

The significance of text, even before the letters, became evident with the Treaty of Waitangi in 1840, the controversial founding document signed by British authorities and 500 Maori chiefs, with which New Zealand became a British colony. Among other things, the Treaty was meant to protect Maori land and interests and grant Maori sovereignty. To this day, it is held in high regard despite the controversy regarding its interpretation and use due to inadequate translation from English to Maori and a resulting misunderstanding of key concepts. In 1975 the Waitangi Tribunal was established for Maori to be heard who believe to have been illegally dispossessed as a result of a breaching of the Treaty. It is a text of authority which Maori and *Pakeha* alike accept. It comes as no surprise, then, that texts in general have the potential to influence even a primarily oral culture, and this is not only the case with political documents, but also with literature.

New Zealand identity, settler identity and Maori identity went through stages of identity construction throughout history. Most of them were dominated and directed by *Pakeha* who had the sources and scientific methods to do research in this field. Until at least the 1930s, *Pakeha* literature was indistinguishable from British literature: it was Anglophile and Eurocentric, barely varying stylistically and thematically from British texts, and they lacked a particularly New Zealand character. McLintock lists the most common types of literature till 1920:

> From 1861 to 1920 New Zealand fiction falls into four main groups. Most writers were either recording pioneer experiences, or exploiting the possibilities of an exotic

setting. In the years 1890–1910 a number busied themselves with preaching for various good causes; some few, from 1890 onwards, attempted to interpret New Zealand life. After 1920 the recording novel died out, while the preaching novel withered, except for an occasional item. The exploiting novel continued to flourish, offering popular entertainment in feminine romances or masculine action yarns. In the period 1930–1960 more writers attempted to realise New Zealand experience truthfully and to interpret it. (McLintock 2006b)

Similarly, literary magazines such as *Phoenix*, even though it suggested the unique potential of a national literature, looked British and read British because "the new journal looked the way an Anglophile education said a modern literary journal should look" (Evans 1990: 80). What was missing quite generally was the willingness to take risks and attempt something new. *Pakeha* New Zealand literature lacked a distinct quality that it was finally given by the journal *Tomorrow* (1934–1940) whose main contributor, the critic Winston Rhodes, encouraged a new kind of literature: "Literature for him was a practical thing that could deal only with the here and now and was therefore by definition local, by definition nationalistic in a regional sense" (Evans 1990: 87). The Caxton Press, established in 1936, was the first to publish books of New Zealand writers, and the tradition of an independent New Zealand literature finally began. The government's literary competition to celebrate the centennial of European New Zealand led to more writing about New Zealand, contributing to the growing nationalism that gave *Pakeha* New Zealanders an idea of who they were, set apart from Britain.

The myths of origin and race that emerged in New Zealand history did not confine themselves to real life. With the development of a distinguished national literature, new myths also arose within the realm of fiction. A popular myth in this new literature is the Man Alone myth, the story of the *Pakeha* underdog, depicting New Zealand life as it was perceived to be for the pioneer: nature and society as a hostile environment in which the tough and self-reliant lone man struggles for survival. The name derives from John Mulgan's 1939 novel by the same title and the theme became particularly popular in literature in the 1950s and 60s. It was a decade later that Maori writers began to use their novels in English as a means to express themselves and display the indigenous perspective of New Zealandness, and

it took more than two decades before Keri Hulme challenged the myth in
the bone people by creating a Woman Alone myth.

Therefore, Maori creative writing developed gradually. The first texts
were collections of oral texts such as sayings and song poems and were
published by *Pakeha*:

> Pākehā published the first books of oral traditions in the 19th century from manu-
> scripts written by Māori. They encouraged Māori into print as contributors to serials
> in the 19th century, and as authors of books and journals in the 20th century. By that
> time Māori were encouraging Māori into print. In the 19th century one motive for
> publication by Pākehā was to preserve the traditional knowledge which must have
> seemed dangerously ephemeral, not only oral but of a dying race. (McRae 1997)

This is not to say that creative writing in Maori did not exist – it did and
was made accessible through Maori journals and newspapers. Sir Apirana
Ngata published collections of Maori song poetry in the 1920s, and forty
years later Ihimaera and Hone Tuwhare published their own poetry, short
stories and novels, thus beginning a Maori literary tradition in English.

From its beginnings, Maori fiction inevitably dealt with traditional
rural life and *Pakeha* contact and its consequences. The first novels in the
1970s were pastoral and non-confrontational, displaying the strong and
inseparable intertwining of life on ancestral land and myth that made the
fiction so harmonious. They lacked the anger and political motivation of
later publications. Novels such as Ihimaera's *The Matriarch* (1986), Grace's
Potiki (1986) and Duff's *Once Were Warriors* (1990) indicate that literature
picked up Maori discontent a decade later and expressed it in new ways.
Until then, Ihimaera and Grace were known for their depictions of rural
harmony and tribal kinship, but it was a harmony that did not seem to
represent the situation of indigenous people. "The basic purpose for writing," Ihimaera said on the subject,

> had been to establish and describe the emotional landscape of the Maori people. The
> landscapes of the heart. I used to think that even if all the land were taken away, our
> *maraes* razed, our children turned into brown pakehas, that nothing could take away
> the heart, the way we feel …

> But increasingly the emotional reality became less and less important to describe and the political reality assumed a higher profile. I could not, in all conscience, allow people ever to consider my work was the definitive portrayal of the world of the Maori. In my attempts to help, I considered I had created a stereotype. Of warm caring relationships. Of a people who lived in rural communities. But what *was* the reality? The reality of 1975 was a hardening of attitudes on both sides. Of inflexibility. Of infighting. By 1975 I felt my vision was out of date and, tragically, so encompassing and so established that it wasn't leaving room enough for the new reality to punch through. (Ihimaera's lecture to the Friends of the Turnbull Library in 1981, quoted in Corballis and Garrett 1984: 13)

There was to be no myth of contented Maori living on their own land anymore because it was untrue. The reality of the difficulties of Maori life as a result of strong *Pakeha* influence and authority no longer allowed a false representation of harmony. Instead, Maori prose became confrontational, angry and in some cases violent in the 1980s.

The injustices suffered due to the breaching of the Treaty of Waitangi, Maori poverty and unemployment, continuing racism and discrimination found expression in fiction eventually. The characters in *Potiki* are in the middle of land negotiations, and even though it is not as violent as other politically motivated novels, "Grace had finally 'joined the ranks of the Maori who believed that justice can only be obtained by direct action'" (Heim 1998: 13). Most violent of all, *Once Were Warriors* presents the reader with the tradition of warriorhood whose origin has been lost, misunderstood and misappropriated. Parallels to the author's own experiences lent authenticity to the subject that others could not attain in the same vein. The idea of Maori–*Pakeha* harmony was irrevocably replaced by a violent literature of survival and a Maori community that fights back and is no longer willing to be oppressed.

After multiple phases of Maori identity throughout history which were dominated by *Pakeha* views and actions, the indigenous people themselves began to be in charge of who they wanted to be. Developing from a people of prehistoric mythical and legendary ancestors to colonial subjects to a postcolonial people with the power to demand a space for themselves – literally and figuratively – the Maori made their way towards the multicultural Aotearoa New Zealand that it wants to be today. Events in New

Zealand politics found their way into fiction in the 1980s, making writing
one of the weapons available to Maori to demand and secure a better future.
Inevitably, indigenous concerns are still to be found in Maori fiction today,
which is just one of the signs of a continuing search for New Zealand
identity on the whole and Maori identity and authority in particular.

2.1.2 National Identity and Historiographic Practice

National identity is continually in the making, a process which historiography attests to. Lorenzo Veracini and Adrian Muckle distinguish three
phases of redescribing colonial history also applicable to New Zealand:

> 1. Indigenous resistance of the 1970s led to a reassessment of indigenous
> agency and collaborative practice.

> 2. New historiographies brought with them debates among those
> who would protect traditional narratives and those who welcome
> the new.

> 3. National/indigenous reconciliation (Veracini and Muckle 2007: 1).

Maori resistance and political protests are ongoing as shown by the 2007
publication of *Resistance: An Indigenous Response to Neoliberalism*. At the
book launch, Tariana Turia, co-leader of the Maori party, said that "all of
us are capable of resistance simply by refusing to be silent about the things
that matter" (Turia 2007). Judging from the range of topics addressed in
Resistance, there is much that needs to be spoken about "to acknowledge
the growth and the blossoming of this seed and its fruit: our own stories
and representations, our own kai [food], our own systems of maintaining
hauora [hours], our legal structures, our capacity to name and therefore
to be; our own knowledge and science – enabling us to be on our own
terms" (*ibid.*). Maori resistance today goes back to the early resistance of
the 1800s and has continued because neoliberalism is seen as yet another
form of colonisation that harms Maori people. Resistance today is still
about surviving as a whole, as a *tangata whenua*, people of the land with a
collective history, not just individually.

While *Resistance* stresses the importance of Maori collaboration and exchange, places like Te Papa demonstrate the redefinition process of national identity in the constant reappraisal of Maori and *Pakeha* interaction and bicultural partnership throughout time. Defined by "hybridity, crossfertilisation and 'tangled destinies'" (Veracini and Muckle 2007: 7), New Zealand should be seen as a country that is able to accept and incorporate cultural difference, and which has more than just one definitive identity. Te Papa's ways of working with history show how both founding peoples are connected and profit from each other. Most of all, the national museum is an example of how such collaboration between the two founding peoples can actually work and not merely be a welcome but unrealisable theoretical construct. The museum's logo, a fingerprint, perfectly expresses the national museum's purpose: at the centre of the fingerprint – a very Western concept of identity –, there is the curl that symbolises the Maori spiral representing an unfolding fern leaf. The essentially Maori is embedded within a Western concept or, to allow for a less hierarchical interpretation, the tendrils of the fern infuse this Western notion of identity.

By representing both founding peoples, Te Papa honours one of the key government goals – *To Strengthen National Identity and Uphold the Principles of the Treaty of Waitangi*. Its collaboration with *iwi*, tribal groups, is a crucial part of this aim and according to the museum's Statement of Intent 2006–2009, "[a]ctive relationships [must be] maintained with a minimum of ten *iwi* or Maori organisations each year".[2] Offering a public national platform for *iwi* to represent themselves, tell their stories and manage their own *taonga* (treasures) shows a respect for the native community and the importance of its preservation and inclusion in a bicultural museum and country. The existence and success of the museum as such prove the thriving partnership that is possible among different cultures and are an active part of the national/indigenous reconciliation Veracini and Muckle speak of.

---

2   Museum of New Zealand Te Papa Tongarewa. *Statement of Intent 2006–2009*. 2. <http://www.tepapa.govt.nz/SiteCollectionDocuments/AboutTePapa/ LegislationAccountability/SOI2006.pdf> accessed June 7, 2010.

Looking at these examples of current practices of writing (about) history, there is a general impression of active participation in the making of history and historic diversity. The emphasis on native inclusion, however, also indicates that there is no equal partnership as yet. In her analysis of New Zealand film and literature, Davinia Thornley comes to the conclusion that nation building remains white and that *Pakeha* notions still form the primary framework:

> This myth of "the Nation" structures New Zealand as a place that restrictively aggregates identity: while these stories appear to valorise mixture, they actually merely *displace* and ultimately *contain* mixture. *Pakeha* rhetoric, or the telling of white stories, remains the overriding organising principle in the management of the nation. The very transmutability of this rhetoric functions seamlessly to move *Pakeha* into the place occupied by Maori, while relegating Maori to a liminal space somewhere between immigrant and Other. In turn, this rewriting of national history allows the *Pakeha* vision of New Zealand the deepest roots of all. (Thornley 2004: 73)[3]

Thornley's critique is valid and she is not the first to note the continuing presence of a dominating *Pakeha* framework. However, her critique denies that any empowering changes have taken place and she offers no solution. The problem of writing about Maori concerns in a *Pakeha* medium has been addressed since the first Maori novels and no satisfactory resolution has been achieved. Some of this criticism has been inverted to show that the *Pakeha* media are best suited for resistance simply because these are methods with which the majority of the population can be confronted, thus rendering them the only media that will allow indigenous concerns to be voiced. Among authors, Ihimaera, for instance, is an outspoken supporter

---

3   Regarding the use of the terms *other* and *Other*: instead of simply constituting the one different from oneself, the idea of the "other" underlying this study is based on Lacan's (1968), and subsequently Spivak's (1990), distinction. Lacan's *Other* is understood as the empirical centre, an absolute that dictates the cultural framework which makes the colonised subject aware of his/her *other* nature. The *other* is constantly identified, marginalised and made dependent on the *Other* by the *Other* itself. Both of them come into existence in the same process of othering and are binaries that the colonised subject in postcolonial fiction tries to disentangle, weaken or uphold depending on purpose.

of this method since the non-Maori genres also give writers the chance to develop their own voice to conventional forms. What is more, traditional Maori forms are no longer sufficient to be of any use in the creation of Maori identity so that the European genres are an extension of what is available. This position is evident in almost all of Ihimaera's critical writing, interviews and lectures on the subject. We are faced with an issue that cannot be resolved given how established these media are. Contrary to criticism, however, this circumstance does not invalidate the use of such media and it must be considered whether the means actually lead to the desired end, which is change.

In an interview in 2005, Ihimaera addresses the issue of writing in a medium that is foreign to Maori and he defends the choice of the English language and the use of Western genres:

> "It was an incredible dilemma," says Ihimaera, "because Maori believe that English is not a sacred language and to try to translate Maori thoughts and Maori values into English is very difficult. Some of my more politically minded friends felt we should maintain the Maori story within the Maori language. But foolishly, or arrogantly, or otherwise, I chose to recognise that if we kept on doing it that way we would end up in a cul de sac. The only way to gain political and cultural and economic power is to work oneself into those power frameworks. For me, that meant writing myself into the frame." (Dickson 2005: 1)

In this manner, the English language can "bear the burden of another experience" (Achebe in Ashcroft *et al.* 2002: 19), the Maori experience, displaying the power of appropriation. The experiences described may then appear less authentic in English than they would in the native tongue, but the chosen language's advantage is the broad readership which will have access to the texts. Therefore, change may be easier to come by with the choice of the most practical medium rather than the most appropriate one at times.

Though rewriting history is a common practice in postcolonial literature,[4] the main concern in the novels discussed here is not the

---

4   Cf. for instance, Colavincenzo's study of myth in Canadian historical fiction (2003) that demonstrates the very common practice of rewriting history in order to challenge authority.

reworking of history. Instead, these authors show a great concern for the present and move towards the future in their writing. Often set in the time of publication, the novels depict the current situation of Maori people with a concern for future social development. Values and traditions from the past gain importance in the present day described in fiction and are the means with which change is made. The past as such is not rewritten, though practices of that time are introduced into the fictional world with the hope of finding their way into the real world through the reader.

Reintroducing Maori myths into fiction is a common practice that connects the characters and Maori readers to their cultural roots. Since the custom of oral storytelling wanes as the old family structures are broken up by the intrusion of the *Pakeha*, stories are no longer told and remembered as they were of old. A return to storytelling reconnects Maori with their heritage; in the novels this reunites the characters with their families and traditions while, on a different level, the authors tell their story to reunite Maori readers with the same traditions and to introduce them to non-Maori readers at the same time.

The novels create a clearer image of Maori culture and New Zealand identity – or rather identit*ies* – that are no longer primarily informed by *Pakeha* opinions of indigenous life. Without a doubt, Witi Ihimaera and Patricia Grace are just two representatives using a significant corpus of Maori myths. In the course of this book, their choice of myths, techniques and their purposes will be introduced and discussed as carriers of indigenous knowledge, customs and values in fiction.

2.1.3 Tikanga Maori: Underlying Maori Customs and Values

In his book *Tikanga Maori: Living by Maori Values*, Hirini Moko Mead recognises the increased need for knowledge of the basic values for the Maori people. Conceived as an introduction to *tikanga Maori*, Maori values, the book gives insight into various aspects of Maori life that are influenced by them. Among these are ceremonies pertaining to social groupings, the sacredness of land and people, prohibitions, and the *tikanga* of the arts, to name only a few. The necessity for such a book is not only determined by the lack of knowledge of Maori values and practices; according to Mead, it is important to find adequate ways to act according to them in today's world. After all, "'Tika' means 'to be right' and thus tikanga Maori focuses on the correct way of doing something. This involves moral judgements about appropriate ways of behaving and acting in everyday life" (Mead 2003: 6). Therefore, *tikanga Maori* should influence all actions as a normative system.

In the context of Maori literature, writers are faced with the problem of language if they choose to write in English and still want to uphold Maori values. Though it is possible to describe events and people in ways that will express these values and customs, it may be impossible to impart the full meaning in English. Many writers have solved this problem by letting their characters sometimes speak in their native tongue and include Maori terms that may express more than their English translations would. "It is worth noting," Mead explains, "[t]hat one's understanding of tikanga Maori is informed and mediated by the language of communication. One's understanding through te reo Maori is different from one obtained through the English language. Reo Maori participants usually have the advantage of prior knowledge and prior experience. This is not necessarily the case for others" (*ibid.*: 2). On the one hand, this is a statement which reinforces how important it is to uphold *te reo* Maori, the native tongue, in order to fully appreciate and understand *tikanga Maori*. On the other, however, it also allows an appraisal of the characters in Ihimaera's and Grace's fiction, who exhibit different degrees of language competence. Their ability or inability to speak Maori thus reveals their respective knowledge of their cultural values and customs as well as the degree of involvement therein.

The novels contain three different types of characters as far as language competence is concerned: firstly, there are characters who have a full knowledge of *te reo* and speak it fluently. They tend to be older generation, Maori elders and oftentimes the following generation. Especially elders have a high status within the community and are familiar with *tikanga* since they are traditionally responsible for teaching the young. Secondly, there are those who remember their parents speaking fluently and who still have some knowledge of Maori, but mainly speak English since it is the language in which they were educated. Living in both Maori and *Pakeha* communities, they speak both languages and may have compromised their native identity, thereby not living fully in accordance with their *tikanga*. Finally, it is often the younger generation who have no language competence in their native tongue due to their education, the urban life, and looser family ties. No longer exposed to the early life on tribal land among their *iwi*, they do not know the customary ways of their people as well as they would otherwise. This is particularly evident in Ihimaera's *Tangi* (*T*) where Tama, a teenage boy, finds it easier to live in the city among *Pakeha* than to return to his family with its ceremonies and rituals that he has not been exposed to for many years.

Inevitably, *tikanga* is not only the foundation of Maori everyday life, but also a basic principle underlying fiction. Within the novels featured here, we shall come across a number of indispensable values which will be introduced in this section. Patricia Grace lists the following values that characterise Maori relationships: *aroha* (love), *manaakitanga* (hospitality), *whanaungatanga* (relationships and loyalty in the family), *nga tipuna* (ancestors), *te tangata* (the importance of people), *te whenua* (the relationship to the land), *te moana* (the relationship to the sea), *te mauri* (the life spirit of every person) (cf. Panny 1997: 4). Mead further adds *mana* (authority, honour and prestige), *tapu* (sacredness), *noa* (the restoring of balance), *utu* (reciprocity or compensation, also revenge), and *ea* (securing of peaceful interrelationships) (cf. Mead 2003: 28–32). The fundamental principle underlying these values is a balanced relationship ensured by certain responsibilities. It is the same with *whanaungatanga*, which contains a set of obligations to secure close relationships within the family. In times of need, one can rely on help from individuals or a group and is expected to be available to lend support when required. Furthermore, it is expected that one remains in touch, as suggested by the connected notion of *kanohi kitea*, which means "a face seen" (*ibid.*: 28) and expresses the necessity to uphold close relationships with the family. Family in this context can also extend to friends who may not be related, but whose involvement with the family and their *marae* is very close nonetheless. *Manaakitanga* (hospitality and looking after people) as well as *aroha* further define relationships between individuals and groups and must be upheld "no matter what the circumstances might be" (*ibid.*: 29). These set duties prove the importance of such values in Maori society.

Particularly Grace's *Potiki*, to take an example, portrays life by the aforementioned values. Not only is life on the tribal land lived peacefully and with a healthy balance due to the people's involvement in the community's interests such as teaching their children about their culture at home; the people also observe the principles of *manaakitanga* when they are confronted with unpleasant events such as Dollarman's visit to negotiate the selling of land. Despite it being clear that the tribe does not want to sell their land under any circumstances, they do negotiate and invite Dollarman to join them, offering their hospitality. This does not mean they like him and it does not keep them from making fun of him, but the point is that they have invited him onto the *marae*. Furthermore, the novel depicts the close relationship between the individual members of the tribe. Toko, for instance, is taken in and raised by Roimata, who is not his biological mother. At no point in this novel is there ever a dispute about family relations since all who live on this tribal land are family, and the task of raising and educating the young is shared by all.

Likewise, *te tangata* and *te tipuna*, the importance of one's ancestors and the people, fundamentally underpin the Maori novels examined here. Each one stresses the importance of family and the survival of the people in times threatened by *Pakeha* dominance. We see how the memory of the deceased is passed on in stories and how one's genealogy is stressed when it comes to the determination of identity. In *Mutuwhenua*, Ripeka's grandmother shows her pictures of her ancestors, telling her about them everytime she visits. Ripeka is certain she will never forget anything she has been told because of her grandmother's insistence on telling these stories. These memories give Ripeka a clear notion of who she is and where she comes from, strengthening her perception of herself as a young Maori woman with ties to her living and deceased relatives.

The importance of *te tangata*, the people, is accentuated especially in Ihimaera's novels, which are often concerned with the survival and revival of Maori culture. A significant example of his innovative fiction and his concern with acceptance and tolerance is *The Uncle's Story*, which not only asks that Maori find their rightful place in New Zealand, but also pleads for the acceptance of Maori within their own community. Emphasising that the threat comes not only from outside, Ihimaera focuses the reader's attention inward among the people themselves, showing that survival and tolerance is also vital within the community. His criticism is not malevolent, of course. On the contrary, it derives from a wish to ensure the life of *te tangata*, which is dependent on their treatment by others as well as themselves.

Furthermore, survival is ensured by *te mauri*, the life force that guarantees the vitality of all things. In Keri Hulme's *the bone people* we see how contact with a mauri leads to significant changes within one of the main characters, revitalising him. A mauri can be in the form of a talisman which then contains this elemental life force: "The mauri is a divine authority by which food may come forth or be preserved in a certain area so that it does not go to another. There is mauri in the land and mauri in waterways such as rivers and lakes. If there is a mountain or a forest without birds, perhaps a river without food [...] then one installs a mauri [stone] [...]" (Ranapiri 1895). Evidently, a *mauri* enables the flow of the life force in the physical world. In addition, it also allows *mana* to flow into objects or people. Mead elucidates that "[m]ana has to do with the place of the individual in the social group. Some individuals are regarded as having a high level of mana and other have varying levels. The word as defined by Williams (1957: 172) has a range of meanings: 'authority, control', 'influence, prestige, power', 'psychic force', 'effectual, binding authoritative'" (Mead 2003: 29).

He explains further that their lineage as well as their work establishes the *mana* of a person. People of authority and high standing have a high level of *mana* that derives from their ancestors (*mana tipuna*) and relations to their *iwi*. The authority they gain from their deeds is called *mana tangata* since it provides human authority, but there is also *mana Atua*, the psychic power that comes from the relations to the Maori gods. At public events, a person's *mana* must be respected and enhanced (cf. *ibid.*: 30). If it is not, this has serious consequences. Usually, these are then dealt with quickly, requiring recompense, but it is more difficult if disrespectful treatment is a consequence of forgotten or ignored *tikanga* over a long period of time. To take an example, Alan Duff describes the abuse of a person's *mana* in several ways in *Once Were Warriors*. Alcoholism, child abuse, and violence against others, especially women, are seen as a result of the disregard for a person's sacredness and the aggressor's detachment from traditional tribal bonds. Mead (*ibid.*: 36ff.) attributes this to ignorance of the individual's place in society and their birthright, as well as their removal from *whanau* (family), *hapu* (sub-tribe) and *iwi* (tribe).

Tapu, another *tikanga*, are spiritual restrictions and commitments that express the *mana* of a person or object. Michael P. Shirres mentions that Maori understanding of *mana* and *tapu* may differ between tribes: "[...] what one writer referred to as *tapu*, another referred to as *mana*. Different words are used for the same reality and the use of the different words itself gives us a better understanding of that reality" (1997: 33). He differentiates between intrinsic *tapu* and extensions of *tapu*, meaning "things which are *tapu* in themselves" (1997: 34) as opposed to the restrictions related to them.

As we shall see in the analysis of Grace's *Cousins*, the head of a person is *tapu* and must not be touched. When Missy's hair is cut off, it is a clear violation of her person, especially as a Maori. Her cousin Makareta, on the other hand, has long hair that she can wind around her head three times, which is an expression of her personal *mana*. Maori carvers such as the one in *Potiki* are also under *tapu* while they work because carving is a sacred occupation. The carving in itself is a *tapu* object that requires certain actions and comes with particular restrictions at the same time. *Noa* is related to the concept of *tapu* and is often regarded as its opposite, which is why anything *noa* (profane) is kept away from the carver while he is at work. (Mead [2003: 31–2] stresses that it is not useful to think of the two concepts as opposites, nonetheless. Both are related concepts that have their place in order to retain a healthy balance between sacred and profane.) This means that women are not allowed to be present and tools or shavings must not get in contact with food since both are *noa*. *Noa*, however, is necessary to restore a balance. "A high level of tapu is dangerous," Mead declares (2003: 31), which is why a state of balance (*ea*) is desired that can only be reached through *noa*. Thus, *ea* is the result of the successful restoration of relationships.

Finally, *utu* is another means through which to reach *ea*. Based on reciprocity and compensation, an unequal state must be balanced. Mead (*ibid.*: 27; 31) speaks of a *take-utu-ea* model to illustrate the point. In effect, there is a breach or claim (*take*) that, once agreed upon, requires compensation (*utu*) to result in *ea*. *Utu* as a concept of reciprocity is important for wholesome relationships and permeates many areas of interaction without being restricted to economic transactions. Further, it justifies the claims for compensation for land theft, which is an important factor in the novels' fictional background since this unlawful confiscation is an aspect of cultural theft and censorship on the whole.

In this respect, *Potiki* most evidently depicts the seizing and importance of land for the Maori people as a source of nourishment and survival. The *whanau*'s negotiations with Dollarman demonstrate *Pakeha* greed and the Maori determination to hold on to the little land they have. While Dollarman offers compensation, the *whanau* knows that it would not be a lasting solution and that they as a people would suffer from the loss in the long run. In other words, *utu* would be required, but the offer is no sufficient recompense and would only result in a *take* situation instead of *ea*.

Components of Maori Identity

Living by Maori values inevitably both presupposes and establishes a notion of identity. As mentioned earlier, being able to trace your *whakapapa* as far back as possible is an important aspect of situating yourself within the community; your lineage tells you who you are and there is a high level of *mana* attached to those individuals who can trace their *whakapapa* to an important well-respected ancestor. As a general definition, "[w]hakapapa provides our identity within a tribal structure and later in life gives an individual the right to say, 'I am Maori.' [...] In short, whakapapa is belonging. Without it an individual is outside looking in" (*ibid.*: 42–3).

This is an aspect of identity that features in many Maori novels to varying degrees. The memory of the ancestor Paikea is of vital importance in *The Whale Rider* (*WR*) in two respects: on the one hand, being able to trace the tribe's origin to him in an unbroken line is a sign of the tribe's strength and endurance. While his descendants are chiefs, the powers that were attributed to him will continue in them and ensure his people's survival. On the other hand, referring to Paikea as the originator of the tribe sets them apart from others and gives them a clear idea of who they are in contrast to them. In this case, their origin not only distinguishes them as Maori as such, but particularly as a specific tribe. As will be shown in the text analysis, it will become clear that there may be contesting influences: Paikea is not the only ancestor who influences the tribe's life; what is more, a female ancestor is responsible for a new streak that ultimately enhances the tribe's strength and influences their future. Therefore, the importance of *whakapapa* in questions of Maori identity is vital and perhaps the most obvious aspect to appear in fiction in this context.

Less apparent is the concept of *ira tangata* and *ira atua*. The former refers to the genetic inheritance from the line of the father and the line of the mother, though the notion goes beyond the purely biological to include a spiritual element. Since Maori trace their human origin from the gods (*ira atua*), the children of the First Parents, they have thus inherited a spiritual quality from them. Although this particular concept is not explicitly found in the novels featured here, it is an underlying principle that finds expression in the myths and stories referred to in the texts. Likewise, *pumanawa,* the idea that characters may be endowed with traits or natural abilities of a mythical or legendary ancestor, appears explicitly in *The Whale Rider*'s female protagonist, as mentioned above.

As a consequence of their *whakapapa*, Maori are born with a right to a certain place. The importance of land becomes clearer when viewed from this perspective: a Maori has a birthright associated with the land. The land is in turn associated with the ancestors and consequently has a value that goes beyond being a source of nourishment or capital. Certain places such as the *marae*, the meeting place, are important locations for the tribe and contribute greatly to individual and communal identity. Having a place to call home and knowing it is there to return to features in almost all the novels yet to be discussed. It is most apparent in passages that describe the custom of burying the afterbirth of a newborn child so it will forever be connected to the land and know where its home is (cf. *ibid.*: 288–9). In *The Whale Rider*, this custom is a guarantee for the main character's return even after a long absence. Quite generally, returns to the *whanau* on ancestral land are stressed in Grace's novel, and even Paikea's uncle eventually returns home after years of drifting from country to country. Such returns are attributed to *turangawaewae*, "the right to a place for the feet to stand" (*ibid.*: 43). Furthermore, it is no coincidence that the word for land and placenta are the same in Maori: *whenua* expresses the connection between the people and the land, symbolising the interdependence of the two. What is more, Maori people call themselves *tangata whenua*, people of the land, defining themselves by the land they belong to – the place where they were born, where their placenta and their ancestors are buried.

Besides the physical aspects of identity based on land, there are also spiritual elements previously mentioned, such as *tapu* and *mana*, that have bearing on the question of belonging as well. The land contains sacred places on land and sea which are thought to be the haunts of spirits and gods or sites of historical importance. The mountains repeatedly referred to in *Mutuwhenua* are such sacred places and any disrespectful behaviour towards them and the ancestral spirits' dwelling there is admonished by the family and punished by supernatural forces (cf. *M* 62).

As a result of the physical and spiritual relationship between the people and the land, it becomes clear that the latter is perhaps the most important element necessary to define Maori identity. Since they are the people of the land, land is not "a personal asset to be traded" (Mead 2003: 273), and ownership or sale is a concept that is not compatible with the Maori belief system. This point underlies the novels and is sometimes addressed specifically as in *Potiki*'s negotiations with the aptly named Dollarman. Ownership is a Western concept, but the indigenous idea of land does not include it. Therefore, negotiations in Grace's novel are futile since it is not within the tribe's power – not to mention their willingness – to sell land.

In 2001, the Ministry of Justice summed up the relationship between the people and the land as follows:

> The importance of the land and the environment was reflected through whakapapa, ancestral place names and tribal histories. [...] The children of Ranginui and Papa-tuanuku were the parents of all resources: the patrons of all things tapu. [...] The way they conducted their lives and the respect they have for their environment and each other stemmed from whakapapa. The system of community co-operation in cultivation and sharing the natural resources inhibited any trend towards individual-ism and individual ownership of land.

More importantly, it goes on:

> The land is a source of identity for Maori. Being direct descendants of Papatuanuku, Maori see themselves as not only "of the land", but "as the land". The living genera-tions act as the guardians of the land, like their tipuna [ancestors] had before them. Their uri [descendants] benefit from that guardianship, because the land holds the link to their parents, grandparents and tipuna, and the land holds the link to future generations. Hence, the land was shared between the dead, the living and the unborn. (Ministry of Justice 2001: 44)

In these passages, the complex connection between Maori and land is made evident, explaining the relations to *whakapapa*, the obligations of each person, and the resulting identification with the land.

Since the ancestral spirits have been mentioned several times above, one can gauge the significance of spirits in Maori belief. Mead also addresses this aspect in his book and introduces further principles that bear on the novels studied here (Mead 2003: 54–9). The living, he says, have *wairua*, a spirit or soul, and *hau*, perhaps best translated as an aura. Ihimaera's *Tangi* depicts moments when the deceased person's *wairua* lingers after death and even becomes visible to members of the family. It is believed that this is possible, allowing the spirit to leave the body even in life, never straying far. *Cousins* features similar moments when the main characters feel and see the presence of relatives, signifying the characters' connection to their cultural heritage. Hence it comes as no surprise that Mata, the one who has been deprived of her cultural roots, only begins to see the *wairua* once she finds her place among her family at the very end of Grace's novel.

Changes in Tikanga Today

According to Maori belief, any talent a person possesses comes from the ancestors and has been passed on between generations. A writer has there-fore received his or her creative talent from parents, grandparents or earlier relatives. Once again, *whakapapa* is responsible for a person's abilities. This leads to Mead's conclusion that "a talent for creativity is not an individual's good fortune but rather it is the fortune of a kin group, of the tribal group, of the community. It follows, therefore, that the results of such a talent should enhance the group [...]" (*ibid.*: 255). While Mead particularly refers to the traditional arts such as carving and weaving in this case, the same can be said about writing, which is also a *tapu* act. Subsequently, the author takes on great responsibility since their work will not only reflect upon them as individuals, but on their tribe as well. As a result, the Maori writer will have more responsibility than the European writer who is solely account-able for his work as an individual. As an artist, the Maori writer will ideally produce work that benefits the group and not just himself.

Furthermore, the origin of any creative act is attributed to the gods and subsequently has a spiritual dimension, though the artist's own contribution is acknowledged in his or her development of the art form. Special *tikanga* requirements have to be observed here that characterise the creative act in progress and once it is completed. Mead mentions that self-taught artists – meaning those who do not learn the art alongside a more experienced artist – "do not necessarily get the tikanga right. They may master the technical aspects of the art form and fail to achieve the same level of mastery over the tikanga. It is preferable to have full control over both aspects" (*ibid.*: 260). Writing might fall into this category of a self-taught art in which the writer should have "mastery over the tikanga" if possible, though it is a personal choice (cf. *ibid.*: 260ff.). Following *tikanga* is said to enhance the creative process and the work of art itself. More importantly, the "creative talent is expected to be used to put the stamp of Maori culture upon the landscape. Some artists accept the challenge to become global in the fields they choose to work in and the media they want to manipulate" (*ibid.*: 263). The same goes for writers like Ihimaera and Grace whose writing has left a mark on New Zealand literature and who enjoy international prominence.

The writing-related *tikanga* as observed at award ceremonies and book launches are, of course, rather new customs that have developed from changes in Maori society and from new requirements in certain areas of creativity. Therefore, *tikanga* prove to be flexible and adaptable though the central values remain the same. It is important to uphold them even in times of change, which occasionally makes old practices redundant or requires the introduction of new customs. Nonetheless, Mead concludes that this is a natural development and that values are continually expanded on to allow their application to contemporary situations (cf. *ibid.*: 353–7). According to Mead, modern life now challenges Maori people to find suitable ways of observing *tikanga* under circumstances that are no longer traditional.

At the same time, borrowing elements of foreign cultures is a natural process, be it Maori borrowing from others or *vice versa*. Mead takes an optimistic stance, regarding this development as natural and favourable. To his mind, if non-Maori members of society borrow certain practices and their *tikanga*, it is a sign of recognition within the community in the same way that Maori borrowing elements of other cultures signals the acceptance of certain aspects.

Throughout his book, Mead emphasises that even though there are *tikanga* that must be observed. It is up to the individual to decide which customs and practices they choose to perform. Furthermore, there are situations in which procedures are unclear due to their newness. All one can do is to examine the matter at hand and ask whether it violates any *tikanga*, though such a distinction may be problematic.

As a result, Maori novels are inevitably concerned with the same issues Mead addresses. In fictional settings, the authors depict their Maori characters' situations, their struggle to live in a changing world in which their *tikanga* seem not to make sense anymore or have been lost to them altogether, and their success or failure in attaining some sort of stability in their new situation. This is the predicament that underlies novels like *Tangi, Mutuwhenua, The Uncle's Story*, and others. Like Mead, the characters (and authors) come to the conclusion that *tikanga* can be preserved even under new circumstances and, more importantly, that they must be preserved. None of the authors featured here appears to disagree with this point, and though the characters do not always agree, they come to learn that it is the better option than to rigidly insist on particular practices or to let them go entirely. Extreme positions are not the answer. Instead, the novels search for a middle ground that is distinctly Maori and yet able to adapt to changes in society.

Characteristically, the novels we will discuss here are explicitly or implicitly interwoven with myths that convey certain *tikanga* and Maori knowledge. Myths, if seen as tales or histories concentrated or distilled over time, contain the essential values and beliefs of the Maori people. Including them within fiction therefore asserts the prevalence of *tikanga* today that cannot be separated from Maori understanding of identity, be it cultural or individual. In order to understand how myths "work" – that is, to appreciate their construction, telling and function – a closer general examination is beneficial. This approach will allow insight into how Maori myths in particular function and whether they take on a different role from that of myths in general.

2.2 Old Tales for a New Future: The Use of Myth in Maori Fiction

According to Laurence Coupe, myths are a common feature in literature, which in themselves can be regarded as mythic narrative due to the creation of texts that represent certain worldviews.

> [...] "mythology", the body of inherited myths in any culture, is an important element of literature, and that literature is a means of extending mythology. That is, literary works may be regarded as "mythopoeic", tending to create or recreate certain narratives which human beings take to be crucial to their understanding of their world. Thus cultural and literary criticism may involve "mythography", or the interpretation of myth, given that the mythic is an important dimension of cultural and literary experience. (Coupe 1997: 4)

Studying myths in connection with literature is therefore almost inevitable, given how they permeate literary narratives. This is especially true in the case of Maori literature of all genres.

A general and very common definition of myths is that they are untrue stories, "discredited and incredible narratives" (Bidney 1966: 4) that contain not a single element of truth: "A purely fictitious narrative usually involving supernatural persons, actions, or events, and embodying some popular idea concerning natural or historical phenomena. Properly distinguished from *allegory* and from *legend* (which implies a nucleus of fact). [...] Also, an untrue or popular tale, a rumour [...]" (*Myth*, OED 1999: 177–8). At the same time, nevertheless, myths are said to reveal ontological truths: a people knows and remembers its origins through the constant telling and retelling of these narratives, believing them to be true. In his article "Myth, Race and Identity in New Zealand", James Belich goes into more detail and defines myths as ever changing ideas that we develop based on our backgrounds, and which emerge through an interlinking of attitudes and theories alike:

> "Myth" is a convenient label, though we should note that these ideas are not merely falsehoods to be debunked, nor texts to be deconstructed, but also important historical refractors and determinants. Modern myths can be seen as fluid cultural motifs, shifting according to time and context and layered such that acceptance of one element encourages, but does not absolutely require, acceptance of another. Each may derive cohesion through dissemination from a common source, but also from atheoretical thinkers with similar backgrounds who make similar choices from sets of options limited by a shared conceptual language. There is an element of convergent evolution as well as of shared descent. Occupying a space between theories and attitudes, myths can draw on the former, but sometimes do so eclectically and inconsistently, knotting strategically contradictory theories together to provide tactical legitimation. [...] Myths interact with theories "above" and attitudes "below", but can lead as well as be led by them. (Belich 1997: 9–10)

On the one hand, this allows myths to develop on their own, emerging gradually and naturally from the history, knowledge and beliefs of the culture in question. On the other, it is still possible to create myths to serve a purpose. The deliberate creation of a mythology can be seen in the way a culture establishes its identity. This was true for the early European settlers in New Zealand, as discussed earlier, and it also applies to the Maori community. Faced with extinction and the overpowering *Pakeha* community, actions are taken to preserve what is left and "renew the value of Maori for Pakeha" (Belich 1997: 22). The narratives of tribal history are both theoretical and spontaneous and can be used to strategically create a homogenous Maori identity that stands against the overpowering *Pakeha* community as it was done in the past. This is still done today even though the image that is portrayed is slightly different and has changed over time, adapting to the challenges of the day. Literature aids the process of creating and recreating identity as will be shown in the course of this chapter and in the discussion of selected novels.

The novelists featured in this study appear to create types of Barthesian *artificial myths* (Barthes 1973: 135) by altering existing myths which are then turned into new mythic stories. Given the fictional nature of these novels, the question of truth and authenticity is of little concern here despite the authors' drawing on popular myths. The novels may not be myths in themselves, but they are narratives of mythic quality nonetheless. This effect is created by the use of features often found in oral storytelling such as repetition and the use of certain key phrases that have a ritual function.[5] The socio-political reality described in the novels, even if it appears only in the background, hinders the reader in perceiving the texts as myths on the whole though some novels contain passages that indeed appear to be new myths. *Potiki* is one of those novels which alternate between myth and reality by presenting the reader with chapters of spiritual significance filled with characters who sometimes seem to be more than human. These chapters are then followed by descriptions of the very real political and economic struggle of the indigenous community.

Here it is important to remember that the Western idea of "real" does not coincide with the Maori concept of "real". We distinguish between the real as what is true, rational and observable while Maori include aspects of the supernatural in their reality. In fiction this finds expression in what we would define as magic realism, but is an established element of Maori realism. "Of course, there is a difference between Maori 'real' and Pakeha 'real'," Alice Te Punga Somerville explains in this context, "whereas a Pakeha realist text might privilege the absence of spiritual dimension (to the extent that its presence is coded 'magic realism'), for example, very few Maori texts exclude this from their depictions of the 'real'" (Somerville 2007: Footnote 32, 110). As a result, the mythic chapters in *Potiki* and other novels create the illusion of oral narration and supply metaphysical depth. The texts are pervaded by aspects of Maori spirituality which are inevitably a great part of the myths encountered, but also of the Maori worldview.

---

5   In "Two Features of Oral Style in Maori Narrative", Agathe Thornton points out two characteristic features found in Maori myths. They are repetition, for emphasis and pace, and chronological looseness. These are features that we also find in Maori novels. Cf. Chapter 3.

The myths we find in the featured novels fall into the following categories: cosmogonic myths or myths of origin/creation myths, myths of transformation/natural myths (including, for instance, explanations for certain geographical features), initiation myths, deity myths (First Parent myths, for instance), and hero myths (the groundbreaking hero, like Maui, who brings change). All these lead to a concept of union, culminating in cultural identity (cf. Leeming 2002: 7–8). Often, the novels combine myths from these categories instead of simply expanding on one of them, depending on their purpose for the plot. At the same time, the novels themselves appear to function as initiation myths in that they introduce the readers to another culture, teaching Maori and non-Maori alike. During the reading process, readers identify with the novels' hero/heroine and share their fictional experiences. Even though this is not as practical an initiation as reality would require, it is as close as literature can enable identification.

Generally, our knowledge of myths can be summarised as follows:[6]

1. They are historical and perennial structures that have been told for centuries and endure due to their timelessness. They contain information coded in mythical terms that serves as an explanation to our world and contains our cultural wealth and spirituality through the ages. Thus, I conclude, myths are a source of cultural memory.

2. Myths have a social function as seen, for instance, in their importance in rituals and ceremonies. According to David Leeming (*ibid.*: 96), "'ceremony' is a word that can suggest the human necessity to tell stories, to make creation conscious of itself through myth and ritual [...]." Therefore, myths bring people together as a social unit by emphasising a common origin and strengthening the bond through ritualised action and speech.

6 Partly based on Lillian Feder's (1980) summary in "Myth, Poetry, and Critical Theory," 53; expanded.

3. The narrative structure of myths expresses the need to control the
fearful and challenging. Mythic heroes and heroines encounter and
test life's conditions in our stead, coming to terms with our environ-
mental limitations. Their attempts to push these limits are our own
desire to overcome them and, as Leeming (*ibid.*: 118) puts it, our need
to move forward.

4. Myths are not unadulterated narratives. Instead, they are accu-
mulated adaptations, which becomes obvious in their varied use in
literature. Myths are adapted for political or religious reasons in literature and real life as the means to a certain end. "Myths," furthermore
"emerge from our experience of reality, from our instinctive need to
clothe that experience in mimetic story and concept. It is also true
that as our experience as cultures and as a species changes, so do our
myths. Old myths (and related rituals) grow and new ones are born
so that we can step out of our merely material lives and project onto a
screen, as it were, our relation to the whole picture of existence" (*ibid.*:
18–19). Myths are, therefore, anything but fixed, rigid narratives and
are subject to change as the society in question itself changes. Similar
to the layering of memories, myths, too, consist of layers of selected
stories.

5. As opposed to fiction,[7] myths are sacred narratives, believed and
"characterized by being anonymous, and so without any determinant
origin" (Ricoeur 1987: 273). Their anonymity stems from the fact that
they are communal narratives, known only as a telling, and have not
been created by one person alone. The anonymity stems from the fact
that an entire community is included in the tradition of telling and
retelling myths. In fiction, this development cannot be imitated fully,
which explains why the novels under consideration here are not myths

---

7   Maori fiction differs from European fiction in this respect since a certain degree of
     mana is attached to it as a work of art, as described in the earlier section devoted to
     tikanga Maori.

in their own right. This last point is illustrated by Berthoff in his essay "Fiction, History, Myth" in which he elaborates the clear distinction between myth and fictional narratives. "Works of fiction, we have every reason to think," he says,

> are *composed* and we know or might know who composed them [...]. Myths, however, are *told*, and we do not know their particular origin. [...] That is, we do not know myth as a making, only as a telling; and there is, with myth, an element of unchangeability in the structure of the telling, the basic terms of which, as spoken, heard, repeated, have the authority of the ritually stabilized. [...] Myths, in fact, are not to be known or encountered directly but only through the performance of tellers, only, that is, in fictive versions, retellings. Perhaps the highest use of fiction is as a way of knowing and replenishing the consciousness of the mythic. But there is always this essential difference between fiction and myth, that in the one mode we know or can imagine an individual maker and in the other we cannot. (Berthoff 1970: 276)

Perceived "as elements embodied in a tradition", as Lévi-Strauss (1979: 18) defines them, myths appear as widely accepted truths within a cultural group, which distinguishes them further from fiction.

Thus, in literature, myths are used in a variety of ways. Firstly, they may form the structure on which the plot and characters are based. This allows for a rewriting of existing myths to adapt them to contemporary needs. In this case, the fictional events and characters resemble those recounted in certain existing myths, following their course. References to the connection need not be made explicit throughout the fictional narrative; the smallest reference to a mythic event or character is enough to grant them mythic status.

In a similar vein, myths appear as the thread – a recurrent theme – along which the story unravels. They are hidden for a great part of the narrative and surface from time to time to point out the universality of the story, the specificity of what is told, or the parallels between the action and the timelessness of myth. In this case, as opposed to the first point, the fiction need not follow the mythic plot in every detail. Ripeka in Grace's *Mutu-whenua* falls into this category: while portrayed as an individual character in her own right, she is undoubtedly linked to Rona of Maori mythology.

These influences create certain reader expectations that may or may not be fulfilled while the plot as a whole is unique.

Thirdly, the use of myths in literature portrays a diffusion of myth and reality that is particularly common in the Maori literature to be examined here. Myth and reality are shown to be interrelated and inseparable, giving readers the impression of being confronted with a mythical tale despite the obvious realistic setting that gradually interweaves more and more with the mythic component. The equal validity of myth and reality enables their simultaneous existence in an approach "to see [mythic stories'] universality as truthful metaphors and to relate them to our current level of knowledge and experience" (Leeming 2002: 14).

Furthermore, myths may be the starting point of a fictional text that develops its own dynamic, departing from the original myth. In this context new mythical structures may be invented that strongly resemble traditional ones. Missy in Grace's *Cousins*, to illustrate the point, is linked to mythical ancestresses from the beginning, but her story goes beyond the myths to depict her as an important figure in the community and in the future of the Maori people as a whole. Her story does not follow the pattern of her ancestresses' lives other than attributing to her certain key characteristics exhibited by these ancestresses.

In *"Trading Magic for Fact," Fact for Magic*, Colavincenzo (2003) further identifies several points that must be considered in the study of myth in fiction. In addition to what has been mentioned above, he identifies the fictional portrayal of historical figures whose lives are surrounded by myths and legends. We find such characters in Ihimaera's *The Matriarch* in which two historical figures are depicted and surrounded by legendary tales that influence people's view of them. Brief mention of such a character is also made in Ihimaera's *The Rope of Man* (*RM*). He remains, however, a marginal reference instead of a central character in the narrative. If he were among the regular cast of characters, the legends and rumours surrounding him would become "legitimate parts of the history, granting them a truth–value equal to what one might call 'the empirically verifiable historical facts'" (*ibid.* 100). This is the case in *The Matriarch* where he appears more prominently.

In connection with historiographic metafiction, Colavincenzo also includes magic realism in the list of the uses of myths in fiction. Even though our featured writers do not rewrite history in their novels, they – like the authors of Canadian historiographic metafiction as analysed by Colavincenzo – may include supernatural and surreal elements in the narrative. While the magic realism of Canadian works such as Thomas King's *Green Grass, Running Water* (1993) opposes historical discourse, the seemingly supernatural occurrences as described in *Potiki*, for instance, oppose the *Pakeha* worldview. This coincides with Colavincenzo's final point that the fiction attempts to "push the ordinary towards the extra-ordinary, or to see the extraordinary in the ordinary" (Colavincenzo 2003: 103), which does not make the fictions myths in and of themselves, but shows signs of mythologisation. The Maori novels, in effect, elevate the ordinary and simultaneously offer an alternative to conventional *Pakeha* notions of existence.

To shed light on these functions of myth, a discussion of certain aspects that influence myth and elucidate its persistence and significance within Maori literature follows. By identifying four key aspects – continuity, variation, hybridity and identity – this allows us to trace the functions of myth in indigenous fiction while offering insight into the construction of myths in Maori novels at the same time.

2.2.1 Continuity and Variation

Kluckhohn (1966: 33–44) characterises myths as workings and reworkings of known stories, the appropriation of existing material to tell the story from generation to generation. Myths are originally orally traded stories that persevered until they were preserved in writing. Given their repeated articulation, myths are not closed narratives but limitlessly flexible and open to modification, expansion and revitalisation. "In other words," then, "all myths presuppose a previous narrative, and in turn form the model for future narratives. [...] Thus myths remake other myths, and there is no reason why they should not continue to do so, the mythopoeic urge being infinite. [...] [T]he notion that we are all of us continually in the making,

and that the certainty and stability of *logos* must always be put into doubt
[...]" (Coupe 1997: 108 –133). Instead of being closed and inflexible narratives, the tradition of myths over the ages is in itself proof of their openness
to modification. Retelling and rewriting occur as stories that are passed on
and myths are particularly prone to change. Each retelling is a step further
away from the original, but it allows for appropriation into other contexts
for new purposes. The past versions form the background before which the
new version is constructed, which in turn allows for yet another version
in the future. No one version is stable or definite, but always in motion,
ever changing.

Roland Barthes offers an alternative to the mythic process when
he speaks of the artificial myth. In *Mythologies*, he states that the way to
debunk a myth is to mythify it in turn by using it as a departure point for
a new myth. Thus an artificial myth is created which then becomes a new
mythology. This way, myths can be robbed of their power – a change of
power relations ensues that is particularly useful in the postcolonial context to destroy and decentralise authority. Given that the featured Maori
writers all use indigenous myths that mean to strengthen instead of subvert
Maori identity, however, the concept of the Barthesian artificial myth does
not apply to them. Instead, the myths that are being written against are
Christian myths in some cases and especially colonial myths, such as the
Noble Savage, which are Western creations demeaning the native peoples
to a lower social standing. In order to free themselves from these colonial
myths, writers juxtapose or even combine them with their own and thereby
create new myths. This attempt is so obviously focused on the significance
of myth that it is unlikely that the intention might be to strip myth of its
power as a whole. Instead, a new myth is deliberately created, the difference
being that it is one containing mainly Maori elements. This has nothing to
do with turning power relations around entirely, but with a fusion of the
familiar and the unfamiliar.

In this fusion the respective myths are continued, though changed from
their original form. Their openness to variation is not to be understood as
a lack of originality, according to Marina Warner: "Every telling of a myth
is a part of that myth; there is no Ur-version, no authentic prototype, no
true account" (Warner 1994: 8). A retelling, then, is just as valuable as the

lost original would be were it possible to trace it. The creative process of telling and retelling, according to Warner, is a mark of every culture's originality and vitality, which is a more positive position than Barthes' need to debunk myth. Like Coupe, she grants the storyteller/writer an active role with "the capacity, as tellers and retellers, interpreters and reinterpreters, to maintain the interaction of myth and history" (Coupe 1997: 189). "Myths," Warner continues, "offer a lens which can be used to see human identity in its social and cultural context – they can lock us up in stock reactions, bigotry and fear, but they're not immutable, and by unpicking them, the stories can lead to others. Myths convey values and expectations which are always evolving, in the process of being formed, but – and this is fortunate – never set so hard they cannot be changed again" (Warner 1994: 14).

The interaction of myth and history is an important one in the postcolonial context. The myths and the way they are used in a certain period allow readers to draw conclusions on the society in question. As the analyses in chapter III will demonstrate, it is possible to distinguish the political and social situation of the time in Maori fictional texts. Whether the novels deal with creation myths, hero myths or others, the tales serve as a reference for collective identity through the verification of a certain worldview and exemplify the way being Maori is perceived and experienced at a certain time in history. The necessary authenticity derives from what Somerville refers to as truth-telling and self-telling that is central to Maori literature and which "is in itself a form of resistance because it unsettles, interrupts, distorts and challenges" (Somerville 2007: 86). Therefore storytelling, particularly the truth-telling she speaks of, cannot help but challenge dominant narratives and unbalance the authority these have had so far. Self-telling in Maori literature, as a consequence, includes indigenous myths and thereby conveys a particular native worldview that is unique and distinguished from standard *Pakeha* convictions. Further, truth-telling in fiction is needed "to make Maori art of integrity," explains poet and playwright Roma Potiki, as quoted in Somerville's article. In order to achieve this Maori art of integrity, she says, "all work must have political self-awareness and the deepest emotional overlay to it. The context must be truthful" (Potiki 1993: 318). Potiki's statement also elucidates Grace's opinion that Maori literature cannot help but be political even if it is not intended to be so (cf. Calleja 2003).

Judging from these remarks, it is inevitable that a Maori text which subscribes to Somerville's demand for truth-telling and self-telling will confront *Pakeha* notions with indigenous concepts. Continuity and temporality within Maori culture, for instance, differ from the Western understanding of time and find their way into fiction in a different way than commonly understood. History is not perceived as the remote past, but as something that effects the present and future in equal measure. This explains the importance of history in fiction and the recurrent use of myths. The human need to ascribe order and causality to the chaos of life leads to the establishing of rituals in all cultures, hence the creation myths and natural myths that explain a people's origin and the laws of the world they live in. Maori believe that time is a spiral, a key symbol that is also found in their art and architecture as the unfurling fern leaf. Given its fundamental significance, it comes as no surprise that even Maori novelists structure some of their work in this form. An important notion in this context is that the spiral prevents "a total rejection of the past" (Webby 1985: 19). Instead, it encourages a revisiting of the past, even makes it essential, and influences the present with the knowledge of the early beginnings. That is why characters are forced to remember or relearn the stories and traditions of their culture in order to be able to begin a new fulfilling life. According to Maori belief, then, there are no endings as such. Each ending is a new beginning, another curl of the spiral, a fern leaf unfolding. The generations are connected from the first to the last and this is their way of keeping the memory of their ancestors alive.

For Maori, life is "walking backwards into the future" (Ihimaera 1998a: 200), which expresses their understanding of time that is also evident in their language. The Maori words for the past are *nga ra o mua*, the days in front; the future is *kei muri*, the time behind. Following this principle, their faces are turned back towards their ancestors as they step forward into the unknown future, honouring those who have gone before them. It is also an idea that furthers the novelists' determination to keep alive the memory of all things Maori. The characters who succeed in combining the traditional and the new, often diametrically opposed lifestyles are the ones who have had to struggle to hold on to the customs of their people. Thus the only way to live without harm to oneself is to remember the past while going into the future. The new beginning becomes a part of the spiral, different from all previous beginnings, and yet connected to the past.

Like the Maori concept of time, myths are said to have a circular or spiral pattern in themselves, hinting at a continuity of subject matter and a recurrence of events in similar forms. In *Fables of Identity*, for instance, Northrop Frye distinguishes four phases of myth which together form a cycle (Frye 1963: 16). The birth phase contains myths of creation, birth of the hero, resurrection, the defeat of darkness and its death. The second is the triumph phase of entering paradise or sacred marriage which gives way to the death phase. Here we have myths of the fall, sacrifice and death as well as the isolation of the hero. The final phase consists of myths of defeat and the return of chaos before the renewed defeat of the dark powers after which the cycle begins anew. So the idea of time as a cycle or spiral is not new or particular to one culture alone.

According to Mircea Eliade, and in correspondence with Maori belief, "'Myth' is, then, synonymous with 'eternal return', with the desire to be at one with a cosmic beginning in 'a continual present', an eternal now" (Coupe 1997: 60). In the context of Maori culture, however, it would also be fitting to say that it is a desire to be at one with a cosmic beginning in a continual *past* that becomes an eternal now. This continuity reflects an imitation of eternity.

Though myths may be given the same chronology that we perceive in the structure of our lives, they hint at a greater pattern that rules over all and determines the nature of things in the present. The never-ending spiral in Maori tradition enables the survival of cultural memory, turning life into a timeless spiral in which all events are part of the here and now. In Ihimaera's *Tangi* and *The Rope of Man* we see this when Tama's parents are simultaneously depicted as the mythic First Parents of the creation myth. Grace, too, includes characters in *Potiki* who are more than just figures of the present: there is the boy prophet, a combination of Maui and Christ, and his virginal mother Mary. The novels combine characters of the now and then, and they also bring together the different lives of the past and the present. What remains after all these elements have been joined is this essence that is carried through time in myths and finds expression in these fictional worlds.

To give the impression of causality, myths need to imply completion. However, if they were completed narratives, there would be no spiral reaching into the present and they would merely serve to explain the past. The selected novels build part of their story on existing Maori myths. They are then linked to events and problems of the present, offering solutions and establishing a link to the early beginnings of this native culture. The old and the new, the traditions of the past and the difficulties of the present are all connected in an attempt to uphold the culture according to its conventions. This includes, most of all, the telling and retelling of myths through the generations, first through oral storytelling and other traditional arts and, increasingly, through writing.

Language as a Reflection of Change
An element that influences the continuation and variation of myths especially in writing is the choice of language. Particularly the English language as the preferred medium in Maori literature is under scrutiny by critics when the writing encourages a return to or a stronger focus on Maori culture. English is the language the majority of New Zealanders, including Maori, speaks and distribution is best possible in this language. Criticism against the use of English appears unfounded if we compare it to similar criticism in other former colonies where English is also one of the official languages. English is as much the Maori people's language today as *te reo* and it is certainly the more commonly used one in everyday situations, but this does not and should not prevent them from giving English a distinct Maori quality. According to Keri Hulme, "a combination of ignorance of the language, and lack of publishing resources, has brought about this current school of Maori writers in English. Writers of double beginning, inhabiting both *Te Ao Maori* [the Maori world] and *Te Ao Pakeha* [the *Pakeha* world], but writing for *Te Ao Hou* [the new world]" (Hulme 1981: 296). Therefore, this new world requires a new use of language.

African writer Chinua Achebe's challenging words – "And let no one be fooled by the fact that we may write in English for we intend to do unheard of things with it" (Achebe 1975b: 7) – ring true for Maori writers as well. By making the language their own, they infuse the dominant tongue with a foreign vocabulary and ideas that are able to represent their worldview to a much greater extent than mere translation. English also appears to offer greater possibilities because it is not bound by the same rules as the Maori tongue. In an interview with Feroza Jussawalla and Reed Way Dazenbrock, Ihimaera addresses the freedom he has when writing in English: "It is profane enough to do whatever I want with it. But Maori, you cannot do whatever you want with it. It is a tapu language. It is the language of the people, it is a sacred language" (Jussawalla 1992, quoted in Skinner 1998: 235). This allows writers like him to do the "unheard of things" Achebe refers to. While central terms of the culture are retained in their original Maori form, the main text is given in the profane language, which is gradually expanded due to indigenous influence.

To Achebe, the language is part of the psyche and must be fashioned in a way as to reflect this. It is not the individual who must change, but the language, the medium of communication. "The price a world language must be prepared to pay," says Achebe with reference to African writing in 1962,

> is submission to many different kinds of use. The African writer should aim to use English in a way that brings out his message best without altering the language to the extent that its value as a medium of international exchange will be lost. He should aim at fashioning out an English which is at once universal and able to carry his peculiar experience. I have in mind here the writer who has something new, something different to say. The nondescript writer has little to tell us, anyway, so he might as well tell it in conventional language and get it over with. (Achebe 1975a: 61)

Again, the African writer's situation reflects the Maori writer's circumstances. "The nondescript writer" is of no consequence, but the writer who has something to say and wants to be heard, must write in a new English to do it well and appropriately. In other words, English needs to be nativised and accultured.

However, the indigenous writer who uses the language of the former coloniser faces problems on different levels. The differences between Maori and English go hand in hand with untranslatable nuances that are difficult to impart in writing. The Maori writer is, then, exposed to two traditions he needs to reconcile within one language. Any innovations remove the "new" English from the "original" and the writer has created a variation of the coloniser's language. At the same time, they have claimed English as their own more than it was before when it was merely an official language Maori had no relation to other than it having been forced on them.

The controversial and challenging function of the "new" English works against the dominant language that – until used, changed and absorbed into another context – will always remain foreign and non-native.

I would like to quote the Indian philosopher Raja Rao and his defence of English as a language that also belongs to the people of his country. "Truth," he says,

> can use any language, and the more universal, the better it is. [...] And as long as the English language is universal it will always remain Indian. [...] It would then be correct to say as long as we are Indian – that is, not nationalists, but truly Indians of the Indian psyche – we shall have the English language with us and amongst us, and not as a guest or friend, but as one of our own, of our caste, our creed, our sect and our tradition. (Rao 1978, "The Caste of English," quoted in: Kachru 1995: 294)

For the Maori people the situation is the same; English as a universal language is part of the Maori psyche and cannot be condemned. The situation differs slightly from the Indian case, however, since the majority of Indians speak their own native tongues while English is restricted mainly to an elite. In New Zealand, Maori speak English while only a small percentage is fluent in the native tongue. This appears as a reversal of the situation in India, but the circumstances are different and still show a remarkable applicability to the Maori situation.

All told, English has long been part of Aotearoa New Zealand, but it is in fiction that this predominance of English is eyed rather critically due to the Maori issues writers often engage in. Still, the justification of English as the primary – though not exclusive – language of Maori fiction holds. In "Language and Spirit", Rao speaks of his engagement in English from the point of view of the writer. "The telling has not been easy," he explains.

> One has to convey in a language that is not one's own the spirit that is one's own. One has to convey the various shades and omissions of a certain thought-movement that looks maltreated in an alien language. I use the word "alien," yet English is not really an alien language to us. It is the language of our intellectual make-up [...] but not of our emotional make-up. We are all instinctively bilingual, many of us writing in our own language and in English. We cannot write like the English. We should not. We cannot write only as Indians. We have grown to look at the large world as part of us. Our method of expression therefore has to be a dialect which will some day prove to be as distinctive and colorful as the Irish or the American. Time alone will justify it. (Rao 1978: 296)

Here, Rao distinguishes between the psychological and the intellectual levels involved in the personal use of language. The discrepancy between intellectual and emotional make-up requires and prompts the creation of what Rao calls a dialect whose development is inevitable if one should neither write like the English nor exclusively as a native.

In fact, Rao's dialect resembles what Chantal Zabus terms the "third code" (Zabus 1995). In the light of Homi Bhabha's understanding of hybridity and the third space, this term appropriately describes the process that languages undergo when they meet in the same text or, on a more general level, in the same place, geographic or other. It is a commonplace in Maori literature in English that the main body of the text is interspersed with indigenous terms. This happens when objects of importance such as the *marae*, the meeting place, are mentioned or if particularly significant Maori concepts such as *aroha* come into play. These terms indicate meaning that goes beyond what is understood by the English translation. In this case, Maori writers use the English language, but create a new version, a new dialect, as Rao would call it, or a third code according to Zabus.

Still, the use of indigenous terms is not enough for the appropriation of another tongue as one's own. It is, nonetheless, the first step towards articulating Maori identity. The English language becomes a tool to undermine Western dominance and it proves, at the same time, to be an insufficient tool to represent native culture and Maori experience accurately in all its richness. Appropriating the English tongue for this purpose is empowering despite criticism that its use marks a move away from Maori culture and towards inauthenticity. The metonymic gap that develops when Maori words or even whole passages are inserted into English further undermines the hitherto dominant voice of the *Pakeha* and Western culture in general. On the one hand, Maori writers thereby manage to introduce their own culture to others in English, the better-known language that allows for a wider distribution of their texts. On the other, they also prove the inadequacy of this dominant language that refuses access to precisely that Maori experience that is the greatest point of difference between cultures and must inevitably always remain undisclosed because it cannot be translated. The English language thus reflects the struggle Maori experience in New Zealand society.

The telling of stories goes beyond the literary and enters a new realm at this stage, making any Maori fiction in English inevitably political. The dominant tongue is challenged and altered to accommodate the alien land onto which it was forced and this relexification process creates a third code that emerges from the power struggle between two languages of which one is dominant. "Relexification," i.e. the use of English words with indigenous structure and rhythms as Zabus summarises,

> takes place [...] between two languages within the same text. Although these two languages are unrelated, they interact as dominant vs. dominated languages or elaborated vs. restricted codes [...]. [...] As a rule, there is a higher incidence of relexifying devices as the work comes closer to orality. This should come as no surprise since such texts are relexified from languages that have remained essentially oral and belong to the vast corpus of oral human discourse, for most languages spoken by humans over the millennia have no connection with writing (Zabus 1995: 318).

The emerging third code, then, contains elements of oral narration, lending itself perfectly to retellings of myth. It also indicates why Maori fiction in English has always had a strong oral quality to it. The Maori language has a long and enduring oral tradition in which speechmaking and storytelling play an essential part that is included in writing as another reminder of Maori culture. As English is suffused with indigenous expressions, the third code is consequently marked by an oral quality as well. Since Maori oratory is regarded as an art with strict rules, the oral quality of texts is not always characterised by the colloquial looseness and openness one would expect. Instead, the narrative is marked by a certain density and urgency that seems to not only result from traditional patterns, but also from the need to express oneself in a dying – but simultaneously very much alive – native tongue. Often, it is the insertion of *te reo* in traditional songs or dialogue that gives life to the narrative as well as a sense of authenticity. Producing a distinct Maori quality, English as the main language of the narrative loses its significance.

This use of language(s) exemplifies the hybridity of the emerging new culture that develops from the interaction of the dominating and the dominated. The third code is just one aspect of the third space that Maori culture has become as it struggles to find its place in-between two different and, in some aspects, contradicting cultures. Hybridity is the only possible result in such a conflict because "[c]ultural identity always emerges in this contradictory and ambivalent space, which for Bhabha makes the claim to a hierarchical 'purity' of cultures untenable" (Ashcroft *et. al.* 1998: 118). The impossibility of "purity" is also based on the continual change within all aspects of culture that do not allow for a going back to some distant original state whose existence is merely assumed. Thus, a purity of myth is equally impossible.

2.2.2 Hybridity in a Transcultural Society

Homi K. Bhabha understands culture as a dynamic and changing force that takes effect when two cultural groups meet (Bhabha 1994: 34), as is the case in New Zealand. When the two collide, a third legitimate hybrid culture develops, which combines elements of both separate groups. In the clash between *Pakeha* and Maori, the indigenous people are not assimilated, but choose which customs to adopt and perhaps even invest with new meaning. This is common practice in Maori literature in English and can be seen in the treatment of religion, myths and the use of language. The struggle to live between two wholly different cultures and not solely in one alone requires change. The individual is then faced with the problem of adapting, rejecting and developing an identity that allows them to live between the two. However, Bhabha points out that the frame conditions within which subjects make these changes remain intact.[8] This would partly explain the criticism Maori writers face as to their writing within a colonial framework without being able to escape it. Ihimaera has been accused of writing for and about Maori with the

---

8   Cf. Monika Fludernik: "Bhabha's hybridity sketches the subversive character of alterity within identity, the way in which hybrid subjects are enabled to manipulate features of one identity frame for the purpose of refunctionalization in another, but he also clearly demonstrated that such manipulation can only reach so far and that ultimately no destruction of the frame conditions is possible." In: "Introduction: The Diasporic Imaginary. Postcolonial Reconfigurations in the Context of Multiculturalism," xxiii.

help of Western literary conventions which even particular Maori features cannot fully make up for. Gareth Griffith (1994) and Jenny Sharpe (1989) both agree that those who speak against the colonial framework inevitably situate themselves within it at the same time. It is a necessary position they must take to be heard. The answer to this predicament, according to Bhabha's understanding of hybridity, is that the frame cannot be destroyed when two or more cultures collide, but elements of each can be appropriated to create something new: the third space.

Therefore, Maori literature itself is a third space. It is the site on which two cultures come together and something new emerges. Literature can indeed be viewed as a ground on which changes take place. It is an experimental, hypothetical playground, true – but it is also the space in which the new can begin and encourage change in the everyday world. Fiction offers insights and possible solutions to the problems in society that the novels choose as their starting point. What is more, reality is the catalyst that makes these fictions possible in the first place. The real battles are fought in the country, the cities, the rural areas, but also on a fictional plain. Similarly, Somerville concludes that, "[t]hus, at the same time that 'reality' has become a part of Maori writing, the writing has become a part of the scope of Maori 'reality'" (Somerville 1997: 79). This, she says, is due to the urge and obligation of "truth-telling" in their fiction that refuses to silence the Maori voice: "[...] Maori writers are writing into/against images of Maori – created by both non-Maori and Maori – that have been unhealthy/unfair/untrue" (Somerville 2007: 98). Each of the novels featured in our discussion is a third space and a space of resistance that you can hold in your hands and flick through, a tangible site of cultural change and growth.

Perhaps the clearest point that justifies Maori literature in English as a third space is the way it combines Western literary practices with Maori elements of storytelling. By choosing the novel as a literary form, writers have already taken the first step into the third space. The novel as a Western genre forms the skeleton upon which Maori literature in English is built. If this literature is a mimetic, though fictional representation of Maori life as it is, then the fiction may legitimately be called a third space in miniature.

So not only does the modern Maori occupy a third space in society, but indigenous literature developed by Maori occupies a third space among world literature in the same way as new literary traditions emerge from hitherto prevailing forms.

It is at this moment of conflict between cultures that the struggle for renewed and meaningful identity begins. The right to write for another cultural group than one's own has not yet been resolved in this context. Complicated not only by the hybrid nature of texts, but especially by the hybrid nature of those who speak or write for a particular cultural group, further complications of identification arise. An author's origin is bound to have some influence on their writing even when he or she chooses a Western medium.

Yet this writing process is an example of the hybrid culture Bhabha refers to, where select customs of both cultures are compounded into a third culture that ascribes new meaning to the chosen elements. This process of restructuring and combining has been particularly evident in Maori literature since the 1970s, describing the difficulties of living between two cultures. The problems that arise from the shifting between cultures are, for instance, a central issue in Ihimaera's *Tangi* and the recent *The Rope of Man* where the protagonist does not embrace one culture alone, thereby denying an absolute sense of belonging until a hybrid state is reached.

In this context of hybridity, Keri Hulme's case illustrates the important questions of who can write for a minority. Her fiercest critic C. K. Stead denied her any right to speak as a Maori based on her *Pakeha* background and literary conventions. Margery Fee (1989) devotes a detailed essay to Stead's criticism, examining what his assessment of Hulme's novel reveals about the situation of minority literature at the time of publication and the difficulties developing because of hybridity.

Both novel and writer have become hybrid and require a new kind of criticism. The problem of hybridity is that it is constantly moving and shifting, adapting and re-evaluating. In her article, Fee suggests that the minority's acceptance of the writer is a valid factor in determining who can write as Maori. She quotes Native American writer Geary Hobson, who determines four factors that should prove helpful in this discussion.

I have modified the points to suit minorities in general: the factors that must all be considered equally when arguing who may speak as *other* are (a) the minority judgement, (b) the neighbouring majority's judgement, (c) the government's judgement, and (d) the individual's judgement. So blood, background, and the individual's chosen way of life jointly determine membership, though none of these is exclusive. According to Hobson, then, Hulme, Ihimaera and Grace are all Maori writers allowed to write as "other" despite Hulme's mixed heritage and the fact that both Ihimaera and Grace speak English, not Maori, as their first language. This proves that the concept of authenticity is anything but clear. Therefore, the complex nature of hybrid texts requires analysis from multiple angles to determine authenticity, as Hobson indicates.

According to Stead, it is not the Maori writer's task to make changes, challenge *Pakeha* conventions or even use them. He interprets the hybrid nature of their texts as failed attempts to convey their life as exclusively *other* without foreign influence. Yet that is not what Maori writers are doing: though the emphasis is on Maori life, there is a connection between minority and majority that is often wanted and encouraged in various degrees. A complete removal of oneself from a Western framework is impossible and unwanted in indigenous writing. If we take into account that understanding a foreign culture always coincides with an involuntary reduction of said culture to match our own familiar frameworks (cf. Sommer 2001: 28), then remaining within a primarily Western framework in Maori fiction is justified as a means of furthering cultural understanding. The Western framework that critics perceive within Maori fiction could be a common ground for understanding, as are the use of English by Maori writers and the references to the Western literary canon.

Subsequently, there are no either/or positions, only blends with individual emphases. Communication between cultural minority and majority is unavoidable and offers a means to strengthen the minority position as long as the majority voice, when speaking for the minority, allows it to speak for itself. Hybridity and the third space are the steps into a future of minority empowerment and an emergence into a wider space with less racial and cultural restrictions in real life and literature alike.

The Textual Dimension

To understand how narrative can influence the strengthening of a culture, it is necessary to look into the textual dimension, beginning with an introduction to Maori writing and history. Generally, tribal stories and occurrences within the community are preserved in tribal histories as it was done before the *Pakeha*'s arrival. Another way to record history existed before the coming of the white settlers and is still used today: the crafting of carvings, tattoos, weaving and paintings, which are elaborated further by oral narration. After writing became available to Maori with colonisation, they were additionally able to record their histories as written texts. The stories of a tribe, however, are *tapu*, sacred and inaccessible to outsiders. The tribal historians keep records and since they are *tapu*, they are not available for research for the most part. Therefore, there is knowledge that remains undisclosed and forms a restricted cultural tribal element. "In the Maori cultural world there are ways to preserve the past other than academic publication," Angela Ballara explains.

> In both [nineteenth and twentieth] centuries there have been tribal historians working away privately or for such institutions as the Komiti o Tupai of the Tanuiarangi Committee, writing down accounts of tribal history, writing and preserving whakapapa books, and serving as repositories of taonga for their people. Their work is often neither published nor known outside their kin group. The fact that the majority of Maori historians do not publish their work should tell us something about Maori cultural attitudes to the sharing of tapu information. Those working from inside a culture, or way of life and system of thought and belief, are bound by its rules. (Ballara 1993: 17)

Maori spirituality – including the myths that are a part of it – is *tapu* and not usually accessible to the uninitiated. Yet, the myths that are known to us are rich and powerful and their importance for Maori spirituality is undeniable. These stories have been made available to an unrestricted readership in collections, scholarly articles, and creative writing.

From a linguistic point of view, oral and written texts have to meet seven standards of textuality (cf. de Beaugrande and Dressler 1981) that, consequently, apply to myths as well: cohesion and coherence, intentionality, acceptability, informativity, situationality and intertextuality. While cohesion and coherence are text-centred, the remaining points are user-centred (speaker/writer – listener/reader). The text's delivery must be efficient, effective and appropriate for communication to succeed. The particularities of Maori oral narration are applicable to written texts as well and, unlike Ruth Brown, I do not agree that "[o]nce Maori oral narratives are on record they are fixed, no longer a dynamic tradition taking on new meanings in new contexts" (Brown 1989: 257). She disregards the fact that meaning may change depending on the individual readers who approach the text from their own perspective, bringing their own experiences and knowledge into the communication between themselves and the narrative. This way, every new reader creates a new context, thereby proving the written text to be dynamic instead of rigid and fixed. What is more, Maori fiction contains a variety of oral elements, proving that even written texts are subject to change and variation, particularly due to the flexibility and openness to interpretation that is commonly attributed to oral narration. These changes and variations take place between texts and also within individual texts. To take an example, different authors may use the same myth in different ways and thus make use of the narrative's flexibility while a myth may also be rewritten and reworked repeatedly within a single text. Ihimaera and Grace each have a preference for certain myths that enter their fiction: Ihimaera's references to Rangi and Papa as well as Grace's use of the myth of Rona have already been mentioned (cf. Alley 1992c).

The fiction is often characterised by an oral quality that derives from Maori oral storytelling traditions and the custom of the highly regarded formal and spontaneous oratory that is based on ancient form and the classical Maori language no longer spoken in everyday situations. Therefore typical textual elements such as substitution, ellipsis, conjunction, reference, and repetition appear in written as well as oral texts. Orality is dynamic, impromptu and tentative with the flexibility to adjust to new contexts, and it is often characterised by rhythm, brief silences, pauses, hesitation and repetition. This contrasts with the rigidity traditionally attributed to written texts. When oral features enter the written text as they do in Maori literature, these narratives become an extension of the oral text because of the additional possibilities the written medium allows. In fiction, particularly passages expressing a strong connection to the Maori homeland, the family, tribe and ancestors are often characterised by a strong rhythm and repetition of important sentences and phrases, proverbs and retellings of myths. Also the inclusion of Maori sentences or songs and whole paragraphs in the native tongue add to the oral quality. This may be due to the fact that Maori culture was primarily an oral one that required no writing until the coming of the *Pakeha*. The language is characterised by its strong rhythm in everyday speech and in songs and chants. Even without hearing the speaker or performer, the rhythmic oral quality easily comes through in the text.

When describing features of oral style in Maori narrative, Agathe Thornton mentions that, in her opinion, myths are still reminiscent of "the ancient oral mode of story-telling" even though they have been fixed in writing at this point (1985: 149). Generally, she says, the narrative is "swift and terse", slowed by characteristic repetition (*ibid.*). This repetition appears to be used in order to create a certain effect on the listeners (or readers): storytelling is a performance that is intent on drawing in the audience, which is supported by the ritual of repetition. The recurrence of certain phrases or words gives the tale and the telling a ritual character that affects the listeners and captures their attention. Perhaps surprisingly, Thornton explains that there are stories such as the tale of Kupe that rely solely on the telling and not a supporting performance, meaning "that the whole effect of the story rested on the sound of the voice" (Thornton 1985: 155). This is comparable to the written story that depends on the narrator's voice and cannot include performance as such. Thus, both a performance as well as a written story involves the listener in similar ways. Augustine Okereke, however, does not share this opinion, as we will see.

Before moving on to a comparison with performance, nevertheless, it is important to note the characteristics of Maori narrative that Thornton describes. As mentioned earlier, texts are thought to be chronological and yet a common feature of many of the novels is the move away from chronology and the appropriation of a spiral structure. A similar method of a layering and repeating of memories is used in Ihimaera's *Tangi* and indicates that there is a particular type of chronology employed by some Maori writers that goes back to an ancient oral storytelling practice that Thornton, however, believes "is not how a modern writer would tell the story" (*ibid.*:

156) because they would be too strongly influenced by European thinking (*ibid.* 171). Yet, contrary to her opinion, writers like Ihimaera do abandon the straightforward chronological method and revert to or approach an ancient mode that can have a number of purposes.

On the one hand, a reason for this preference may be a return to Maori origins that includes the renewed use of oral storytelling practices that might have been abandoned over the years. On the other, such practices can be used as an open turning away from methods spread by other cultures. Two more reasons can be distinguished here: firstly, the story is presented as a whole, so to speak – beginning and resolution are given at the start so that the tension and curiosity as to how the end comes about is only gradually revealed and "can be savoured at leisure" (*ibid.*: 158); secondly, the method is employed to satisfy the audience and inform them of the story's important points as a means of informing the listeners – there is a question and there is an answer. There may be repetitions of the question as a reminder of the original point of the story that prompted the telling or to assert the chronology of events if an event that has to be explained first precedes the question. Once the introduction has been delivered, the question may be repeated before the rest of the story is told. A point that is not mentioned here, but which comes to mind, is that placing the end at the beginning represents the traditional belief in the interrelationship and wholeness of all things. Thus the ending is inherent in the beginning and *vice versa*. On the whole, Thornton's article emphasises the practical side of Maori oral storytelling: a storyteller gives the information when it is needed, the tale is mostly sequential, the oral style is paratactic and consists of a chain of statements. As we shall see at a later point, writing is both different and similar to these traditional oral storytelling methods.

In her conclusion, Thornton emphasises the connection between oral storyteller and audience, implying that it must differ from writer and reader. She does not explicitly exclude writers in her article, but she mainly refers to the oral storyteller in the course of her analysis. What is more, she discusses performances and tales that were obviously performed at an earlier stage. Since such a storyteller enhances a tale by reacting to the audience, the appositional style that Thornton includes as a characteristic of Maori narrative is a direct result of the interaction with the audience (*ibid*.: 173–4). Inevitably, such contact is impossible with the readership for the most part as the writer may only guess the reader's reaction.

In a similar context, in her essay on performance and text, Okereke insists that "[o]ral literature is by definition dependent on a performer who formulates it in words on a specific occasion – there is no other way in which it can be realized as a literary product" (Okereke 1998). Even though her essay deals with the recording of oral performance in writing and is therefore a highly specific analysis, some of the introduced ideas are applicable to the more general study of differences between oral and written media. She correctly points out that a performance can never be recreated in writing to have the same effect on a reader as it had on a listener. In more general terms, nonetheless, looking at Maori novels and their oral features – thus in literature only – this requires modification. It is true that oral literature depends on a performer who speaks with regard to the situation, the audience, the emotional state and other factors that influence the performance. In writing, however, this is also possible. Writers have a target readership, so their writing suits this particular group. Especially Maori literature has a specific and comparatively small readership that makes it possible for writers to anticipate reaction and expectations. In their work, writers will know which issues are on the reader's mind and will be able to direct and influence them in similar ways as a speaker would direct the audience. Admittedly, there is a greater distance and a sense of indirectness between writer and reader as opposed to speaker and listener, but if one looks at the most powerful passages in Maori novels, they are just as strong as speech and can resonate within the reader.

Okereke calls writing "a printed text, devoid of life" (*ibid*.: 44) when, in fact, she is referring only to the text which records a performance and acts as a copy. An original text, however, can be equally as powerful as oral performance. Even though Okereke is clearly in favour of the oral arts, one must admit that storytelling is a cultural event as well as art, be it oral or written. In her analysis of performance versus the written record, Okereke insists that

> [t]he tale exists only in its performance; what this implies is that everything that causes the tale to come into being must be taken into account in its analysis and

understanding. Therefore, the actions of the narrator, the narrative process, the medium of narration, the audience (its constitution, action, and reaction), the moment of narration, the place of narration (including its social and cultural significance) all come into play in determining the nature of a tale. (*ibid.:* 40)

All these points apply to the printed original text as well. The tale exists in the telling, spoken or written. The narrative process, its medium, the writer's stylistic peculiarities, the readership and its constitution and expected reactions, the time of publication, the fictional setting as well as the place of publication and distribution are equivalents that characterise the story and are too similar to Okereke's points to allow for such a strong distinction between oral and written text. Even the impossibility of retelling the same story in the same way is not the sole prerogative of oral storytelling: most notably, in Ihimaera's *Tangi* the crucial passages mythifying Tama's parents appear in several variations throughout the story, linking them to the First Parents. It is only the well-known beginning of the myth that remains unchanged towards the beginning and end of the novel, embracing the story much like Rangi and Papa embraced each other. The story that unfolds between their bodies, is the story of Tama's existence in spiritual darkness and the gradual recovery of his *maoritanga*. Like the bodies of mother and father, the passage holds the narrative together:

> My mother was the Earth.
>
> My father was the Sky.
>
> They were Rangitane and Papatuanuku, the first parents, who clasped each other so tightly that there was no day. Their children were born into darkness. They lived among the shadows of their mother's breasts and thighs and groped in blindness among the long black strands of her hair.
>
> Until the time of separation and the dawning of the first day. (*T* 26 and 204)

Flanking the text this way, Ihimaera uses the space in-between to write and rewrite myth, experience, and a return to Maori customs. In this context, the textual body itself within the repeated use of the myth is a visible third space in which transformations orchestrated by the author take place. Imitating the development Bhabha identified between cultures, a space that is not visible as such, the novelist makes the process visible on the page. Inevitably, the means by which such a process is depicted in writing must rely on narrative techniques. Therefore, as in oral storytelling, there are in writing "the performer or narrator, the mode of transmission (language and technicalities), and the audience" (Okereke 1998: 42).

Evidently, this combination of written and spoken media and their techniques is not only characteristic of Maori writing, but also of the development towards hybridity on the whole. Hybridity itself is not fixed but open and varied. Bhabha insists that colonialism produces hybridisation which then leads to an undermining of colonial authority itself because the *other*, though denied authority, has the power to transform. Colonialism enables resistance in the first place by encouraging mimicry, which makes the colonised subject "not quite/not white" (Young 1995: 147): "If it is in some sense reassuring for the colonizers," writes Bhabha with regard to India's colonisation,

> that Indians become in certain respects "English", the production of mimic English-men also becomes disturbing, for "mimicry is at once resemblance and menace". The mimic man, insofar as he is not entirely like the colonizer, white but not quite, consti-tutes only a partial representation of him: far from being reassured, the colonizer sees a grotesquely displaced image of himself. Thus the familiar, transported to distant parts, becomes uncannily transformed, the imitation subverts the identity of that which is being represented, and the relation of power, if not altogether reversed, certainly begins to vacillate ... The surveilling eye is suddenly confronted with a returning gaze of otherness and finds that its mastery, its sameness, is undone. [...] Mimicry at once enables power and produces the loss of agency. (Bhabha 1984: 127)

This might be what some critics of Maori fiction forget: the often-criticised Maori writing within a Western frame is positive because it is resistance and should not be viewed as compliance or assimilation. What Maori writers do is more than just mimic existing Western texts: by creating hybrid forms and a hybrid style with the help of both Western and Maori resources, they resist more actively than mimicry would allow. This is evident in Bhabha's definition of hybridity as "[...] a *problematic* of colonial representation [...] that reverses the effects of the colonialist disavowal, so that other 'denied' knowledges enter upon the dominant discourse and estrange the basis of its authority" (Bhabha 1985: 156). Consequently, whenever two or more cultures collide, there will be change, fusion, and the emergence of something new that challenges the authority of existing texts.

Robert Young agrees with Bakhtin that in a hybrid text, an utterance contains more than one "language" and therefore carries yet another dimension within it. He quotes Bakhtin who explains that,

> [w]hat we are calling a hybrid construction is an utterance that belongs, by its grammatical [syntactic] and compositional markers, to a single speaker, but that actually contains mixed within it two utterances, two speech manners, two styles, two "languages", two semantic and axiological belief systems. [...] It frequently happens that even one and the same word will belong simultaneously to two languages, two belief systems that intersect in a hybrid construction – and consequently, the word has two contradictory meanings, two accents. (Young 1995: 20–1, from Bakhtin 1981)

Maori myths and particularly the vocabulary and grammar have this doubling effect in literature that adds an underlying second language and belief system to the English surface layer. Myths, untranslated native terms and unusual syntax in English subvert the Western literary frame. Maori writers are aware of the power this hybrid approach has and can use it in a subtle manner that allows the underlying layer to come through regularly in their syntax, choice of words and topic. Others may emphasise the hidden "language" in ways similar to Grace's approach in *Potiki* that goes beyond mere relexification and the creation of a third code, whose ending is entirely in Maori, leaving the non-Maori reader frustrated.

This textual dimension of hybridity is further complicated by translations from Maori into English. Myths are hybrid constructs due to their constant retelling, but also because of their transfer into another language. English lacks the vocabulary to adequately convey nuances inherent in the original Maori telling of stories due to the extent of allusions and metaphors and concepts foreign to another culture. In Maori fiction in English, then, there are lacunae which may remain undetected by non-Maori speakers. To make up for these absences, new words appropriated from English or created in Maori emerge to fill the spaces and possibly even expand the original thought. If this does not happen, the lacunae remain. In both cases, however, it becomes clear that there is a language problem that can only be bridged to a certain extent. A fully accurate translation is impossible between the two cultures, given that language develops only to describe what is known in a given culture, but not necessarily in another.

Consequently, the fusing and contesting that Young speaks of with regard to Bakhtin's organic and intentional hybridity[9] is contained in myths themselves and the language(s) in which they are told. Since translations of Maori myths into English were encouraged by ethnologists in the Colonial era, it is quite likely that many of the collected myths of the time were mis-translated or manipulated, knowingly or unknowingly, in the early stages. Like classical songs in Maori, according to the McLintock's *Encylopedia of New Zealand*, myths

> [...] have been recorded in a number of books, with variations in the words from one book to another. This was inevitable, because they would go from lip to lip among the people throughout the land; on reaching some tribes a word or a name would be varied; and, because of the long period during which the circulation went on, some words were dropped or some were added. With a European as recorder, or a Maori not sufficiently literate, some of the words were wrongly spelt. (McLintock 2006c)

As mentioned previously, the myths we know today are bound to be different from the originals, and especially the English versions will differ from the Maori ones. In Maori fiction in English, this confronts us with hybrid texts pervaded by Maori and English cultural elements. There is a double complication in the oral and written traditions as they progress through time and the difficulties of translation from one language into that of another culture. The fusing and contesting that takes place within myths or any other literary text are examples of the hybrid nature of New Zealand cultures and their languages.

---

9   Cf. Robert Young, *Colonial Desire*, 22: Bakhtin distinguishes between two kinds of hybridity: the organic that fuses, and the intentional that contests. "Hybridity there-fore, as in the racial model, involves an antithetical movement of coalescence and antagonism, which the unconscious set against the intentional, the organic against the divisive, the generative against the undermining. Hybridity is itself an example of hybridity, of a doubleness that both brings together, fuses, but also maintains separation."

Intertextuality as Transformative Practice

It is therefore clear that narratives are influenced by other narratives. In this context, intertextuality is a two-fold theory that is concerned with texts and can also go further into culture and politics. Apart from establishing certain relationships between texts, intertextuality may also have a political function, as Mai observes in his article "Bypassing Intertextuality": "In [Kristeva's] eyes it is a *politically transformative practice*. In the last resort, hers is a political concept which aims at empowering the reader/critic to oppose the literary and social tradition at large" (Mai 1991: 41). Incidentally, Maori novels are intertextual in both ways by relying heavily on other texts and by encouraging a change in society at the same time. The texts that enrich these novels are oral stories of the Maori tradition and written texts from the Western canon, but also from within New Zealand itself. For instance, *the bone people* incorporates several works of the Western canon such as *Robinson Crusoe* and *Ulysses*, and it also uses and inverts the almost Jungian archetype of the New Zealand *Man Alone* myth pervading much of its literature since the 1930s.

In this context of relationships between texts, Frank Schulze-Engler clarifies that,

> [o]ne of the most basic assumptions of "intransigent" intertextualism is that individual literary texts form part of a universe of texts that is – implicitly or explicitly – regarded as a cultural continuum, since texts are always in dialogue with other texts which they seek to re-write, re-model, or replace. [...] As Manfred Pfister has quite rightly pointed out, the only "texts" and "pre-texts" allowed in this literary universe are poetic texts themselves – and, of course, not just any poetic texts, but preferably those belonging to a "Great Tradition" that has produced the "Western Canon". (Schulze-Engler 1998: 6)

Readers and writers are able to recognise and use these texts although a connection need not be discernible. Nonetheless, given the need for political change felt by Maori that brought about the urgent publication of novels in the 1970s and 1980s, the links tend to be easily recognisable in heavily intertextual novels so as to keep the purpose in the reader's mind at all times. Coming from the "Great Tradition" of poetic texts, Maori novels are based on the Western form, but their hybrid content removes them from that tradition at the same time. While the Western frame remains, the text is multicultural, hybrid, *other*. The texts are still "a mosaic of quotations" (Kristeva 1980: 66), but now the quotations are no longer exclusively derived from the "Great Tradition" alone and are from another great Maori tradition that challenges the dominating canon. The "politically transformative practice" of intertextuality therefore operates in this third space of Maori literature in English.

It is possible to transform and to challenge because the distinction between coloniser and colonised is inevitable and the one cannot exist without the other. As Bhabha insists, colonialism's othering process inexorably brings forth that which will oppose it. When discussing Anglo-colonial literatures, Horst Prießnitz compares the confrontation between coloniser and colonised to a speech situation in communication theory:

> Seen in terms of intertextuality and communication theory, the cultural situation of a colony can be regarded as a dialogue between at least two speech partners. The speech situation is constituted by a colonial cultural context, whatever its nature, from a particular historical period on and under specific political circumstances, being subject to the influence of the original British cultural text. Because the colonizer is deemed to be more politically sophisticated, the imported and transplanted original cultural text is also accorded a pre-eminent role to which indigenous colonial cultures have reacted in very different ways. [...] Colonial status thus proves to be a dynamic process of cultural confrontation between the British original text and the very diverse colonial contexts in which a shared language and system of values it embodies function as a communicative medium. (Prießnitz 1990: 35)

The coloniser's cultural text, then, is the dominant text forced on the colonised who then retaliate with their own in the coloniser's language. There is a clash of cultures, languages, traditions and values that must be resolved in the coloniser's tongue that, to a certain extent, denies opposition due to untranslatable indigenous terms. This frustrating process, however, is what encourages resistance and makes it necessary. In this dialogue between coloniser and colonised, the original language is permeated by indigenous words and expressions that create the third code, laden with new meanings and cultural influences. This development may affect both sides, changing the European and Maori cultural texts at the same time.

The question is whether a language can indeed carry cultural values, given the intertextual quality of cultural texts. In *An Encyclopedia of New Zealand* from 1966, an entry on the Maori language concludes that "[i]t is almost impossible to interpret and translate correctly into English this language, which is so full of allusions" (McLintock 2006c). The Maori people's insistence on the preservation of their native tongue and the conservation of specifically Maori and untranslatable expressions hint at the belief that values are inherent in the indigenous language. Certainly, our selected novels are intertextual narratives influenced by texts from many traditions – English, Maori, Christian, and *Pakeha* – and interspersed with Maori terms that carry meaning beyond what can be translated into English.

In "Intertextual Strategies: Reinventing the Myths of Aotearoa in Contemporary New Zealand Fiction", Janet Wilson touches on writing practices applied by Maori writers like Ihimaera and Grace from the very beginning of their careers:

> In New Zealand since the Seventies, writers who have adapted intertextual strategies have focused more on myths and legends of the Maori oral tradition, and those of the Pakeha New Zealand literary tradition, than on European texts of the colonial encounter. Writers of the Maori Renaissance have engaged in a two-way cultural exchange – assimilating European texts and genres to their stories and recovering earlier legends and myths of the pre-European past – as both political act and self-empowering process. (Wilson 1998: 271–2)

Myths have therefore become a primary tool used for political transformation, realising that "[d]ecolonising the European fictions does not invoke a simple reversal of centre and periphery, but a dismantling of the constitutive components of such potent characterizations" (Brydon and Tiffin 1993: 78). Confronting European texts with indigenous alternatives thus weakens the European frame, offering new possibilities for expression and bringing with it a re-evaluation of power.

Interestingly, Wilson points out that Maori authors are not writing back to Europe, but to Aotearoa New Zealand and its own traditions by remaining focused on writing traditions within their own country instead of using European literature as a point of reference. This seems especially useful considering New Zealand's search for an independent and particularly

"Kiwi" identity that clearly distinguishes New Zealanders from everyone else. In an interview from 1985, Ihimaera also addresses this point: "[W]hat we're in fact trying to do is to use European formats to reveal ourselves to a wider audience [...]. [L]et's face it, with American influences, and the whole pervasive subjection of all cultures to internationalism, what you've sometimes got to do is give your own culture a new currency, a value which young people can respect" (Wilkinson 1985: 99).

Particularly, Maori myths provide an alternative to European literary traditions and carry with them an unmistakable indigenous quality that has been imprinted on Maori literature in English. It was common practice for novelists from the start to include excerpts from myths or *karakia*, traditional songs or prayers, in their prologues or as an epithet that introduces the reader to the world depicted in the novels: *Potiki* begins with Maori verse and a mythic prologue, and *Tangi* includes an entire poem the author wrote for this purpose. Wilson (1998: 274) further comments that the custom clearly marks the author's allegiance, be it political or cultural. Moreover, quoting such well-known traditional texts before the actual novel also introduces Maori form into the European genre. This practice imitates the ritual custom of ceremonial speeches, which begin with a ritual chant, the acknowledgement of the ancestral house, Mother Earth, the dead and the living. A *waiata* is sung to suit the occasion and remove *tapu*. Like these customs of speech with their strict protocols, the chosen epithets are an acknowledgement of the author's origin and the context of the work.

The myths that contribute to the intertextuality of the novels are in themselves full of references. Due to the oral tradition of myth and their persistence and development over generations, they have acquired layers of meaning deriving from the many retellings. As hybrid constructs, myths are intertextual narratives that further complicate the nature of hybrid texts. Maori novels become intertextual narratives through the use of myth in a double sense: the inclusion of myths becomes intertextual practice in the novel and, additionally, they bring with them an inherent intertextuality harking back to the old days of oral storytelling long before writing. Those myths contain a more "natural" intertextuality, if you will: they have a social function in bringing people of a tribe together and explain their origin while the type of intertextuality found in the novels is a carefully constructed one with not only a social, but also political function. Their use is carefully planned and serves a more far-reaching purpose than the mere telling of myths.

Stories told at a family gathering do not usually have the same agenda that Maori novels have, but both are useful for the construction of identity. Storytelling among the tribe serves to bond the individuals to their community, explaining origins and remembering ancestors, which leads to a clear cultural identity on a smaller scale, one that is important for life in this particular community. It is a private identity. When included in novels that are available beyond the boundaries of a specific cultural group, however, the myths and the narratives in which they are embedded become public and obtain a political function and force. Having entered the public sphere, the novels counter dominant discourses because they are different and challenging by offering a new point of view and demanding attention and equality, at times explicitly, – an equality that allows them to maintain their difference.

2.2.3 Memory and Identity

In her article "Dispelling the Spells of Memory: Another Approach to Reading Our Yesterdays", Uma Parameswaran identifies three points that writers and critics of the South Asian diaspora should keep in mind. These points can be modified to suit the context of Maori writing and the issues of identity (re)construction because the problems that writers of the diaspora face are comparable to those that indigenous writers face in New Zealand, barring the geographical distance to their homeland. There is instead a psychological distance due to *Pakeha* influence and social changes in the past that may evoke a feeling of homelessness similar to that which expatriates experience. In this respect, Maori in New Zealand and people of the diaspora share the loss of the original homeland and a sense of displacement in a new or changed environment. Looking at available Maori writing, it becomes clear that some aspects coincide with Parameswaran's demands. The question is how great the focus on each point is within the fiction and non-fiction in question.

Claiming a Space within the Centre: A Maori Literature of Memories

The purpose of Parameswaran's demands is to create a literature that has a place among the dominant national literature and leaves the periphery to which it has been designated so far. One does not simply have to break with the illusion that a country's culture consists exclusively of the dominant output in literature, art, film and the like; in fact, both as writer and critic, one has the obligation to work against the dominant view to point out differences and further a positive development that allows the marginalised to gain entry into the centre. According to Parameswaran there must be a negotiation between the old and the new inhabited space: "[We] just have to make room for ourselves within that space and not on the peripheries, no matter how spacious and independent the alternative cultural space. The centre is not a space of exile, nor is it the original homeland that never was. The centre is here and now, the place [...] on which we stand. [...] There will always be an interplay of tensions, but it will be empowering, and not crippling as it would be were we to face in any other direction" (Parameswaran 2003: lii). So, the minority writer has no other choice but to claim a space within the centre and, as a result, changing the power play that exists between margin and centre. The new space enables the writer to speak from a new location that will be heard because it is embedded within the existing dominant structures. This applies to the place of Maori writers as well as to writers of the diaspora. It is the here and now that is important and requires change and a reformation of power structures.

Adapting Parameswaran's (2003: lvi) demands to make them applicable for the New Zealand context, we are left with three barely modified points to establish a strong Maori literature among foreign influence:

1. Maori writers need to introduce and establish archetypes and cultural allusions out of their own historical experiences, and make them part of the national literary culture. As will be demonstrated at a later point, Patricia Grace and Witi Ihimaera both especially do so in the third phase of the Maori novel.

2. Those who study Maori writing need to see where Maori are located in the texts, and why they have been located there.

3. Critics need to educate themselves and others on how to read New Zealand in indigenous writing so that the memory and culture of the Maori people can become a prominent part of national literature.

As will be demonstrated in chapter III, these points have been integrated into the production and the study of Maori literature to different degrees. It seems, however, that the extent to which writers and critics propagate and are aware of the necessity for a Maori space in New Zealand waxes and wanes from time to time. While the 1970s produced pastoral Maori novels that represented a harmonious tribal life in the country, these were the first steps into the right direction that led to a more aggressive literature in the 1980s. Part of the writing from the 1990s onward appears to have lost its drive and has expanded to include other issues of the day. Once again, the anger of the 1980s is lacking and has been replaced by a striving for harmony in the present day, which is harmony mainly in urban areas unlike the 1970s rural focus. This return to harmony can be explained by New Zealand's wish to be a truly multicultural country with equal opportunities for all, but it might also derive from a lack of confrontational and more aggressive novels that represent the current situation. On first sight, it might appear that Maori political activism is restricted to the real world and non-fictional sphere for the most part today. Either there is too little such creative writing or it finds no publishers since the heyday of fiercely political fiction has passed. At the same time, however, there is political fiction in the early twenty-first century that has a new kind of fierceness that does not require force. Instead, there is a clear, more developed political agenda propagated by peaceful means.

Myth and Myth-making as Frameworks for Identity

Literature, therefore, need not be as forceful as that of the 1980s to create a place for Maori writers. So instead of writing fiction that is explicitly political and overpowers the creative aspect of fiction with its openness and variety of approaches to topics, myth offers the opportunity to place the problem within a greater context, as Cupitt suggests in *The World to Come*. "We can add," he says, "that myth-making is evidently a primal and universal function of the human mind as it seeks a more-or-less unified vision of the cosmic order, the social order, and the meaning of the individual's life. Both for society at large and for the individual, this story-generating function seems irreplaceable. The individual finds meaning in his life by making of his life a story set within a larger social and cosmic story" (Cupitt 1985: 29).

Considering that myth-making is "primal and universal", it comes as no surprise that Maori writers have taken it upon themselves to use existing myths and elaborate them, alter them or write their own. The fact that the most overtly political narratives by Ihimaera and Grace were published in the second phase of the Maori novel during the 1980s goes to show that there was a time and demand for such fiction during that period. It did not, however, manage to proceed into the following decades in quite the same manner. Instead, the aggression that is palpable in Ihimaera's *The Matriarch* (1986) is merely surpassed by Duff's violent *Once Were Warriors* (1990) in the following decade. Despite the success of these novels, subsequent publications are tamer in this respect, relying on the power of myth, tradition, genealogy and a mainly peaceful resistance.

The use of myth in novels would not, according to Cupitt above, be a hindrance for further development. On the contrary, it encourages – perhaps even demands – the perpetual telling and retelling of stories, their continual creation, because this energy to move forward is inherent in myth's "story-generating function". The original myth, be it the tale of the First Parents, the many stories of Maui's adventures or other often-told tales, is the larger framework within which the individual Maori creates their own story. Writers do so by choosing particular myths that underlie their stories and form the fiction's framework; furthermore, they offer this framework to their readers who may choose whether it is an exclusively fictional framework or one that is relevant for their lives today as well. Since the question of identity is ever evolving and the cause of much insecurity, myth-making may be one solution through which not only the fictional characters, but also the readers can come to an understanding of who they are and who they want to be. As Stuart Hall insists, identity is anything but certain or easily defined. "Identity," he says, "is not as transparent or unproblematic as we think. Perhaps instead of thinking of identity as an already accomplished fact, which the new cultural practices then represent, we should think, instead, of identity as a 'production', which is never complete, always in process, and always constituted within, not outside, representation. This view problematises the very authority and authenticity to which the term, 'cultural identity', lays claim" (Hall 1990: 222). He, too, stresses the process and the lack of a steady definition. In fact, the process is the definition of identity. As such, identity does not seem to exist, but only as an ongoing process of searching, selecting, and creating. As mentioned earlier, it is the frame constructed by myths old and new that is one of the ways in which identity may be constructed. Therefore, myths and the process of myth-making function as pointers to – and as a reflection of – the process of identity construction. To put it simply, myth has a clear practical function.

Similarly, Cassirer argues in *The Myth of the State* that myths have an emotional foundation that serves a practical social function. They unify a community by displaying harmonious common origins. These myths, then, have no objective truth or value of their own because they are "a direct expression of human feeling rather than of intellectual thought" (Bidney 1966: 9). There are, however, other opinions, as Coupe summarises in his study of myth: "Traditionally," he says, "there have been two opposed theories of the interpretation of myth [...]. One assumes the perspective of perfection, translating narrative into the terms of truth, *mythos* into *logos*. The other sees myth as a matter of permanent possibility, trusting in the ongoing power of *mythos* itself. One is bound to hierarchy; the other is open to a horizon" (Coupe 1997: 100).

In the case of Maori literature, the latter notion of myth as open is most appropriate. In Ihimaera's *The Uncle's Story* the dangers of the hierarchy of myth are depicted in several passages that show how Sam is hindered by the apparent rigidity of the myths underlying his culture. It is only once he discovers the interpretive possibilities inherent in myth that he is able to be himself and live as he wishes. In all other novels, myths are considered to be open from the onset though occasionally characters appear who hold fast to a single interpretation of their myths, thus contrasting with the main characters who do not share this belief in the same manner. Such a contrast proves the necessity to be tolerant and to allow for other, new interpretations and ways of thinking. Ideally, the new approach will lead to better integration and understanding between generations, cultures, men and women, and people of all sexual orientations. In this respect, myth does have an emotional basis and social function, as Cassirer states. Nevertheless, this does not consequently mean that there is no truth or value in myth itself. We must assume that myths originated due to a necessity of some sort – to explain the world we live in, to remember and pass on values and rules, cultural beliefs and traditions, for instance. In much the same way in fiction, myths are valuable for a writer's various purposes, as we will discuss in the following chapters. Myth may not be the only component that can be used to analyse questions of culture and identity, but Ihimaera and Grace have chosen it as their ideal means.

Cultural Identity in Transcultural Times

As tales containing fundamental beliefs and truths, myths contribute to Maori cultural identity even in times of transition. The circumstances require reinterpretation, which results in the retelling of myths from different angles and with a different focus. Gradually, the process will lead to changes in the perception of oneself as an individual or a group since the underlying beliefs transported in myths may have been altered in the new telling.

Such a time of transition in New Zealand emerged with the first coming of the *Pakeha* and has continued to this day. The two cultures struggle to be reconciled in order to enable a peaceful coexistence, which for a long time meant assimilation rather than mutual acceptance. Yet even living side by side creates difficulties, not to mention any attempt to equally embrace two or more cultures as one's own identity. We must assume that each culture comes with its own unique fundamental concepts that exclude any others. "However rational you are," Bhabha explains,

> [...] it is actually very difficult, even impossible and counterproductive, to try and fit together different forms of culture and to pretend that they can easily coexist. The assumption that at some level all forms of cultural diversity may be understood on the basis of a particular universal concept, whether it be "human being", "class" or "race", can be both very dangerous and very limiting in trying to understand the ways in which cultural practices construct their own systems of meaning and social organisation. (Bhabha 1990: 209)

As is evident here and in previous discussions of hybridity, Bhabha resists the idea that different cultures can be brought together since each has its own values and understanding of life that ultimately exclude any other belief. Each culture therefore has its own concepts that are incompatible with others or at least limited in their ability to be merged, thereby rejecting any universal compatibility or classification. As a result, it is necessary to examine cultures from within, without using another culture's concepts as an underlying model that will give insight into the former. As Bhabha rightly points out, an approach guided by expectations formed on the basis of another culture would be dangerous since this might lead to misrepresentation. At the same time, the interpretation could be limited by the restrictions of the model that may not apply to the culture under scrutiny.

On the one hand, it appears as though cultural identity cannot be established with the help of direct comparison with another that does not allow space for difference. On the other, identity cannot be established through the process of othering, which would be the diametrically opposed alternative, as Bhabha explains: "[The postcolonial perspective] insists [...] that cultural and political identity is constructed through a process of othering. The time for 'assimilating' minorities to holistic and organic notions of cultural value has passed – the very language of cultural community needs to be rethought from a postcolonial perspective" (Bhabha 1990: 219). Subsequently, it is impossible to replace one cultural identity with another. As a result, Maori people would not become *Pakeha* by assimilation, and this – according to Bhabha – is not the point in the first place. On the contrary, any exposure to another culture leads to the creation of a third space with, as he demands, its own language, selected cultural beliefs and customs, and so forth. What is needed, then, is a hybrid or rather transcultural society that exists in its own right though it chooses some of its elements from existing cultures.

Here, one might say, otherness unifies. It is exactly this otherness that distinguishes one from the other and determines one's identity by exclusion. Though it may be unclear what you are, it is easier to distinguish what you are not. You may be Maori, but not quite; you may also be *Pakeha*, but not quite. In this example, elements of each culture are joined while others are dismissed and the gaps are filled with something new that belongs neither to the one nor the other. The third-space culture thus draws on memories provided by the two original cultures while reinterpreting and also adding something of its own.

Consequently, memory features as an indispensable defining aspect of identity construction. The memory of particular myths, for instance, supplies us with our particular worldview due to myths' inherent metaphysical explanations that crucially define who, where and why we are. These explanations define our culture and determine the way we think, perceive, and remember. Thus myths shape cultural identity and motivate certain ways of thinking, expectations and experiences. At the same time, nonetheless, they also have the potential to rebel against established concepts.

At first sight, Maori mythology has the features of a grand narrative – a large-scale theory claiming universality. As it depicts and explains existence while at the same time incorporating rules and experiences, it influences the Maori worldview and shapes cultural identity based on its tales. The grand narrative is a concept defined by Jean-François Lyotard as a narrative type of knowledge common in ancient societies where the storyteller's status in the group is considered to guarantee its truth (Lyotard 1984 [1979]). Given their claim to universality, grand narratives are characterised by their abstract quality that makes them applicable to a number of situations. They hold collective beliefs and focus on the greater scheme instead of individual tales, through which they become fundamental for the community concerned. Here, grand narratives exceed any anecdotal value that stories generally may have and become foundational myths and thus history.

Even though Maori mythology is the grand narrative of the indigenous community itself, it would not be considered as such from a global point of view. The grand narratives commonly discussed in postcolonial and cultural studies are Western ones that displace and marginalise any other narratives that exist outside them. A claim to universality seems impossible, however, since any narrative is created and enabled by power structures. Hence grand narratives are untrustworthy and one-dimensional, disregarding the existence of cultural multiplicity and the variety of human experience. Beside a supposed History with a capital H, the reality of smaller histories is easily ignored. Maori history and mythology therefore cannot be considered a *grand récit*, but rather a *petit récit* that exists alongside those Western narratives that have claimed superiority thus far. Therefore, a large-scale universal theory does not exist. Instead, human experience is varied and complex, refusing any theory that attempts to summarise it. The resulting focus on alternative stories and other truths in postmodernism, postcolonial, and contemporary cultural studies devotes itself to the specific and local instead of the universal.

As Ihimaera insists in an interview after the publication of *The Uncle's Story*, Maori must breach the European frameworks that direct their lives and learn to live within Maori frameworks (Dickson 2005: 2). Many sections of the novel explicitly address the problem of European or *Pakeha* dominance, forcing the characters to make a stand and fight for the Maori structures that are being oppressed: "We occupy the borderlands of White society. We live only by the White man's leave within White structures that are White driven and White kept. [...] We must disconnect from the White umbilical" (*US* 320). Very much aware of their marginal position within New Zealand society, the Maori people still need to take an active part in the preservation of their culture even in the new millennium.

Clearly, Maori identity is still too strongly shaped by European standards. The recurring theme of *Pakeha* supremacy even in novels from the twenty-first century attests to the difficulty of debunking enduring grand narratives. Even though the first novels drew attention to the problem and the following publications depicted the improvements achieved in the last thirty years as well as the remaining problems, the latest novels are still critical of developments and encourage a continued pursuit of the necessary cultural reinvigoration. To this end, the novels employ Maori myths and legends that are still valid to this day and can be shaped to suit the current situation. This is the case in books like *The Whale Rider*, which is still popular today. In it a heretofore unconsidered interpretation of a myth is used to promote a changed view of women and power in the Maori community. *The Uncle's Story* from the beginning of the new century offers yet another reinterpretation of myths that have hindered Maori in the modern world. It appears that the myths remaining in Maori memory still have the potential to challenge European grand narratives and therefore feature greatly in fiction as frameworks within which indigenous life is not only possible, but also successful alongside other cultures in an ever changing world.

Memory, as a consequence, is an essential element of myth and its reinterpretation in current fiction. After all, it is the persistence of certain memories that allows grand narratives to endure and also *petits récits* to come to the fore. In the context of narrative reinterpretation, the study of memory is particularly suited due to memory's own susceptibility to change. As will be illustrated in the following chapter, narrative and memory share fundamental characteristics and functions that make them compatible in fiction and warrant an analysis of the Maori novel and the role of myth and memory within it.

2.3 Memory in Narrative: In Search of a Maori Identity

Underlying the discussion of the forms and functions of memory are Astrid Erll's research on the representation of memory in literature in *Kollektives Gedächtnis und Erinnerungskulturen* (2005) and Ann Rigney's (2005) objection to the plenitude and scarcity model of memory. Drawing on Maurice Halbwachs, Pierre Nora as well as Jan and Aleida Assmann, Rigney's distinction aims at a cultural view of memory based on an Assmannian understanding rather than the plenitude-loss-restoration model that preceded it. From her point of view, literature would be an example of a medium through which memory can be preserved; not as a second-best solution to oral communication of memory as Halbwachs (1991 [1950]) would see it, but as a natural process in our time. She understands memory as a cultural rather than a psychological process that requires a range of media. Based on the number of available media today and the absence of participants in the event or circumstance that is meant to be remembered, Rigney encourages a re-evaluation of these media as culture-shaping processes which are, consequently and inevitably, memory shaping.

The Loss of Original Plenitude

The "original plenitude and subsequent loss" model assumes that memory is something fully formed in the plenitude of experience. Therefore, it needs to be preserved while as many first-hand experiences as possible are available and the participants in a given event are alive and able to share their stories. While alive, memories are passed on orally in the form of stories. This way, even those who were not participants in the remembered events have a part in the process of remembrance, leading to an exchange of living memory that goes back only as far as the living participant can remember. The exchange takes place between those who remember and those who are listening (cf. Erll's definition of *Generationsgedächtnis*; 2005: 16). With time, however, these memories are lost between generations as the participants die. "At a certain point," Rigney explains, "the only way for the memory to survive is for it to be written down" because what Halbwachs referred to as "lived experience" in *La Mémoire Collective* is finite (Rigney 2005: 12). "The written medium," she continues, "allows things to survive, then, but in doing so it aggravates the loss of original plenitude by carrying 'lived' or 'internal' memory into what Halbwachs calls the 'external' sphere of history" (*ibid.* 13). It appears that, by leaving the private (internal) and entering the public (external) sphere, preserved memories acquire a different quality and become part of an unreachable past. Instead of being available through living participants of the event, memories are now only retrievable through written documentation, which is a public medium. Assmann's cultural memory proper (i.e. memory after the participants' death; cf. J. Assmann 2002: 48–66) would then be memory in the public domain, available to everyone from what we have heard or read instead of experienced ourselves. It comes as no surprise, therefore, that writing is considered a second-best medium to the direct oral communication through which memory was kept alive before. The Maori people have encountered the same problem since the rural-to-urban migration that spread families across New Zealand and reduced the opportunity for regular face-to-face contact and storytelling. Many Maori novels have taken up the task of creatively passing on communal stories and local legends in the absence of oral communication.

Before there can be memory, however, there is forgetting, and so a scarcity of memory. Memory is never rigid and stable: "Instead, it is an active and constantly shifting relationship to the past, in which the past is changed retrospectively in the sense that its meaning is changed. [...] [T]he point is that memories are always 'scarce' in relation to everything that theoretically might have been remembered, but is now forgotten" (Rigney 2005: 17). Consequently drawing on Jan and Aleida Assmann's research on cultural memory, Rigney prefers "a social-constructivist model that takes as its starting point the idea that memories of a shared past are collectively constructed and reconstructed in the present rather than resurrected from the past" (Rigney 2005: 14). Erll agrees with this point and explains that only that which is important for a particular group is effectively remembered:

> Particularly similarities and continuities that demonstrate that the group has remained the same are emphasised. Participating in the process of collective remembering indicates that the one who remembers is part of this group. [...] Collective memory [...] is geared towards the needs and concerns of the group in the present. Therefore, this is a strongly selective and reconstructive process in which distortion, a changed attribution of significance, and even fictionalisation are possible. (Erll 2005: 17, translation NM)

Therefore, the Maori novels that incorporate memories in the form of myths, legends, tribal history, customs etc. have chosen aspects that are of importance for their particular purpose while ultimately emphasising being part of the Maori community. Here, the factuality of the selected memories plays a minor role due to the significance of a cultural identity. While the memories are used to explain or express something particular in the present, it is necessary to pick suitable memories which are then combined in ways suited to the purpose. The act of selecting and combining is a creative act in itself and part of the fictionalisation Erll indicates above. Quite generally, there is no doubt about the fictionalisation of memories in this case since we are dealing with novels. As cultural products, creative writing has the potential for change beyond the fictional sphere by insinuating itself into the reader's thought and perhaps even into society if the fiction is able to make an impact.

Returning to Rigney, she further distinguishes her approach from previous theories of memory by asking what the consequences are if, as she believes, "external" sources of information are the norm rather than the exception (Rigney 2005: 14). This question is important given the growing world-wide communication network, the easy availability of sources, and the continual loss of eyewitnesses. These sources are no longer original memories, but reconstructed memories made available to the public. Depending on their place of origin, the culture they spring from and the current circumstances, they will differ from original memories and take on new shapes that are relevant for the present. If we assume that information is made available when there is a need for it, it follows that memories available to the public through various media serve a purpose at the time of their emergence and will be influenced by a number of criteria that ultimately shape them. Finally, "every person and every historical fact, when entering into a collective memory, is transformed into a doctrine, a concept, or a symbol of sorts. When appropriated by a collective memory, it acquires a social significance, it becomes an element of a given society's ideational system" (Assmann 2001: 19).

In a similar vein, writers create the mentioned doctrines, concepts and symbols in collective memory through their fiction. The work, absorbed into the literary canon, influences the reader's perception and may also lead to action. Fictional events and characters can therefore have an impact similar to that of historical events and people. Since fiction works on an ideational level from the beginning and is inherently symbolic, the similarities between fiction and reality as far as social significance is concerned are striking. We may assume, however, that the fiction emerges primarily when there is a need for its particular kind while the occurrences of historical events and people may be chance encounters or at least less strategically planned than a novel in comparison. Behind fiction there is a clear purpose, but events in reality cannot be controlled in quite the same manner throughout. This, nonetheless, indicates that fiction is capable of a strong influence on society.

Fiction and reality, it would appear, share the capacity to supply society with concepts, perceptions, and ideas and may subsequently shape memory. Thus the myth of Paikea, the Polynesian ancestor of the Ngati Porou tribe, who arrived in New Zealand on the back of a whale, turns into a story of destiny and social change in Ihimaera's novel *The Whale Rider* (1987).

An historical event is fictionalised so as to address current issues among Maori. The new use of the myth emphasises that the memory of Paikea is still strong and important, but at the same time a change in perception is introduced by the shift from a male-centred hierarchy to a tribe that will be led by a female descendant of Paikea one day. Within the fiction, there is thus an example of a change that anticipates a similar change in reality. The male mythic/historical hero Paikea is the symbol for Maori strength and endurance; the fictional girl Paikea is symbolic of the same, additionally emphasising the resilience and power that is within women. There is therefore a move from historical reality to fiction that encourages a further step from fiction to reality today in order to effect change in society. So as to be experienced, the situation and its possibilities are first depicted in literature, the external source.

Significantly, much of memory today comes from external sources and is therefore a product of representation rather than experience. "When it comes to the formation of cultural memory in the modern age, moreover," Rigney emphasises,

> the role of mass media and the new digital media (including local internet sites) is undeniable and, however one may judge the quality of the information conveyed, these modern media need to be taken into account as an integral factor in the production of cultural memory today. [...] The role of texts and other media and hence the degree of vicariousness obviously increases as the events recollected recede further in time. This suggests that it makes more sense to take mediated, vicarious recollection as our model for collective memory rather than stick to some ideal form of face-to-face communication in which participants are deemed to share experience in some direct, unmediated way. (Rigney 2005: 15)

Literature, then, is one of these many media that cannot be ignored. It is a creative medium of collective memory that invariably reworks memories, myths and legends in the process of storytelling in a particular context. The importance of such a varied reworking of memory, its reduction and expansion over time, prove to be a vital part of cultural identity and bonding. "Communality, in other words," Rigney concludes, "is based on the exchange of memories. The price of communality is a loss of literal accuracy, and hence of the plenitude and highly personalized memory [...]"

(Rigney 2005: 15). Finally, memory has moved from the personal to the communal and collective.

Cultural memory[10] gradually develops through communication in the public sphere in a variety of mediated forms. It does so in stages that Rigney has identified as selection, convergence, recursivity, modelling, and transfer. In the following, these stages shall be discussed to offer a better understanding of cultural memory as applied in the text analysis.

2.3.1 Five Stages of Cultural Memory

The selectivity of what we choose to remember or consider worthy of remembrance harks back to the scarcity of memory that is but a fraction of all memories available in theory. Instead of viewing this selectivity as negative, however, Rigney suggests we regard it as an essential factor that can tell us something about present conditions among a particular cultural group. "Cultural memory can [...] be described," she says,

> as a "working memory" which is continuously performed by individuals and groups as they recollect the past selectively through various media and become involved in various forms of memorial activity, from narrating and reading to attending commemorative ceremonies or going on pilgrimages. In the very act of recollecting in public we consciously or unconsciously select those things, from the totality of everything which might have been said, that are somehow relevant to the present. The partiality of remembrance is not merely a shortcoming, then, but also one of the preconditions of its being meaningful for particular groups of people. (Rigney 2005: 17–18)

J. A. Barnes's (1990: 52–3) concept of structural amnesia describes the selectivity that is practised in oral cultures that have no writing through which

---

10   In this study, cultural memory is regarded as a specific form of collective memory. While the latter is a general collection of biological, cultural, social, and psychological aspects that influence our conception of the historical past, the former is specific to one particular culture and its conception of itself even in the present. Admittedly, this is a fine line. Collective memory includes a personal aspect – one's own memories – that cultural memory rarely has due to its focus on the distant, mythical past. At the same time, it is valid for a larger group such as a society or nation.

to save memories: in such societies, only the most relevant information is passed on orally because there is a limit as to how much collective memory can hold. The lack of further media with which to store information makes it necessary for the oral culture to neglect what can be done without while maintaining the most important information only. Finally, in *Searching for Memory*, Schacter (1996: 52) determines that "[w]e remember only what we have encoded, and what we encode depends on who we are – our past experiences, knowledge, and needs all have a powerful influence on what we retain". Selection is, therefore, an inevitable process dependent on individual and cultural factors.

Selection as a first stage of the preservation of memory leads to the convergence of memories which need not be related as long as the participating group considers them relevant for conservation. The convergence of memory replaces the variety of memory that exists while eyewitnesses of an event are still alive; in other words, convergence signifies a maximum of meaning in a minimum of signs. The Maori novels discussed here can be viewed as a collection of superimposed memories (of myths and legends, real events etc.) that coalesce into a (sometimes mythical) narrative into which current concerns can be integrated. According to Pierre Nora's (1997 [1984–1992]) concept of sites of memory, texts, among other objects and places, can become such locations of memory in which collective remembrance and historical meaning are centred. The advantage of literature is the way it lends itself to a constant cycle of telling and retelling. This recursivity of cultural memory forms its third stage, referring to the repetition, revisiting, and retelling of memories even across different media. Here, the continual retelling encourages shared frames of reference even among people who are otherwise unconnected.

A novel, or the way authors choose to rework memory in it, form just one model of remembrance with specific methods and characteristics that may be appropriated by others for similar purposes. The results may vary, leading to another model that varies to a certain degree from the original, as it were. In this case, the process of remembrance depends on the novel and its requirements as a medium. Generally, what is remembered is the result of tensions between the desire to remember and the availability of memories – some things are lost or only partially remembered. Also, the relevance of certain memories does not guarantee their memorability because what is remembered and how depends largely on the media available for public expression on which they are modelled. However, as Rigney points out, once a model has been established, it can serve as an example for further ways of remembering: "Models of remembrance [...] are repeated, transformed and appropriated in new situations with the help of 'mobile' media. This means that one act of remembrance can stimulate comparable acts in other situations and within different social frameworks. The language in which memories are articulated is recycled, providing an intellectual hook with which relics of the past can be 'fished' out of the archive and brought into working memory" (Rigney 2005: 23). By encouraging a process of remembrance somewhere else, then, the model crosses borders and goes beyond the framework of a nation, a culture, or a people.

In the case of Maori literature, the first Maori novel became a model for other fiction of this cultural group. Its incorporation of myths and indigenous customs, its choice of language(s) and the structure of the narrative all lent themselves to writers as models of remembrance. Of course, every novel differs, but many are modelled on the very first as the original form. That is one of the reasons why the works of the early phase appear to have the same agenda and similar ways of presentation. With time, an original model of remembrance changes as writers develop their style. New issues, settings, and types of characters are added to their stories. What remains, however, are the "repeated, transformed and appropriated" models Rigney speaks of above. The first novel made a beginning; the following did not copy, but explored other related ways of remembering, such as Duff's depicted approach in *Once Were Warriors*, which sets itself apart from other Maori novels by its violent reinterpretation of the warrior origin of the indigenous people. It is suggested that the young have not forgotten their origins as a warrior people, but it is their inappropriate approach and misinterpretation of this that leads to gang violence and a vicious cycle of crime. Duff's novel insists that remembering alone is insufficient: the memories are there, the origins known; what the youngsters and even their parents lack is a capacity for appraisal and conducive decision making. Unfortunately, by singling out and focusing on the warrior aspect of their Maori identity, the characters ignore any integrative properties of their culture.

Finally, what the chosen novels present is the need for a wider outlook that is able to encompass more than one family, one tribe, or one culture. Similarly, aside from being models valid for one particular culture, models of remembrance may also be available to others outside of this group. Depending on the memorial forms among other groups, a model of remembrance may be shared. Rigney explains that "[t]his means among other things that the pasts of particular groups are given cultural shape and expression in relation to each other, and that models of remembrance may be exchanged among groups with a similarly marginalized position within the public sphere" (Rigney 2005: 24). This transfer and the translation into another group's situation are yet another stage of establishing and defining cultural memory. The models are anything but rigid. Their flexibility allows their appropriation not only for different situations, but also for different groups. This means that literary techniques for the representation and storage of memories may be shared between writers of different countries with similar historical experiences. The model may be shared among Maori, Aboriginal and African writers, to name a few, given their common colonial history and the urge to return – at least in writing – to that which was forgotten or ignored.

As literature is a creative medium, it is more flexible as a cultural framework for remembrance than something as fixed as sites of memory like memorials. While a memorial is an unchanging symbol surrounded by the stories told of whatever it represents, one might say that literature itself is memory. In its material form it is a site of memory like any memorial, but it is also the collection of memories in itself at the same time: literature tells its stories on its own without the necessity for outside contributions since the tale is already between the book's covers. Additionally, literature can indeed encourage remembrance outside the book among its readers and will do so, which is the point of any site of memory. "By virtue of their aesthetic and fictional properties," says Rigney with reference to literary representations,

> they are more "mobile" and "exportable" than other forms of representation, whether in translation or the original, and are certainly more mobile than actual memory sites [...]. Certain stories travel and, increasingly within the modern world, they do so beyond the boundaries of the immediate community and beyond national boundaries.

As such they may be instruments par excellence in the "transfer" of memories from one community to another, and hence as mediators between memory communities. (Rigney 2005: 25–6)

Maori literature may not enjoy the same wide distribution that more established literature does, but it is available and does cross global borders. Books can be spread more easily today than ever before thanks to technology, contributing to the memory transfer across cultures that Rigney addresses. That such a transfer is possible and necessary – even within fiction – can be seen in novels like Ihimaera's *The Rope of Man*. Here, the setting is no longer restricted to New Zealand and goes beyond borders. There is a strong global orientation evident in the story that is exemplified by Tom's work as a journalist. Partly set in Great Britain and addressing the overseas experience of Maori people, Ihimaera clears a path for memory transfer between countries. At the same time, this offers the opportunity to appropriate models of remembrance abroad to enrich both contemporary Maori literature as well as Maori experience.

In conclusion, cultural memory is subject to a selection process and alterations through retelling and merging. As a basis of cultural identity, cultural memory undergoes the same continual changes that are attributed to identity and it is equally as varied and in flux. The ways in which memory is processed can be imitated by other cultures that choose them as an appropriate model, whereby the framework spreads and is no longer particular to the original culture. As described above, this development can be reproduced in fiction, which points towards the similarities between memory and narrative. Both appear to be subject to the same methods to manifest themselves in thoughts and writing, reality and fiction.

2.3.2 Memory and Narrative: A Comparison

For experience to become memory, first a process of narrativisation is required because, as Jerome Bruner points out, "[w]e organize our experience and our memory of human happenings mainly in the form of narrative – stories, excuses, myths, reasons for doing and not doing, and so on" (Bruner

1991: 4). Fiction represents particularly the individual memory of characters who not only experience, but narrate. Literature and memory, Erll (2005: 143ff.; 165–6) explains, are connected in several ways: literature can create an understanding of the past and demonstrate how memory works by reconstructing the processes involved. Memory is a symbolic form that appears to use techniques also found in literary texts.

The selection Rigney referred to previously is the beginning of a creative process that requires more than simply the separation of the chosen items from their original context. They must be processed – by being put into new contexts, for instance – in order to eventually become memory. In her analysis, Erll (2005: 144–7) distinguishes three points in which literature and memory coincide: firstly, both use techniques of convergence; secondly, they share narrative processes and, thirdly, they use genre-specific models to encode events.

As discussed earlier, convergence brings together and focuses memories of the past and may even combine memories that were originally unrelated. Convergence, as a literary element, is created by the use of intertextual references, for instance, which concentrate meaning symbolically in the text. These references can only be recognised if the reader is familiar with the respective culture's customs and interpretative techniques, Erll points out in her definition. Even though Maori novels often offer obvious pointers for the unfamiliar reader, books such as *Mutuwhenua* refuse to reveal convergence too explicitly. The readers are confronted with strange events in the story that hark back to ancient times and old myths which may only be hinted at because they are understood among the cultural group concerned. The references, however, are subtle or even expected to be known without further explanation, which leaves unfamiliar readers frustrated with their little knowledge of Maori culture and the inability to fully follow the narrative in all its richness.

As mentioned above, memory and literature make use of narrative strategies. Since memory has a limited capacity and is only able to contain a restricted number of items, it is forced to be selective. A text, too, needs to restrict itself to the most relevant information that is needed in the current situation. The selected items must then be combined sensibly to achieve meaning: what a particular memory signifies is determined by its arrangement within the text among all other textual elements. Meaning is conveyed through narrative emplotment, the symbolic transformation of unreflected pre-narrative experience into reflected explication (cf. Polkinghorne 1988, quoted in Erll 2005: 87). This retrospective selection condenses and intensifies events while others are forgotten since the selection process focuses only on what is relevant for the current situation in which the memories are coherently narrated.

Subsequently, only once memory has been turned into narrative are we able to discern meaning. Here, Erll emphasises that the narrativisation of memory should not be mistaken for fictionalisation, however:

> The world of collective memory is a *world of narratives* in whose frameworks the past has been transferred into meaningful structures to a large extent. (This does *not* mean that it is a world of "fiction". Fictionality is one of the privileges of literature as a symbolic framework [...].) Such narratives of memory range from the mandatory myths that constitute the background of cultural memory to those meaningful everyday stories that determine the immediate objectives of communicative memory. (Erll 2005: 145–6, translation NM)

Therefore, memories are made available to us as meaningful narratives and are thus constructed, though not invented. An example of memory as narrative is conversational or group remembering that is an integral part of Maori culture as depicted in fiction, which is taken from customs of Maori tribal life. When Ripeka's grandmother repeatedly shows family photographs in Grace's *Mutuwhenua*, it is to remind Ripeka of who she is, what her family stands for and what Maori life is meant to be. The gatherings in the meeting house so often found in Ihimaera's novels are an occasion for the telling of stories. Here, past events are related and passed on to those who have not witnessed them. As in fiction, the way memories are narrated can depend on who the listener or reader is, what situation reader and narrator find themselves in, and what kind of narrative aesthetics underlies the telling.

Narrative aesthetics are partly determined by the chosen genre. In literature, Erll maintains, narrative engages with genre-specific models to create worlds that memory also makes use of. This is due to the socialisation and enculturation that makes such models readily available to members of society exposed to certain genres. These may then be used to interpret memories and arrange them in ways that make sense to those who remember. Genres offer particular strategies of narration and their motifs, structures, and ways of emplotment that can be seen as strategies to allocate meaning. Consequently, the choice of Maori novelists to write from their point of view in a particular genre has important implications for the interpretation of memory.

To write from the Maori perspective and to write in opposition to existing fiction, expectations, and social and cultural conditions requires the adaptation of familiar genres. The writers featured in this study have chosen the novel, among other things, in which to express ideas and concepts. These Maori concepts, however, are unfamiliar to most non-Maori readers of the genre and necessitate a look into the narrative from a different point of view – in other words, the writers create another, a strange world in a familiar genre. At the time of publication, the average *Pakeha* reader of Ihimaera's *Tangi* would have had difficulty with the unabashed lyrical density of its prose, the use of Maori terms and perhaps the unusual spiral structure of the narrative that is characteristic of some other novels that followed in *Tangi*'s wake, moving seamlessly between past and present.

On the one hand, the novel as a genre therefore fulfils particular expectations, but on the other, Maori writers not only conform to them – they encourage change. When writing against reader expectations, the genre-specific models that shape memory are altered as well. This remains in line with Erll's conclusions, though it does suggest a certain amount of flexibility that postcolonial writing entails. A change of the genre-specific models that shape memory consequently involves a reshaping of the narrative and any expectations associated with it. She admits that the reshaping of genres is a response to new challenges in literature and the study of memory (Erll 2005: 146–7). She also points out that experiences which are difficult to express and interpret – such as the Maori experience – may use existing genres so as to make sense of them in the first place. Collective experiences may be shaped to suit the novel as a specific genre, or these experiences may shape the genre itself, thereby giving those experiences a particular form and offering a particular guideline for interpretation.

Literature, nonetheless, differs from memory in its fictionality, though that is not to say that memory is always accurate and objective. Reality may be used in fiction, but it then becomes symbolic, a sign that takes on new meaning; imaginary elements, in turn, become real (cf. Iser's study of fiction and the imaginary [1991]). The combination of the real and the imaginary in fiction structures our understanding of things, but its objectivity and factual correctness is restricted. Fiction's characteristics such as the ability to combine reality and imagination or the creation of alternative realities clearly distinguish it from reality. This in itself does not distinguish it from memory, however, since memory and the way it is structured may well mirror the structure of fiction. Moreover, in literary form, writers are able to make use of the restrictions and functions of memory in a number of ways. Simulating memory's operating mode, impressions can be presented to the reader in a fragmented fashion to resemble short-term memory without being semantically encoded. Repetition, one of the main features of Maori storytelling, allows recall and retains information more easily. As in the case of long-term memory, fiction retrospectively attributes meaning to events, based on association and current needs.

What is more, literature allows a concentration and layering of experiences to an even greater extent than memory itself, says Erll. This complexity and ambiguity is especially characteristic of representations of the past in fiction (Erll 2005: 148). The compressed and highly symbolic character of Maori myths encountered in the novels is just such a representation of the past whose layering of experiences corresponds with a layering of meaning and interpretations. Depending on what the fiction demands, myths can thus be reinterpreted and given new meaning that is added to already existing layers. Myth's richness is therefore so complex and ambiguous that it gives access to various interpretations. This circumstance, for instance, enables Ihimaera to successfully combine traditional knowledge with the controversial issue of homosexuality in *The Uncle's Story*. Despite the clash of cultural beliefs that rejects gay men and women, Ihimaera's novel makes use of myth's complexity as a toehold from which to access a new interpretation of traditional myths. Without the richness and flexibility of myths, such a tale of tolerance and acceptance would not be possible.

Finally, it becomes clear that literature contributes to what may be remembered while at the same time being able to depict how things are remembered individually or collectively. Each of the chosen Maori novels offers a glimpse into these two aspects of remembrance. They combine experiences, events, and particularly myths that create fictional realities which already are or may yet become part of collective memory. As in much of postcolonial literature, this approach may also allow for the rewriting of dominant texts and memories, bringing the marginal to the fore.

2.3.3 Cultural Memory in Maori Fiction

Even before the 1970s, *Pakeha* dominance in New Zealand led to the urge to strengthen Maori culture. Choosing literature as one medium through which to introduce it back into society's consciousness was an important step for the Maori people, considering how important writing is in Western cultures. The novel as a popular and widespread Western genre offered a wide readership that could be introduced to the marginalised culture as soon as Ihimaera's *Tangi* was published in 1973.

Though the representation of Maori customs and traditions was an objective of Maori literature from the start, it was not the only one. Due to the dissolution of traditional tribal structures that came with the rural-to-urban migration, there was a realistic fear of a loss of culture. Ultimately, literature featured not only as an introduction to native culture for *Pakeha* readers; the primary purpose was geared towards Maori who may have been removed from their heritage for a variety of reasons. Literature became a medium of cultural memory, so to speak.

The contents of cultural memory and its meanings are passed on through specialists such as Maori elders. All that can be regarded as part of the foundation of the Maori community – like their myths and legends – becomes part of the wealth of cultural memory. In an essay on collective memory and cultural identity, Jan Assmann defines cultural memory as the summary of "a specific stock of texts, images and rites of every society and every epoch in whose 'care' the respective society stabilises and communicates its self-image, and which supports the group's awareness of unity and particularity through collectively shared knowledge, preferably (but not exclusively) of the past" (Assmann 1988: 15, translation NM). With reference to his delineation, Erll (cf. 2005: 28–9) further expands the definition:

this type of memory is essential for any group's construction of identity because the related events are the basis of its existence, as expressed by Jan Assmann. Furthermore, it is a retrospective construct that reconstructs events from the distant, possibly mythical past in the present. According to Assmann (1992: 76f.), the past is transformed into myth based on fact or fiction.

These myths of cultural memory serve as a repository of values and truths that can determine action according to the culture's norms, and a culture's interpretation of itself in contrast to others. In this sense, cultural memory also incorporates a political dimension that the novels in this study touch on. The resulting cultural memories are highly stylised, ritualised and bound to certain media since they are dependent on a long-term tradition to convey meaning. Such media may be texts, songs, carvings, or ceremonial traditions, to name a few. As mentioned earlier, it is the specialists' task to pass these memories on, thus indicating an organised body in charge of their perpetuation. Due to this level of organisation, cultural memory creates a clear set of binding values for the group. Finally, cultural memory is marked by the way it reflects the group's situation and their self-image.

Maori culture can be considered as what Jan Assmann calls a hot culture in *Das kulturelle Gedächtnis* (1992). The Maori myths of the distant past describing the creation of the world and the coming to Aotearoa, for example, form an understanding of a collective past. At the same time, these myths are also used to determine and interpret the present and the future. Most Maori writers incorporate myths in their fiction as a basis of a past that connects all Maori people. At the same time, these stories give a direction to characters who seem lost: in *Tangi*, Tama has a feeling of purpose only once he is confronted with his family traditions again, and in *Mutuwhenua* Ripeka decides to stay true to Maori customs even during her married life because she is unable to live entirely like a *Pakeha*. A contented future seems impossible without these myths and the knowledge they convey.

In such hot cultures, memory of these myths remains active, but not rigid. On the one hand, it can interpret the present as a time enriched by memories of the mythical past; on the other, it may also be a hindrance by insisting that the past was richer and better than the current situation. Both

Ihimaera and Grace appear to have a wistful view of some lost customs. They do not, however, condemn the present. Instead, they insist that the past is not lost as long as the stories remain and a memory of the early beginnings of Maori life is retained in every Maori. The current circumstances are not as they should be and pose problems for them, but the novels suggest that – though it is a difficult task – the present can be improved by the repossession of Maori traditions, thereby leading to a better future. To clarify, the novels never suggest that the past on the whole was a better time and the present is entirely out of order. If it were, a rebellion would be necessary on a much greater scale than the individual struggles depicted in fiction. Characteristically, the protagonists require greater Maori influence, but not a life entirely apart from the *Pakeha*. On the contrary – Ihimaera's later novels in particular advocate co-operation between the two cultures that will eventually lead to contented co-existence. Grace's novels, however, often focus on Maori life to an extent that *Pakeha* culture is almost entirely left aside. Yet, this does not mean that the author calls for a rejection of the *Pakeha*, but instead strongly encourages a return to Maori customs and beliefs. Judging from their fiction, all three writers believe that the myths and memories of the past will enrich the present.

As discussed earlier, as a medium of cultural memory, literature can render visible the process of remembering in narrative form, whether collective or individual. As Rigney's five stages of memory indicate, texts can become locations of memory in which collective remembrance and historical meaning are focused. Here, the advantage of literature is the way it lends itself to a constant cycle of telling and retelling that reflects indigenous oral storytelling. Since the continual retelling encourages shared frames of reference among people who may even be unconnected, I suggest that books can be the beginning of a new memorial phase that is established through recursivity. This applies to the featured Maori novels in particular: they are read, but that is not the end of it – they are discussed, written about, and expanded on in much the same way that memorials are. They are the beginning of a phase that demands an exploration of the subject matter due to their presence in a given culture. By choosing and refusing to depict certain aspects of the past, literature is able to blend particular memories that are then stored by the readership. Maori novels have thus become *lieux de mémoire*, cultural products or phenomena collectively associated with the past and (national or cultural) identity. These sites of memory function on the three levels that Pierre Nora (1998 [1990]: 32f.) distinguishes: the material, functional and symbolic dimension. As books in print, Maori novels are available in a material form, and they are written and printed for a purpose. Hence, on a functional level, they offer versions of the past that are made accessible to the public. At the same time, they may be written having a political agenda in mind, to encourage action, or quite simply to inform. On a symbolic level, some of the novels are attributed with symbolic meaning either as early as their publication or later. Intentionally endowed with symbolic meaning, the novels obtain this additional level that sets them apart from others. They thus take up a special position in society, allowing them to feature in collective memory.

As sites of memory, the fiction encourages certain views of the past or even rewrites existing versions. What it does not do in Maori literature, however, is change fundamental myths on the whole. They remain as they are, although a novel's plot may hark back to known myths. The stories of the past should not be changed, and the three writers' work proves this point: no one changes the myths incorporated into the novels. The only thing that differs is their interpretation. The best example is *The Uncle's Story*, which demonstrates how myths can restrict lives. Nowhere in the novel is there a change of existing myths while they are recounted in the course of the narrative in order to demonstrate the characters' situation. What can be changed, nonetheless, is the interpretation – a realisation that one of the protagonists comes to only gradually. Seeing himself disappearing in *Te Kore*, the mythic nothingness and place of eternal darkness, it takes Sam a long time before he finds "a pinpoint of light" that eventually leads to "showering *Te Kore* with light" (*US* 240–1). This experience, contrary to his traditional knowledge of *Te Kore*, is the necessary change of the myth that gives new meaning to his plight and enables him to live a life that is frowned upon in his community. Furthermore, while reinterpretation is one possibility, Ihimaera also emphasises the necessity for new stories that will blend the lives of those who would otherwise be rejected with the lives of their fellow men and women. Maori culture is an inclusive culture, so as soon as traditional views lead to exclusion, there is a need for re-evaluation and new stories that will ideally become memories themselves with time.

Apart from the subject matter at hand, Maori cultural memory finds expression in the use of myths as already mentioned, and also in the language of each character and the narrators. Sharing both English and Maori allows a new approach to writing and storytelling, as we discussed. Cultural memory is therefore influenced by several factors in and outside the depicted fictional worlds. The three phases of Maori writing each contain representatives of approximately each decade since the first novel with changes evolving from one phase to the next. These changes represent the active properties of memory which, like identity, is never static.

Going through gradual transformations, Maori cultural memory in fiction guides indigenous identity. Thus, Grace's character Ripeka in *Mutuwhenua* expands her image of herself as she grows from child to adult and from Maori daughter to the wife of a *Pakeha*. The stories of the old days that her family told her remain with her throughout her life, but she learns to look at them from another perspective due to her confrontation with a *Pakeha* world. Yet those stories that express what it is to be Maori are kept in her memory and allow her to see herself as Maori instead of the *Pakeha* girl she wanted to be when she was younger. The mysterious Maori stone artefact she and her cousins found one day when they were little represents Ripeka's deep connection with her roots despite her rebellion. While she tries to behave like other white girls, the stone always remains a precious item of which she thinks in important moments, but never speaks of. She feels the need to tell her *Pakeha* husband about it even though she cannot explain why – the artefact is such a great part of her indigenous identity that she feels she can only be understood completely if Graeme knows of it. Being a sacred item whose significance the Maori remember, it stands for the main character's deepest core that can only be known by someone with the same roots.

In most novels, it is a lack of cultural memory rather than an excess of it that is the cause of problems. Ripeka grows up with a wealth of stories and indigenous knowledge and is able to choose how she will use them in her life, but other characters like *Tangi*'s Tama are deprived of such influence. Lacking indigenous experience and knowledge, such characters are eventually lost, insecure and without a clear identity.

What the authors offer is a gradual unravelling of cultural influences that eventually point the way towards a focussed cultural and individual identity with the help of indigenous myths, beliefs and practices. Beginning with a plea for a return to Maori roots in the novels of the first phase, the literature steadily nears a tolerant transcultural understanding of Maori identity that is firmly based on indigenous cultural memory and the appropriation of traditional customs and beliefs.

2.3.4 Memory and Identity Revisited

Part of the difficulty that the protagonists in Ihimaera's and Grace's novels are confronted with is what Erll (2005: 119) refers to as synchronic plurality. Living in a multicultural society, the characters are faced with a number of cultural norms deriving from different cultural memories valid for each respective cultural group. It is almost impossible to combine two distinct sets of cultural memories since each has its own myths of the past that supply the group with norms and values. This difficulty is what characterises the protagonists' actions and is the source of their problems. Since a person able to combine two or more sets of cultural memories would be a rare case in which norms and values would no longer retain their respective primacy, the fictional characters struggle until they find a way to integrate one set within the other to a certain extent. What becomes clear in the novels is that rarely any are able to completely adopt both Maori and *Pakeha* culture to the same degree. There always remains a certain tension even after a suitable approach has been found.

Tama is an exception in the second half of *The Rope of Man*, represented as an older character than the ones we have encountered previously: he knows who he is and that he has found his place not only in New Zealand, but in the world. The calm that defines his actions in the last half of the novel is in stark contrast to the confused young man we see in the first half, struggling to be true to his Maori heritage in a dominantly *Pakeha* world. At the same time, this calmness sets him apart from characters in earlier Maori novels. The older Tama, now called by the Western acquivalent name Tom, appears to have found the solution that is best for him. The fact that he is called Tom instead of Tama signifies his recognition of the inter-relationships between the cultures of New Zealand and exemplifies how one culture can influence him without driving out the other. In the novel, he is both Tama and Tom, who is at home in his own skin no matter the name. Unlike the young man Tama once was, the adult Tom is confident and knows exactly who he is as an individual and a member of his tribe. A name may be a person's first pointer as to their identity – it is especially important in a cultural group that is proud of its lineage and gains *mana* from it –, but it is superficial compared to the many other cultural influences that shape and change individuals.

Ultimately, by accepting the sets of values from two (or more) cultures, Tom has made his place in the world. He did not simply find it, but actively created it since it was a struggle for him in his younger "years of wandering" (*RM* 54) in a "nasty, racist, homophobic, sexist, miserable bloody society" (*ibid.* 215) that required his participation. In this respect, Tom is the most accomplished character and his struggle has come to an end. If we look at previous novels, their endings never offer a real conclusion with a solution. Instead, one hurdle has been overcome, but it is clear that this is only the beginning even though it is a first essential step towards a clearer individual and cultural identity. *Mutuwhenua* ends before we know whether Ripeka's decision to have her daughter grow up with her grandparents in a Maori environment leads to the results she hopes for. At the end of *Tangi*, Tama decides to take charge of his siblings after his father's death, but we do not see whether he keeps his promise – in fact, we only realise in the sequel that he does not. *The Uncle's Story* has an ending full of possibilities and hope, yet we cannot know if the characters are successful in their quests.

Whatever the outcome, one thing is clear: the characters are subjective points of intersection in whom the many different identities that exist within their community touch. In them, the plurality of options – cultural, collective, individual and so on – coincide and influence the construction of identity. Each option carries with it specific memories that relate to sex, ethnicity, age and so forth. Although the characters are points of intersection, they are rarely compounds of all influences since, as mentioned earlier, being able to accept two or more different sets of cultural memories entirely would deny their inherent need for primacy.

Fiction as a Medium of Cultural Memory

Literature as a medium of cultural memory thus becomes a mediator between the individual and collective dimension of memory, says Erll: "This way, personal memories can only become relevant on a collective level through medial representation and distribution. This is particularly evident in the case of contemporary witnesses. Their experiences only become an element of collective memory through interviews and the publication of their correspondence. Conversely, the individual only gains access to socio-cultural schemata through communication and the use of media" (Erll 2005: 123, translation NM). The representation of memory in literature and other media therefore encourages their institutionalisation in collective and cultural memory. The media are used at home or in schools and universities, for instance, furthering their canonisation. The prominence of the Maori novels featured here derives from such – perhaps unexpected – canonisation: unexpected because they managed to break into the literary market that was dominated by *Pakeha* and Anglo-American writing at the time. In the course of the Maori renaissance, Maori fiction had the chance to make a name for itself, leading to a steady surge of indigenous writing since the 1970s. The opportunity readers then had to become acquainted with Maori culture through literature written by Maori themselves instead of having to resort to second-hand *Pakeha* reports made an impact on the understanding of this seemingly foreign culture.

"Media are not neutral carriers of foregoing information relevant to memory," Erll insists. "What they seem to encode – versions of reality and the past, values and norms, concepts of identity – they often create in the first place" (Erll 2005: 124, translation NM). Consequently, the move from exclusively oral or artistic storytelling to writing enabled a far more detailed depiction of the past than before and would have opened up a variety of medial constructions of the past unknown without the new media. These available versions of the past determine the construction of identity on an individual as well as collective and cultural level with the help of a variety of media of which literature is only one. It is safe to say, in the context of this study, that the Maori novel has influenced the perception of Maori culture from within and without.

Therefore, the works of Ihimaera and Grace are cultural texts that save information relevant for Maori culture. They portray views of Maori life and beliefs that are made available to readers through distribution. Books may be collective texts on the one hand because they circulate among a vast number of readers, or cultural texts on the other due to their capacity to store information. Regardless of literary characteristics, texts become cultural texts because of the way society treats them: the novels presented here are essential works of the New Zealand literary canon and are read at home, at school and university. They have been read since their first publication and still are today. Subsequently, they have influenced the view of Maori life and offered an approach to Maori experience. As part of a canon, the novels are considered to convey concepts of identity, and collectively shared norms and values that are important for New Zealand society.

Maori readers can identify with these cultural texts and subscribe to the values and beliefs they impart. Since New Zealand is a multicultural society, Maori literary works take on an interesting role as cultural texts – like society itself, they are divided: one part of them subscribes entirely to their cultural importance while another part cannot do so to the same extent. Despite accepting and keeping them within the canon, a compromise is made so that Maori content can be contained within a Western form that will allow the work to be accepted within that canon. Rather than a compromise, it can be seen as transcultural development instead. It is clear that *Pakeha* readers will not be able to identify with a Maori text in the same way due to a lack of personal experience. Yet there is no doubt that Ihimaera's novels, for instance, are important works ranking as high as works by the best *Pakeha* writers. This is due to the fact that even non-Maori readers are aware of these texts as cultural texts, and their acceptance of them as important works of New Zealand literature allows for a basic identification with them as New Zealand texts portraying the nation's culture in all its variety.

According to Erll, these texts can only take on their status as cultural texts if their status as literary texts is reduced. Therefore, literary aspects move into the background while the text is centred on a general (timeless) truth that goes beyond the literary text's contemporary interpretation. Identification with these texts would then encourage an increased interest in further "knowledge about heritage, identity, norms and values, and a search for truth" (Erll 2005: 157, translation NM). Thus cultural texts are not merely consumed, but prompt action as well.

In this context, with reference to Ricoeur, Erll (2005: 153f.) speaks of an "iconic enrichment" of reality that is triggered by the reading process. Literature thus has an effect on the reader's perception of reality, leading to actions that are also influenced by what he or she has read. These actions, says Erll, change "cultural practice and, therefore, this reality itself". She continues, "Literature influences the collective understanding of the course and meaning of past events, interprets the present, and raises expectations for the future. Even actual action – ranging from altered forms of everyday communication to political action – can arise from this collective reconfiguration" (Erll 2005: 153, translation NM). This is clearly the case with Maori literature, especially the novels that carry with them the energy of the 1970s Maori renaissance. Furthermore, cultural negotiations, in Bachmann-Medick's opinion, take place outside the text in which difference is presented so that it requires the reader and the space outside books to make sense of these conflicts. The interaction between text and reader encourages the discussion of cultural hybridity beyond the fiction (cf. Bachmann-Medick 1996: 273ff.)

Essentially, the way literature is received depends largely on institutions that may hinder or support the distribution of texts. Since the Maori renaissance was in full swing by the time the first novel was published, Maori contributions were greatly encouraged. Governmental support in publishing and the fierce demand for Maori recognition, among other things, proved to be beneficial for indigenous literature. Public authorities discourage certain interpretations while encouraging others, a process that determines how a text is viewed, and influences the actions that arise from it. The focus on Maori culture and its furtherance certainly led to the inclusion of Ihimaera, Grace, and other writers in the national literary canon. With this came a particular approach to Maori, their situation, needs and perspective. Their fiction and non-fiction are examples of the Maori perspective relating to contemporary political and social issues that need to be addressed. Thus their writing contains a political angle that may well have been attributed with more importance than was originally intended by writers. However, given the time of Maori political activism in which their novels, poems and short stories were published, it was inevitable for the political message – next to their literary quality – to become the focus and certainly one of the significant reasons of their success.

Given the importance of the Maori novel within New Zealand society from the beginning, it comes as no surprise that its genuine portrayal of Maori identity allows the novels to function as models for the construction of identity. The iconic enrichment of reality through fiction in this case determines the type of cultural identity Maori assume and *Pakeha* are made familiar with. Things such as the presence of myth in everyday life, the presence of the ancestors even after death, the significance of *tikanga*, the importance of *te reo* are all embedded within the fiction and blend with reality. This way, Ihimaera elaborates, Maori can finally tell their own story and challenge the distortions brought about by non-Maori texts. At the same time, the described fictional resistance also contributes to the construction of Maori identity and encourages change in the world outside literature:

> Maori writers have played a major role in the stories we [New Zealanders] tell about ourselves. They have also made it easier to "see" Waari [Ihimaera's pseudonym for Maori subjectivity]. Their major corrective has been to Write the Maori Story from the Inside. To construct a Maori world that is *validated* by *authentic* Maori experience. To offer characters who are not bit players in Pakeha texts (as villain or plot device or exotic colouring or, worse, friendly sidekick) but the main characters – heroes, heroines and, yes, even villains – in texts of their own. To offer themes of decolonisation, antidotes and antivenemes which unpoison the stories which have been told about us. (Ihimaera 1998b)

In this light, there is reciprocity between identity construction in fiction and reality: while writers work with elements that are identity forming in reality and exemplify them in fiction, the stories themselves portray identities and their construction that readers may draw from in return.

CHAPTER THREE

He Tuhinga Pakimaero: The Novels

In *The Stepmother Tongue*, John Skinner divides New Zealand literature into two categories. He subsumes Ihimaera and Grace under the group New Literatures in Old Worlds, whose writers live in a society whose stability was disrupted by British imperialism. These writers use English as an alternative to their native tongue in which they would be proficient enough to write as well (Skinner 1998: 15). Skinner does not address that Ihimaera is said to have been more accomplished in English than Maori and that Grace herself states in an interview (Calleja 2003: 112) that she cannot speak the language, which might question this categorisation. Nonetheless, Ihimaera writes in Maori even though the majority of his contributions have been in English.

On a very general level, however, Skinner's categories are appropriate and he does concede in his book's "extroduction" that not all writers in former colonies are easily placed within his classification. The difficulties evident in this system are yet another reminder of the complexity of categorising writing in multicultural societies. On a very basic level, his categories apply if one requires a superficial, first-glance classification. The writers and their work are far more detailed and oftentimes resist this process, which is a characteristic of their writing of survival and resistance.

For our analysis, the body of work has been divided into three phases, roughly circumscribing a decade each. This is not a random division – each decade has altered, compounded or encountered new concerns that are subsequently addressed in fiction. Naturally, since the end of a decade does not inevitably mark the end of literary concerns and techniques or the beginning of something entirely new, some of the novels of one decade may be included in the phase mainly containing novels of another. The last phase, for instance, includes work both from the 1990s and the new millennium.

The main criterion here is the subject matter of the novels rather than the time of publication. A novel such as *Once Were Warriors* would therefore be included in the second phase, which is otherwise dominated by 1980s fiction due to its content – the social criticism inherent in Duff's depiction of violence and the inescapability of this vicious cycle – despite its publication in the 1990s.

Phase one of Maori writing comprises novels in English exclusively from the 1970s and examines the first novels by Grace and Ihimaera. The second phase includes Grace's *Potiki* and more of Ihimaera's work, which are both increasingly political, and critical of Maori-*Pakeha* relations in the 1980s. There was a degree of meekness in the earlier decade's writing that is now replaced by a fierce demand for change that stems from the newly attained steadier position of Maori writers and changes in society. While the previous decade saw the introduction to indigenous writing and created a foundation for it, the following years made use of the secure footing resulting from it. If the first phase is viewed as the foundation of the Maori novel, then the second can be compared to raising the walls of the home that the writers are attempting to construct for their fiction in New Zealand.

Finally, the last phase marks the completion of the basic structure while being open to further development. The novels of the late 1990s and early 2000s share the concerns of earlier decades even now, like the difficulties of being brought up in different, possibly opposing cultures. Furthermore, they also introduce new issues such as the Maori attitude towards homosexuality or the position of the Maori individual in New Zealand and beyond in this new age. Especially in Ihimaera's case, the novels appear to open up and include a more global perspective than before. Since 1973, the novel has moved from the tribal community to an urban setting, and eventually further to comprise New Zealand as a whole and as part of the world, diffusing national borders without a loss of *Maoritanga*.

3.1 *Te Tumu*: The Foundations – What It Means to Be Maori

In the 1970s, Maori began to re-establish their culture that was in the process of being forgotten with time. It became clear that there could be no going back to the past as it had been, but that the present had to be considered for a better Maori future. This led to the fusion of old and new, of Maori and *Pakeha* views and culture that also found expression in fiction. They did not expect that the revival would be easy and harmonic, but the longing for harmony especially comes through in the novels of the first phase of Maori writing in the 1970s. Later, the novels became more political while others focused on the individual, personal consequences of the changes taking place in New Zealand society. Since these shifts in society have an impact on the individual, the featured writers have chosen either a group or a single character to exemplify the effect of cultural change in a multicultural society. However, it is presented more as a separatist bicultural society consisting of Maori and *Pakeha* in the first phase rather than the actual multicultural or indeed transcultural country described in later novels.

In 1998, Ihimaera explained how the Maori people cannot rely on what comes from outside of their own culture if they want to live as Maori and not as the products of colonisation. He says, "New Zealand's brand of multiculturalism had indeed derived from 'anti-Eurocentrism' and 'cultural relativism'" (Ihimaera 1998a: 195). So even though the country itself had developed its own cultural politics, it was being influenced from outside and measured against Europe and other Western countries. But what does it mean for the native minority in their country? "All this," says Ihimaera, "had forced us to establish our own verities. To take our compass bearings not from abroad but from ourselves" (*ibid.* 196). Yet, at the same time, you cannot ignore the cultures you live alongside, he says. You must be aware of "[...] the subversive nature of Maori culture and of its struggle to represent itself within the framework of European ideology. [...] From this I discovered Myself in relationship to the Other and that the very fact of being Maori meant that whatever I did would always be a subversion of the main discourse" (*ibid.* 197). Combining the native beliefs, mythologies and histories with elements of *Pakeha* culture proves difficult, but it must be done, as Ihimaera's own work suggests. Consciously writing against the main discourse helps "society regain belief in itself and put away the complexes of the years of denigration and self-abasement. And it is essentially a question of education, in the best sense of the word" (Achebe 1975c: 44).

In this first phase of the Maori novel, the main concern appears to be a reminder of the cornerstones of Maori life so as to encourage a focus on its very roots. In "The Novelist as Teacher", Achebe remarks in a similar vein that "I would be quite satisfied if my novels (especially the ones set in the past) did no more than teach my readers that their past – with all its imperfections – was not one long night of savagery from which the first Europeans acting on God's behalf delivered them" (*ibid.* 45). There needs to be a reminder of the good that is found in traditional Maori life especially at a time when more and more of the young people leave to study or work in the cities. Removed from rural life, they adapt to a *Pakeha* environment or, in many cases, fail. The inadequacy of *Pakeha* society finds expression in the novels of the first phase that deal with the struggle between the two lives the characters have to lead. Moving between countryside and city, the prevailing impression is that they need to choose one over the other because they cannot have both.

In 1975, Witi Ihimaera published his article "Why I Write" in which he explains his motivation and the politics behind his work and speaks of the New Zealanders' dual heritage. New Zealand is a land for which there are two different maps, he says. One is the white man's map, the other is the Maori map. In the course of history, the overpowering *Pakeha* map took over. To him, even a *Pakeha* has a Maori heritage because s/he lives in this country alongside indigenous people and their culture even if s/he is rarely confronted with them:

> The pakeha map is dominant, its contours so firmly established that all New Zea-landers including Maori are shaped by it. [...] [M]ost New Zealanders remain unaware that they have a dual cultural heritage and not a single one. Their attitude is still predominantly separatist, which is surprising for a country which prides itself for its amicable record of race relations. For instance, ask who discovered New Zealand and you will be told Abel Tasman. But the answer, as given by Maori history, is Kupe.

> And that, quite simply, is why I began to write. To make New Zealanders aware
> of their "other," Maori, heritage. To convince my countrymen, with love and anger,
> that they must take their Maori personality into account. (Ihimaera 1975: 117)

Ihimaera's early work is political simply because he writes about the struggle
the Maori people face, and this circumstance always implies social criticism.
His focus, however, are not primarily the social difficulties at this stage.
Instead, it is the difficulty of "retaining our emotional identity" (*ibid.*) and
knowing who you are and what your cultural roots are. For this reason,
Ihimaera's work is essential for our discussion.

Maori culture is mainly conveyed orally through rituals, speeches and
ceremonies, but, now, this is no longer enough. For one thing, the tribal
family, the *whanau*, no longer lives together as closely as it used to. People
have moved to the cities where there is promise of a career and the rurally
based culture's roots come loose. Furthermore, the Maori language is being
lost. Many children no longer speak the language of their parents, and a
loss of language means a loss of a vital part of one's culture. Only with the
1987 Maori Language Act did the native tongue become one of the two
official languages of New Zealand. Before then, English was the only language spoken and taught at school and used for official purposes. Fiction,
however, employed *te reo* even in English works. This is a custom that can
be observed from the earliest novels until today. Such use of language has
a variety of functions: it can exclude the non-Maori reader and show what
it is like to be outside a certain cultural sphere; an indigenous term may
convey something that is impossible to convey in English, a concept that
is unique to the culture and defies translation; it can preserve the native
tongue. The first step to preserve a culture is to keep its language alive,
among other things in literature and speech.

Oral literature, nonetheless, soon no longer sufficed and "Māori people
quickly saw the advantages of writing and printing for conveying ideas, in
their own language and in English" (Swarbrick 2006). Ihimaera is one of
those authors who use writing to keep this culture alive:

> [...] our own tradition of oral literature is not enough to carry our culture into the
> future, and a certain amount of force has had to be applied to Maori elders on one
> hand and Pakeha editors on the other to allow opportunities for the Maori written

word, even if the results do make them wince. As well as there has been some pres-
sure from people who want me to write what they want; I hope that writers who are
Maori never succumb to any expectations other than the ones they carry themselves.
(Ihimaera 1975: 118)

In other words, what it takes is an innovative perspective and an original
strategy to develop one's own literature. It may derive from what is already
there and dominant, but it is flexible enough to allow for new influences.
Even though most Maori writers use English as their chosen language, their
novels are very distinct from those of European writers in subject, theme
and symbolism, structure and language. The use of the native tongue is well
thought out within the novels themselves: "Language conditions the way
people perceive, the way they think, and in many works of Commonwealth
fiction, language becomes the symbolic representation of ancestral heritage
and home. Thus to lose a language is to lose touch with one's ancestors.
Yet loss of the ancestral tongue is all too often a hallmark of the multicultural situation, and this loss or threatened loss is reflected in the style,
and becomes a significant thematic concern, of writers [...]" (Beckmann
1981: 117). Even in the novels it becomes clear that not all Maori characters
are able to speak their ancestral tongue. Its loss is palpable and a reminder
of what is at stake. The featured novelists may write primarily in English, but their work is interspersed with Maori words and phrases, some
of which are left untranslated. Grace even ends *Potiki* entirely in Maori
without supplying any translation whatsoever. In doing so, she reclaims
her language and forces others to delve into the Maori culture through
the preference of a dying native tongue. At the same time, she seems to
say that some things cannot be conveyed but in their original and unique
language, that there are no words in a foreign tongue to express that which
constitutes *maoritanga*.

    This emphasis on language is important and not unusual in ethnic
literatures: a language transports the values of a culture, the traditions
and beliefs. Especially in the case of a primarily oral culture such as the
Maori one in which oratory is held in high regard, the importance of the
native tongue cannot be underestimated. It is part of the writers' aim to
re-introduce that which is about to be lost. Cliff Watego points out,

each author [...] emphasizes that the first step in assuring that the qualities of this culture are to be maintained in a future that is already conditioned by past and present attitudes is to re-educate the young in the ways and values of their people. Only then can this generation have a firm appreciation of [...] Maori identity, and gain the spiritual strength and dignity necessary to transcend the critical judgement which unjustly focuses the weight of opinion in favour of the material advantages of white society. (Watego 1984: 493)

This re-education begins with the reintroduction of language in many cases because it is regarded as a crucial element of identity.

The ways of the *Pakeha* can only serve as temporary solutions, says Watego. Even though the Maori are threatened by the loss of their culture, it would be wrong to substitute them with *Pakeha* ideals to recreate one's identity. In his opinion, what the novelists try to make clear is "that although change has become an accepted fact of Maori life, any compromise between Maori and *pakeha* ideals is really only a superficial contract based on day-to-day pragmatism; it neglects the deeper, more significant aspects relating to the Maori spirit which forms the crucial link in preserving the Maori's culture and their identity" (*ibid.* 491). There is adaptation, but not always assimilation, especially in the novels. The Maori culture remains very distinct and at the heart of the characters, no matter how great *Pakeha* influence may be. However, there is the danger of giving up on indigenous ideals due to the "tailored solutions to 'Maori problems'" (*ibid.* 491) that the *Pakeha* world offers. Eventually, in the novels, the native culture is embraced and recognised as the main, if not only, heritage.

The conflict the characters face evolves from the need to reconcile two very different cultures and identities. It is the individual's task to create a new individual identity that allows for both to coexist. Significantly, this is something each character has to come to terms with on their own; it is not a group's task. In fact, the group is there to uphold the indigenous culture only. Watego states that *Pakeha* society is harmful to the Maori and his quest for identity. Nevertheless, it cannot be avoided and reconciliation must be sought. In the early novels, this meant a definite preference of the Maori heritage and a turning back to indigenous culture, often after a detour into the *Pakeha* world which proves to be insufficient or hostile. "All these novels," Watego summarises the characters' crisis, deal in some way with the individual's finding the best possible reconciliation between himself and society. Partial fulfilment of this quest presents a danger to the individual himself, for society is in a constant state of flux, and for the individual to remain at a level of insight that takes into account only causes or results of such changes isolates that person to one area of human experience. From the point of view of the indigenous novelist, avoiding this quicksand of thought and opinion and accommodating himself to perpetual change is absolutely necessary. Indeed this condition is the most difficult for the individual to sustain, since it prefigures a predicament that required him to sustain a cultural identity (which is based on subsistence) yet adhere to a tradition of change (based on progress). (*ibid.* 495)

Even though identity is usually perceived as constant, the characters need to expose themselves to change in order to adapt to the requirements of a given time. This seeming contradiction is what causes the crisis at the heart of the novels ever since Ihimaera emerged as the first Maori novelist.

3.1.1 Witi Ihimaera's Tangi (1973)

Ihimaera's *Tangi* has had a profound impact on New Zealand literature as the first Maori novel. It is the augmentation of his short story by the same title in the collection *Pounamu Pounamu* (1972). There are two earlier versions of the short story: the unauthorised "The Faraway Side of the Hour" in *Te Maori* 1:6, and another published in *Contemporary Maori Writing*, edited by Margaret Orbell in 1970. In 2005 a new, slightly altered version of the novel including a sequel set in the early twenty-first century was published under the title *The Rope of Man* to celebrate the author's career as part of the Ihimaera Thirtieth Anniversary Collection featuring revisions of some of his work.

In his review in *Te Ao Hou* in 1974, Paul Katene ended with the question, "Is *Tangi* really the long awaited novel by a Maori?" (Katene 1974: 60) and he was proved right by the book's success. Katene notes that it is a novel which Maori relate to because it is a vital part of their culture that is being presented here. At the same time, he says, "[r]eaders unfamiliar with the tangihanga will, nonetheless sense that something totally new has been added to the literature of this country – a new insight – a new depth plumbed. *Tangi* is not only a personalised vision of the author, it is the personalised experience of a people – it is the heartbeat of Maoridom, told with great subtlety and sensitivity within a framework that remains peculiarly Maori" (Katene 1974: 60). The novel became a milestone in New Zealand literature, a novel that introduced the Maori worldview and the problems of those days to the country and, subsequently to the world, in its own very distinct language.

The novel was not written in Maori and thus does not circulate only among the native communities. Written in English, it ensures that those Maori who can no longer speak their native tongue or have become too far removed from their heritage have a significant piece of their culture in writing. At the same time, choosing this language, Ihimaera presents a part of his culture to a much wider readership which would not know much, if anything, about Maori life. In *Introducing Witi Ihimaera*, Corballis and Garrett go so far as to assume some of the changes between the *Tangi* versions "seem to have been dictated by a desire to make the vocabulary more accessible to contemporary Pakehas" (Corballis and Garrett 1984: 24). What is more, with the emergence of Maori writing in English, the world is presented with something that has been there for a long time: "The Maori viewpoint has always been accessible, to Maoris that is, and to those who understand the Maori language; in this sense it has been a 'hidden' literature for many years. But it was not until the early 1960s, and via written English, that Maori literature began to unfurl the views of the people, until then participants in virtually the largest underground movement known in New Zealand, into the world of light" (Ihimaera and Long 1982, quoted in: Corballis and Garrett 1984: 41).

Despite the European influences on his writing, Corballis and Garrett attest to his clear "Maoriness of tone", "[a]nd so we return to the point that Ihimaera is not simply a Maori writer; his work owes a good deal to European precedents. He has consistently practised what he has preached: a 'dual heritage', biculturalism" (*ibid.* 67). In *Tangi*, Ihimaera first sets to work on this idea of biculturalism, but it is not yet as much in the foreground of his work as it is in later novels. In his study of Ihimaera's works and political outlook till 1987, Ojinmah identifies three chronological phases: the pastoral phase to which *Tangi* belongs, the transitional phase including *Whanau*, and finally the political phase begun with *The Matriarch*. In *Tangi*, Ihimaera is more concerned with the emotional aspect of cultural conflict rather than the political side that inevitably influences the characters' lives.

Therefore, it comes as no great surprise that the early *Tangi* includes a poem – a genre that may affect readers more immediately than prose – that is no longer included in the 2005 Reed publication of the novel. This poem expresses the importance and hints at some of the characteristics of Maori writing in general and at the time of publication in particular:

TANGI

My mother was the Earth,
My father was the Sky.
They were Rangitane and Papatuanuku,
the first parents, who clasped each other so
tightly that there was no day. Their children
were born into darkness ...

This is *Tangi*, a poetic drama in prose, about
a young man and his father.
This is *Tangi*, an account of death, but also
an affirmation of life.
This is *Tangi*, describing simply and
sincerely, the Maori values placed on life;
and on aroha, love and sympathy for each
other.

This is *Tangi*, a vivid expression of the
village family unity of rural Maori life.
This is *Tangi*, written in the hope that such a
life, and the values of that life, will never be
lost.
This is *Tangi*, the first novel written by a
Maori to be published.

Haere mai, haere mai, haere mai.

The poem's structure and language introduce the reader to what we may expect from a Maori novel and also makes clear that the style will be close to that of the Maori oral tradition. Katene describes *Tangi's* uniqueness in his review: "The style follows the Maori oral tradition in its persistent use of mytho-poetic elements; its personifications; its dramatic and lively juxtaposition of images; its sudden changes of moods and colour – light and shade. Word groups and word sounds play an important part in recall, in emphasis, or to act as pivotal points for transitions from laughter to tears – from sunlight to darkness; from present to past" (Katene 1974: 60). We see how Ihimaera incorporates some of these elements in his poem as well, combining his Maori tradition with the language and literary style which used to be viewed as predominantly European.

The poem's first stanza is a retelling of Maori cosmogony and is a ritual opening which brings us to one of the novel's main themes: the omnipresence of myth and its importance in life. The poem places us at the beginning of all things, the beginning of the Maori world and also the opening of the novel. This stanza is followed by a characterisation of the story to come, a narrative about the children's relation to their parents. In the course of the book, the real parents are often likened to the mytho-logical First Parents, emphasising the connection between myth and real life: the two are inextricably connected. Finally, towards the end of his poem, Ihimaera gives his reasons for writing *Tangi* before the ritual clos-ing line: "the hope that such a life, and the values of that life, will never be lost". The poem's exclusion from the new version of *Tangi* appears to be due to the changed focus and new philosophy Ihimaera chooses to depict in 2005. The poem complements the style of the Maori oral tradition that the writer employs in many passages of the novel, and which he abandons for the most part in his rewriting.

The main event the novel revolves around is the *tangi*, the funeral. The homecalling of the *whanau* to farewell the deceased is one of the most profound events in Maori life. "The tangihanga," Mead says, "is an example of an intricate and public cultural event. It is a complex of several tikanga which are interrelated and underpinned by a body of matauranga Maori and a set of beliefs. The number of people involved in it can vary between a modest 100 to 10,000" (Mead 2003: 12). Ihimaera's depiction of a *tangi* brings the changes within the Maori community to the fore. The *whanau* is no longer as close-knit and geographically close as it used to be, and the young have had to decide whether to live with their family or seek their fortune in the city. Yet despite the geographical separation, that which connects all Maori people is still intact: the bond that their heritage provides cannot be severed and the *tangi* is proof of this. This tribe's period of mourning lasts three days and everyone has come to honour the deceased.

Tama, the novel's central character, is the deceased man's son who has left the *whanau* to pursue his career as a journalist in the city. With the ambitions that force him to move away from his family and their customs, he must try and combine his *maoritanga* with *Pakeha* requirements. They are often conflicting concepts and ways of life that put a strain on Tama's relationship with his family.

His parents do not hold him back from pursuing his dreams, but at the same time they expect him to uphold the traditional values and beliefs of his people. When his father dies Tama feels guilty for not having been home to help him instead of moving to the city. He knows it would have been the oldest son's duty to be with the family. With his father's death, Tama remembers it is now his duty to be the head of his family, help his mother, and teach his brother and sisters the meaning of their *maoritanga* to which he must return himself. This also means he will have to leave the city and abandon his beginning career.

Loyalty in the Face of Change

Change is one of the main themes encompassing the entire novel, the dissolution of what once was and which can no longer remain. Living in these times requires of the Maori to adapt as well as keep up their traditions so as not to lose their cultural identity, and we see them struggle with this in the novel. While Tama's parents do not hold him back, it is clear that they would rather have him home to help with the farm instead of living in the city where they fear he will be corrupted by *Pakeha* ways. The city changes people just like it does the girl Tama sees on the train to Wellington. While she assures her grandmother that the distance will never change anything between them and that their hearts will always be one, the girl who passes the time singing Maori songs during the journey becomes a cigarette-smoking city girl when Wellington comes into sight (cf. *T* 195).

The city is depicted as a necessary evil for Tama's family. They move there for better opportunities, but there is not enough work and the father must leave his wife and children for long stretches of time to work elsewhere. Furthermore, factory life is unhealthy for Tama's mother, who loses her baby (*T* 66), and, most of all, it is a lonely life in anonymity. Like the Maori girl in Tama's neighbourhood who jeers at him with her spiteful calls "Maori boy! Maori boy!" (*T* 76), Maori children forget the importance of their heritage and perhaps even that they themselves are of a different cultural background than the *Pakeha* around them. The Maori youths who have to compete with *Pakeha* drop out of school and few of them continue as Tama does, who "took a firm step forward into the *Pakeha* world" (*T* 78) and managed to find his place in it. However, no longer being in a Maori environment makes him lose part of himself: "But because the world I was growing up in was a Pakeha one, it was difficult to retain my Maoritanga. Even when I was trying to be humorous about it, there'd still be an ache in my heart. Sometimes, I even forgot my Maoritanga and its values. I remember how shattering it was, when I realised it. [...] It was more difficult to live in two worlds as I grew older. The Maori part was so easy to forget. Not being Maori, but what being Maori meant; the customs, the traditions, Maori aroha" (*T* 78–9). In the novel, leaving the ancestral land also means leaving your cultural background and a part of your identity behind since the only "[h]ome was Waituhi" (*T* 84). Tama's family eventually returns there, having "discovered an old truth: that they belong to a particular piece of earth, and that it is their responsibility to find that place, to re-enter and repossess their birthright" (Corballis and Garrett 1984: 33).

Yet, even life in the country is no longer what it used to be. The younger generation moves away, most children no longer speak Maori (cf. *T* 59), and the land, too, changes: "an old colonial home now stands [...] [where] there used to be a Maori stockade upon that hill" (*T* 115) and the outside *Pakeha* world is intruding even into this small space. The most startling evidence proving that the Maori people have realised that times are no longer as they were can be seen in the new decoration of the Rongopai meetinghouse for

Te Kooti, rebel leader at the time of the Land Wars. Instead of the usual traditional carvings, the interior is painted:

> It was one of the very few painted meeting houses remaining and still beautiful to look upon, despite the decay brought by wind, rain and sun. But when it was finished, the elders came and were shocked at what they saw. The young men, in decorating the house, had departed from the traditional designs. The old reverence and dignity had gone. In its place, the young men had blended both Maori and Pakeha art and scenes of life together. For the elders, this was not right. But you told me, Dad, that perhaps even then, the young men had seen that the old life was ending. And this meeting house for you, was a symbol of the twilight years of the Maori. (*T* 116)

Evidently, there is no going back to life as it was and Maori cannot avoid or stop these changes. In an article on Ihimaera's fiction, Hartwig Isernhagen further analyses the changes that are apparent in the repainted meetinghouse, which make it a bridge between old and new. "The fusion of disparate elements in the paintings is, of course," he says,

> first of all an image of historical loss and the reference to the mythical prediction concerning the white face behind the Maori face is a reference to a myth of colonization and/or destruction. But it is also a reference to a traditional myth and, thereby, a statement of continuity, and the fusion can also be interpreted as mediation, the process of history that is indicated by it as a reconciliation rather than a loss. What is perhaps even more important, though, is that regardless of the concrete values attributed to the historical process, there is change and continuity with the past – both of which the *whanau* had been in danger of losing. (Isernhagen 1984: 194)

The change that has entered indigenous life therefore requires a new way of thinking and some way of preserving *maoritanga*. As a result, Ihimaera points out that Maori customs are particularly important and must remain with you even when you are no longer in your native land. Whether you live in a city far from your *whanau* or not is unimportant to a certain extent – the Maori ways must be kept to honour your ancestors and remind you of who you are by remembering the past, both historical and mythic. Even though the *Pakeha's* influence cannot be prevented, it should not lead to the loss of cultural identity Maori fear. As the repainted meetinghouse shows, there is a certain degree of blending between cultures.

Tangi portrays Maori life with all its customs and values as Ihimaera states in his poem's last stanza. It becomes clear that the author himself fears the loss of this rural life and all that is connected to it. As Ihimaera says, "My concern is for the roots of our culture, the culture we carry within ourselves and which makes us truly Maori. It is a culture essentially rurally based, with toes firmly gripping the soil, and so I write about the rural Maori rather than about the Maori in urban areas where – so I've been informed – all the action is" (Ihimaera 1975: 117). Ultimately, the people's *maoritanga* is at stake, their *whanaungatanga*, kinship and family responsibility, and *manaakitanga*, reciprocal assistance to one another. *Tangi* is a literary means by which to preserve as well as present them to those who are not familiar with them. The *tangi* is the one thing that still presents most clearly what it is to be Maori[1] and, therefore, "Witi Ihimaera finally fixes Tama Mahana in a situation that demands his undivided loyalty to his Maori heritage" (Watego 1984: 494) in the course of the novel.

"That is the Maori way": Maori Customs and Cultural Difference
At times the novel appears repetitive when the author emphasises the importance of *maoritanga*. Especially in Tama's conversations with his father, it becomes clear what is expected not only of him as a son but also as a member of his *iwi*. It is his task to return home and be there for the family, particularly after his father's death, and this is something his father prepares him for on several occasions while still alive. "You're the eldest, Tama," he reminds him. "If anything happens to me, you come home straight away. The eldest always looks after the younger ones of the family. I was taught that as a child; I teach you the same thing now. If I should die, you come home to your mother and your younger brothers and sisters" (*T* 21). It is stressed throughout the novel in conversations between the two men even after death that "[t]hat's the Maori way" (*T* 29). It is the Maori

---

1   Ihimaera quoted in Martin (1983: 54): "I looked for the one major physical institution that Maori people retain in the most positive way and found it in the tangi, our ceremonial of mourning ... virtually the only institution we have for conveying our feelings about being Maori."

way of giving yourself to the *whanau* and not to be selfish; it is the Maori way of being a family:

> [w]hen you went out getting kina and paua at Makarori Beach, you stopped off at other houses to ask if anybody else wanted to come with you. When you returned home, you told everybody to come to your place and have a good kai. If somebody got married, you didn't wait for an invitation, you just went to the wedding, because you were a member of the family. And if there was a tangi, you stopped whatever you were doing, no matter if you were working in some flash factory or at some flash job, and you went home to help out. One of the family had died and the tangi, it was the homecalling. (*T* 120)

Everything is done together; the family stays together even if they are separated geographically because family bonds remain. These bonds gain their strength from the mythic history, Maori heritage, ceremonies, rituals, songs and dances. There is a connection that binds the family of the living and continues even in death.

The novel describes how tribal family bonds are very strong and extend from the living world into the world of the dead. "That is the Maori way: not to talk of one family for we belong to each other, not only family living but family dead" (*T* 30). There is no distinction between the dead and the living other than the dead not being present in the same way. However, the spirits linger for some time like Tama's father who comes to see his son until the day of his burial. During these visits, he reminds him of his duties, calling him home, making sure he does not forget what a Maori son must do. On the one hand, Tama's conversations with his deceased father indicate his guilt and deep sense of loss, but it is also part of Maori belief that the dead remain in the world until their burial when, according to their mythology, they leave Aotearoa New Zealand at Te Reinga, the very tip of the North Island, to return to their ancestral Hawaiki. Keri Hulme explains this belief, among others, in her article "Myth, Omen, Ghost and Dream":

> It is thought that when someone dies, they make their way down to the far northern tip of New Zealand, to Rerenge-wairua (the leaping-off place of spirits) at Cape Te Reinga. As they go, they leave signs of their passage; northern tribes believe that if you are from an inland area you will leave bracken or nikau, from a coastal area,

seaweed. Other tribes believe that you tie knots in the grasses. Whichever, eventually the spirits arrive at Te Rerenga-wairua, slide down the roots of the last pohutukawa tree in the land, into a kelp-fringed hole in the sea, and make their way to the borders of the night. (Hulme 1984: 32)

Pakeha and Maori views on death differ greatly. In *Pakeha* society, death is a taboo, something that cannot be spoken of aloud and is approached with fear. "Why do they whisper, why are they afraid?" Tama asks himself. "Oh my friends... Yes, you must only speak in whispers. Don't shout. If you shout, Death may come for you, angry that you speak of Him without reverence. He may think you mock Him. So speak in whispers, only in whispers so that He does not hear. He is everywhere like God. Better not say His name at all. Then He will pass you by and lift the shadow of His cloak over someone else." (*T* 8)

This notion of death is difficult for Tama to understand. His *Pakeha* friends in the city treat him the way they treat all who have lost someone, and it is an approach that makes them appear embarrassed, ashamed and helpless when faced with death, as Tama realises: "I look at them but they turn away from my gaze. Is Death so shameful, friends? [...] Why are you afraid?" (*T* 19) Like his boss Mr. Ralston, who, as a character, serves as a representative *Pakeha* in this novel's concern with death, all white people are helpless and clumsy when faced with the passing of a person (cf. *T* 69). In passages like these, the *Pakeha* readers are confronted with their view through the eyes of a Maori and the colonised are shown as superior in their understanding of life, death, and family.

In Mead's explanations of values, customs and rituals that characterise a *tangi*, he admits that not all Maori today are as unafraid of death and the dead anymore as Ihimaera's novel suggests. They may share the same beliefs, but they may not be comfortable with them:

> These people cannot come to terms with the belief system. For them, it is all too real and their lives are affected, not positively, but negatively. The wairua [spirits] become ghosts that haunt them and frighten them. However, a majority of Maori live happily with images of their ancestors all around them in a carved meeting house, with the wairua of the ancestors above them, with the bones of their ancestors at the burial ground near by and surrounded by their living relatives. All are part of the reality of being Maori. All elements are parts of the whole and death itself is not a frightening

experience. Some say it is but another dimension of life. Even the children who attend tangihanga and participate in the whole ceremony accept that death is something we need to understand. It is manageable because we have tikanga to guide us and help us through a crisis and a reality of life. (Mead 2003: 148)

The notion of death being a part of life that must be understood and that the transition from one state to the next must be conducted properly is foregrounded in Ihimaera's novel once Tama arrives and finds himself forced to take on a prominent role as the eldest son of the deceased. He may not be familiar with the ceremony, but he is guided through it, simultaneously being guided back into the Maori belief system on the whole.

The endless spiral of new beginnings is also present here. Someone's death is not the end of all things and sorrow may be relieved by happiness. Though it might seem inappropriate to sing, dance and joke at a *Pakeha* funeral, it is presented as a common and very natural thing at the *tangi*. Even crude jokes are made at the funeral of Tama's father, jokes that would be unacceptable at such a gathering in *Pakeha* society. Stories are told in remembrance and no one is offended if they are rude. Laughter and tears are closely related. Mead explains why this light-heartedness is an essential part of the *tangi*: "The rest of the evening is given over to light entertainment to take the kiri mate [bereaved family] further into their transformation from a highly tapu state to a gradual reduction of it. This is a transitional stage and an important one because of the high level of stress that has been upon the kiri mate" (Mead 2003: 140). As the story shows, death is a part of life and it is treated as such, without fear or shame. The *tangi* becomes a celebration of life, not merely a ceremony of death. Since it is a highly ritualised event that is *tapu* and requires the observation of strict protocols, Mead emphasises the need to return from this sacred stage to a profane, *noa* state. In order to do this, the light entertainment, singing and laughter are necessary elements used at the right time. This way, a better understanding and full appreciation of *Tangi* can be gained by the knowledge of the *tikanga* involved here.

During the *tangi*, the family reminds Tama that life does and must go on, and that he should mourn deeply, but also to make his way back into the joys of life. He sees his *whanau*, "there they were, these same people who had mourned him, happy now" (*T* 195). All they do springs from their traditions, rituals and the deep knowledge of the ways of life and death, and all this expresses a clear affirmation of life. Their songs are those of their people, both happy and sad. They are reminders of their past and the lives of their ancestors, a new bringing to life at a time when death is so prominent. The *tangi* brings forth the *aroha* and the strength of the Maori people.

Making the Past Live in the Present:
The Connection between Myth and Reality

Where does this Maori strength come from? A great part of it springs from the close relationship to the land, most of which was taken from them with the arrival of white settlers and during the Land Wars. This relationship becomes clear in the way the characters are described in several places, revealing the richness and significance of nature. Tama says, "There are obsidian splinters at my heart, tearing at the greenstone landscape of my mind" (*T* 28), and he compares his father to a giant Kauri on many occasions, a tree that is sheltering and firmly rooted in the earth (cf. *T* 29). Now that his father is gone, Tama himself must be that Kauri for the family.

The most beautiful comparison with nature in the novel evolves from the myth of Mother Earth and Father Sky. Tama repeatedly speaks of his parents as "My mother was the Earth. My father was the Sky" (*T* 204). Mother and father, Earth and Sky, echo throughout the novel, emphasising the qualities of the two and nature, especially landscapes, are used to describe the person (*T* 152). This method emphasises the Maori relatedness to and dependence on the earth and harks back to the mythological creation of the world at the same time. In *Tangi*, this is the most lyrical way of portraying *maoritanga*.

These descriptions also prove how inextricable myth and reality are in Maori life, depicting the closeness of myth and one's own heritage. In an interview with J. B. Beston, Ihimaera said, "I try to use Maori myths, to make the past live in the present" (Corballis and Garrett 1984: 34). Similarly, Tama's life cannot be separated from myth, and so he turns the myths of his people into personal variations to describe events in his life. Particularly, this occurs at the most traumatic time when he mourns his father's death and loses one crucial pillar of his world. He is reminded of his own place in this universe in relation to his family.

To him, the mythical parents and his own are one and the same and the creation myth becomes a personalised myth instead. With time, Tama personalises it even more, creating further variations until, when he is ready to take his place as head of the family, the myth blends completely with his own life. So he says to his father,

> E pa, I shall greet you every morning. Every day I shall wake with my mother the Earth, arising from the strands of her hair to spread wide my arms with aroha for you. When snow falls, I shall catch the flakes and press them to my cheeks. When it rains I shall let your tears fall upon my lips. I will not fear your thunder for I know you love me. But, e pa, bring the light soon. Let me laugh...
>
> And my mother Earth, do not weep, for I shall comfort you. I am your son, the son of Earth and Sky. Although the sky has been wrenched from you, I shall make you happy. I will give you grandchildren and they will sing and thread flowers in your hair. (*T* 53–4)

In the course of the novel, Tama has mythologised his own parents and always sees them in the light of the First Parents.

The creation myth, however, is not the only one employed within the scope of this novel. There is the myth of Maui who slowed down the sun and battled with it to make the days longer (*T* 63), and then there is also the myth of the deceased soul that descends into the underworld at Te Reinga and returns to Hawaiki (*T* 73). All Maori rituals and ceremonies revolve around the recalling of ancestry and mythology as we see in the detailed description of the *tangi*. It is held in the *marae*, the meetinghouse which is also an ancestor: "– This house, it is the body of an ancestor, son. See the koruru, at the top of the entrance? That is the head. The arms are the maihi, the boards sloping down from the koruru to form the roof. See the ridgepole? It holds up the roof and is the backbone. And there, inside the house, those panels are the ribs..." (*T* 14). Tama's father teaches him – and the reader – that ancestry is never forgotten and made manifest even in the form of a building. This is another way of recalling one's heritage beside song, dance, and ceremonial speeches, one that is present at all times. Therefore, the *marae* is a physical memorial that is the centre of Maori rural life.

Tama is often put into the same situation as the reader with whom he is introduced to Maori culture. He learns of his people's history based on the legends and myths that have been passed on through generations, such as the legend of the seven ancestral canoes that came from Hawaiki to Aotearoa and became the first tribes to settle in the new country. The recitation of their names his father taught him is like a ritual incantation, one that Tama later says is calming to his heart. Another example of the introduction occurs after his father's death when Tama sees the *piwakawa* twice, the bird connected with death and the myth of Hinenuitepo "whom all men must follow into Rarohenga, the world after death" (*T* 92). Knowing his father has been taken to Rarohenga, in his sorrow Tama tells the story of Hinenuitepo and of "Maui who tried to bring immortality to men" (*T* 104) by killing her, and who was betrayed by the *piwakawa*'s laugh. While telling these stories and reminding himself of the beliefs of his people, Tama as a character functions as Ihimaera's tool to instruct non-Maori readers. We are introduced to the mythic world that is more historic than mythic in Tama's eyes, we are led into the Maori world that is so foreign to ours and are shown the interrelatedness of myth and reality. Even a phenomenon as scientifically explicable as the Napier earthquake is given a mythic meaning: "Once, not long ago, the sea rushed over this land the train traverses. That cliff face felt the sting of the sea's spray. Then Ruaumoko awoke from the breast of Papatuanuku, and split the earth with his awakening yawn. With his fiery hands, he pushed up the land and toppled the city which has been rebuilt there" (*T* 108). Not only events of the distant past are given mythic explanations – even contemporary occurrences can be interpreted as events springing from myth.

Though this way of thinking may appear unusual to non-Maori readers, the novel introduces such myths repeatedly in the course of the story, juxtaposing the foreign readers' experience with that of the Maori people. This way, the differences between the two are brought into focus, emphasising the importance of myth in Maori culture. It cannot be ignored because it is such a vital part of their worldview, and because this is so, it should not be forgotten and must be preserved for the world but also for Maori themselves.

Similarly, the *tangi* is presented in a way that will open up a new world for the non-Maori reader. The cultural intricacies are shown in the rituals revolving around the funeral, and particularly the ceremonial speeches, songs and dances are expressions of Maori beliefs. Once again, Tama becomes the person with whom the readers are introduced to this culture and they are taken by the hand in the same way Tama's relatives guide him through the *tangi*. Ihimaera supplies us with translations he places alongside the Maori songs, giving the original language its rightful place, but also allowing foreign readers to understand and get a glimpse of Maori life. However, in some cases the language is not translated and phrases are left only in *te reo Maori* so that the reader has to guess the meaning from the context. This, too, is a means of returning the language to its rightful place and giving it the attention it deserves as a language that stands alone in an independent culture. This is an example of how Ihimaera uses the English language and claims it as part of Maori identity today. The code-switching in his fiction corresponds with Bhabha's idea of hybridity in which the coloniser's language is used for an indigenous purpose, thus altering the language and working towards the creation of a third code. As the analysis of later novels will demonstrate, such use of language persists even until the third phase of the novel.

Significantly, Ihimaera uses the Maori language for the most private moments in his novel. The first chapter is marked by simple syntax and the "diction is designed to reflect the separation of the speaker from the wholly Maori world", says Beckmann in his analysis of *Tangi*.

> [...] His orientation is toward the *pakeha* world, and the language of chapter 1 reflects this. [...] In the *pakeha* world Tama speaks in English, reverting to the Maori only when the ties of love and grief pull him home in his mind. [...] The reference to the *whanau*, the extended family, fixes for us the cultural background of the central character, while his warm attitude toward his home is also made clear.
>
> Conversation between the Maori siblings is largely in English but the most caring moments, the most intimate words are recorded in Maori and then translated: "Turi turi, Ripeka, I call. Hush now" (p. 4). [...] Similarly, the representation of uniquely Maori customs, habits of mind or behaviour are lent authenticity by the use of Maori words which are then translated where necessary and possible. (Beckmann 1981: 125)

The chapters containing the most extensive use of Maori language are the ones devoted to the *tangi*. Aside from the reason that the ceremony is a Maori ritual being conducted in *te reo*, the native tongue is most frequently used here because it is an intimately emotional moment in the book. To involve the reader, Ihimaera offers translations within the text which are directed at both the reader and Tama, the young man who is now drawn back into the culture he abandoned.

In the translations, the *waiata*, the songs of mourning and grief, address a "you" which we understand to be Tama. However,

> the "you" is an invitation to the reader to identify himself with the grievers and the ceremony. Also, since "you" the reader-outsider is also "you" meaning Tama, an implicit recognition is made of Tama's psychological distance from his *whanau* at that point in time.
>
> Ihimaera thus achieves the multiple effect of lending authenticity to the *tangi* by using the Maori first; rendering the Maori comprehensible to a nonspeaker by translating; avoiding a stiltedness about this by the use of the "you" meaning outsider-reader; identifying Tama as something of an outsider because of the identification with the *pakeha* "you"; and finally indication in all this the real grief of the mourners and the even larger Maori principle of *aroha*, love, by making it possible for the outsider to share in this most intimate moment of grief [...]. (Beckmann 1981: 126)

So much is conveyed in the use of this simple pronoun that Ihimaera employs to re-educate Tama.

Ihimaera draws on the customs and rituals that he is familiar with and which are not merely memories for him, but real experiences. However, he is aware that for some of his people these things are becoming no more than memories of a past and that there are also people outside of his culture unaware of the Maori way of life. Faced with extinction, Ihimaera writes to show how Maori live, or should live. In 1975, two years after publishing *Tangi*, Ihimaera wrote an article in which he explains his three focuses in writing. "My first priority is to the young Maori," he says,

> the ones who have suffered most with the erosion of the Maori map, the ones who are Maori by colour but who have no emotional identity as Maori. My second priority is the Pakeha – he must understand his Maori heritage, must understand that cultural difference is not a bad thing and that, in spite of the difference, he can incorporate

the Maori vision of life into his own personality. Thirdly, I write for all New Zealanders to make them aware of the tremendous value in Maori culture and of the
tragedy for them should they continue to disregard this part of their dual heritage.
They can accept or reject that heritage if they want to, but they must at least have
the opportunity to choose. (Ihimaera 1975: 118)

Evidently, Ihimaera writes with a finger on society's pulse. It is not merely
the Maori pulse, but one consisting of mixed blood flowing through one
vein. His work is always contemporary with an eye towards Maori-*Pakeha*
relations and the difficulties that exist therein. He may not offer definitive
solutions, but he encourages tolerance and an incorporating worldview,
creating awareness and presenting opportunities that may be more important than ready-made answers.

"This is where it ends and begins": The Role of Memory
"We say that the past is not something that is behind us. The past is before
us, a long unbroken line of ancestors, to whom we are accountable. We say
that it is like walking backwards into the future" (Ihimaera 1998a: 200).
By walking backwards into the future, Maori step into the future with
their eyes on the past, keeping their ancestors in sight and honouring their
achievements. It does not mean, however, that they cling to the past and
ignore or strictly oppose the changes that have come with the *Pakeha*. It is,
nonetheless, this looking back and keeping alive of cultural memory that
is central to Maori identity.

Ihimaera uses layers of memory to structure his novel and thereby
create a fictional repertoire of cultural memory for the reader. Recollections are part of the mourning process that Tama goes through before
and during the *tangi*. There are three story lines that make up the novel
and exemplify its emotional, social and mythical levels: firstly, Tama's
emotions and reactions to his father's death till his return to Wellington after the funeral; secondly, his family's history, and thirdly, the myth
of Rangi and Papa. Thus the novel is interspersed with flashbacks of
different kinds: there are memories of the *tangi*, childhood memories,
and recollections of myths which all join to form this fictional repertoire,
moving seamlessly back and forth between past and present, and following
the traditional spiral pattern Ihimaera deploys in *Tangi*.

Throughout the novel, Ihimaera emphasises the traditional Maori spiral of simultaneous beginning and ending. "This is where it ends and begins" is the opening line of *Tangi* he repeats in different variations throughout the novel. Wherever Tama goes and no matter what he does, he is aware of the end also always being a new beginning. However, it is not a circular pattern, as one may deduce, but a spiral. The course of events is not repeated endlessly and identically because changes are inevitable. "The tangi marks the end of one life, the beginning of another" (*T* 157), and Tama willingly accepts the new course with the knowledge he gleans from his heritage: "I am Tama Mahana, and my father is dead. This is the end of my journey but it is also my journey beginning. It is a journey out of the upheaval of the tangi. The tangi is over. The hands of the clock stand at the beginning of another hour" (*T* 194). Every beginning opens up a new chance, a new perspective, and is a further step into life.

Myths are part of the characters' memory and add to the novel's layers. These myths are not perceived as untrue tales, but as part of a prehistoric past. This reality of myth helps to explain how ethnic literatures use myth "as a relevant pattern of interpretation for reality [...]," Isernhagen points out. "This is true both on the level of character and action and on the overall level of the book's appeal to the reader: characters use myth to comprehend their realities and texts constitute themselves at least in part along the lines of myth. [...] It is also a very clear attempt to fuse the divine with the historical, or even the political, and this may contribute to its usability in contemporary contexts [...]" (Isernhagen 1984: 189–90). Such use of myth indicates the need to go back into the past to use the knowledge derived from it to master the present. This is the case in *Tangi,* where "[i]t is not that the myth structures the series into a whole, but rather that it transcends its fragmentariness" (*ibid.* 194), thereby forming the spiritual backdrop to the story. In this manner, Maoridom is significantly emphasised and identified as the core of the fictional characters' lives through their relation to indigenous mythology. It is with the help of his knowledge of myth that Tama is able to return to his *whanau* and take his place amongst them again. Also, it helps him to cope with the identity crisis he finds himself in after his father's death.

The focus on Tama indicates that *Tangi* is a novel that depicts individual and not primarily group identity. Tama is the central and focal character for the most part of the novel to illustrate how much he has been separated from life in the *whanau*. His inner struggle is repeatedly emphasised by the referrences to myth that contrast with his chosen *Pakeha* lifestyle. In *Tangi*, therefore, "myth is used [...] as a means by which a narrator-protagonist situates himself in a field of present tensions through reference to mythical precedent. [...] The centrality of myth is [...] based on the restriction of the narrative to one centre of consciousness" (*ibid.* 195). It is Tama's experience as an individual relearning what it means to be Maori that we see. The tribal family appears firmly rooted in their culture and tradition while Tama is the one whose ambitions forced him to leave. Since indigenous identity is bound to ancestral land in much of Ihimaera's work, his novels are characterised by "[...] the deep, almost religious sense of place" (Martin 1983: 54). Consequently, in the case of *Tangi*, those who remain in Waituhi suffer no danger of being drawn too far into the *Pakeha* world, thus avoiding its influence for the most part. Alone and away from home, however, Tama struggles to uphold the Maori ideals and the only thing that manages to bring him back is his father's death, resulting in Tama losing the person who was a point of reference in life. Lacking this reference now, it is the land and the people who must remind Tama who he is as an individual in the world, showing that a community, the tribe, and the family are central to this process of identification. As a Maori, Tama is not primarily an individual, but a member of a larger group connected by blood and history. As a result, the myths of his people form the backdrop for his way of thinking even when he is separated from them. They are so ingrained in him that he cannot stop referring to them despite his awareness of the rational *Pakeha* worldview.

Speaking of Tama's inner turmoil and the novel's structure, Murray S. Martin observes that "[...] the organisation of the novel not only reflects the pattern of the tangi, but provides a structure that sustains it where the series of parallel events accompanied by the collapse of time would otherwise overwhelm its meaning, and matches Tama's own psychological vacillations in contemplating his future" (Martin 1983: 54). The *tangi* as a deeply rooted ritual performs the same function as myth in Ihimaera's novel.

Both determine the text's structure that reflects Tama's way of thinking and worldview. Isernhagen says, "For Ihimaera, one might say, myth exists in a social domain, as convention, and it is, therefore, both 'mere' construct and reconstruction of reality, both imposed and given" (Isernhagen 1984: 192). Myth underlies the action. It is that which gives meaning and shape to everyday life and determines what the characters do and how they go about this. At the same time, myth helps to interpret life in much the same way Tama uses it to come to grips with his father's death. Myth is history and a reservoir of events, traditions and rituals that are elements for the (re)creation of identity.

In this respect, Ihimaera has taken on a certain responsibility as a Maori writer. His critics say that he should be more radical as a minority writer, and he becomes more and more political with every novel. "His stories, Bill Pearson notes, 'have disappointed some Maori activists who think writing by Maori should advance the cause of Maori rights: "middle-class Maori", "Pakeha pet", are some of the names he has been called'" (Ojinmah 1993: 3). Corballis and Garret see his role on a more basic level that does not require politics: "At the level of myth, the novel demonstrates that the spiritual strength of this culture may be regained by its recreation in fictional literature. Ihimaera becomes, at this level, the traditional artist whose task it is to resuscitate the myths that bind his culture together" (Corballis and Garrett 1984: 35). His responsibility as a writer is that of a preserver of cultural identity. It is this treasure trove of myths which, as a great part of Maori identity, Ihimaera delves into and uses in his work, connecting them to the present day in a way that offers an idea of how life in a country of different cultures could function.

Ihimaera selects myths of significance in cultural memory that are identity shaping by firmly embedding the characters within a cultural tradition. The tales merge within the fiction to create a body of stories of origin and belonging that are told over and over again – within the novel itself, but also within Ihimaera's complete oeuvre – as a means to create and uphold a sense of identity. The fictional models of remembrance have the potential to be transferred into Maori reality and thereby coincide with Rigney's (2005) stages of cultural memory. *Tangi* itself has become part of Maori cultural memory, albeit as a fictional depiction of indigenous life in

1970s New Zealand. Promoting a self-image that is firmly rooted in native values and beliefs, the novel takes on a role similar to that of the Maori elder who is responsible for the teaching of traditions and indigenous knowledge. Despite the changes encountered in the modern day, the novel promotes a return to tradition as a way to approach the future. Finally, *Tangi* continues what the Maori short story began prior to the novel and enters the literary community with a detailed glimpse into the lives of young Maori caught between their heritage and the lures of the *Pakeha* life.

3.1.2 Patricia Grace's Mutuwhenua: The Moon Sleeps (1978)

In 2006, New Zealand Prime Minister Helen Clark honoured Patricia Grace as a writer who has made an outstanding contribution to her country's literature. "Patricia Grace's work," she said, "has played a key role in the emergence of Maori fiction in English. A writer of novels, short stories and children's fiction her work expresses Maori consciousness and values to a wide international audience" (The New Zealand Book Council 1998). The author published her first novel *Mutuwhenua* five years after Ihimaera, and became the first Maori woman novelist.

Credited for her use of polyphony and realistic voices in fiction, Grace's novels and short stories also stand out for their storytelling techniques that derive from Maori tradition and intertwine several storylines, usually told by different characters in the same way that stories would be told in the indigenous community. After having read the work of writers such as Frank Sargeson and Amelia Batistich whose fiction conveyed a first distinct New Zealand voice, Grace became aware of the different voices that could be employed in writing (Calleja 2003: 110–11). Her novels often have strong female characters because, as the author explains, "I come from a culture where women are strong" (Calleja 2003: 111). This is evident especially in *Cousins* (1992), which follows the lives of three girls in different environments from childhood to adulthood. Their voices are strong, and especially a unique one, that of a girl's unborn twin brother, is exceptionally vivid. A similar unborn character narrates part of Grace's *Baby No-Eyes* (1998), based on the Maori belief that both deceased ancestors and the yet unborn have a presence and a voice that Grace includes as part of the storytelling process (cf. Calleja 2003: 116f.).

That such a voice can be part of the telling coincides with the Maori belief that the human body is more than just that. In "Myth, Omen, Ghost and Dream", Hulme explains that there is the physical body, which in itself contains a number of properties such as *hau*, the "'breath' or 'essence'" and *mana*, personal power. But then there is also what she calls "an unseen double, a soul-shadow, your own spirit", *wairua*. The *wairua* "can detach itself while you sleep, and go visiting. It can go to the realm of the dead and return with news [...]. It can go among the living [...]. It can even make itself known while you're conscious – sometimes you are attracted to someone you don't know, who later turns out to be *whanauka* (part of your relation-group), and then you say, 'My *wairua* knew you before I did'. If your *wairua*, through natural death or a too-sudden waking, becomes detached from your body, it can then be thought of as a *kehua*, a ghost" (Hulme 1984: 33). Taking it further, the ghost then has a voice as well, enabling it to remain part of the story and allowing it to contribute.

Grace's female protagonists tend to have resolute, confident voices and are strong characters due to their culture and their place in it. The only exceptions are characters who do not yet know where they belong, such as Mata in *Cousins* (1992). *Mutuwhenua* contains the voice of a female character who, despite her insecurities, is strong and willing to have an active part in determining how her life shall be. The story depicts the life of Ripeka, who sometimes calls herself by the *Pakeha* name Linda. She marries Graeme, a *Pakeha* schoolteacher, much to her grandmother's and initially her father's disapproval. Early on in her marriage she realises that the ties to her culture and family are too strong for her to be happy where she is now. However, she finds a way to live with both cultures she is connected to.

Ripeka was not always aware of the differences between people of different races and the way their cultures influenced and separated them from others. As a child, she is friends with a *Pakeha* girl whose difference she does not see until one day at a school performance. "I remember two things about the concert," she recollects.

> The first was the girl with the violin. I say "the girl" as though she didn't have a name, or as though I didn't know her. Her name was Margaret, and she was, had been, my best friend [...].
>
> Then suddenly there was a new Margaret. A girl I didn't know and hadn't seen before. Wearing a ribboned frock, sleek stockings, and buckled shoes, with her gold hair falling softly on to her shoulders. And gold sounds drifting and swooping and lifting from under her bowing hand.
>
> [...]
>
> I prepared for our bit, still enveloped in the soaring notes, and at the same time noticing the nakedness of my own feet stranded on bare boards. And soon it was our own music breaking in on the afternoon, on the soles of feet and the palms of hands. (*M* 12–13)

This is a self-conscious and traumatising moment for Ripeka, which coincides with the trauma of her first menstruation. Both her body and mind mature, it is the day she grows up, leaves her childhood behind and discovers that there are things in life that are not as simple as they used to seem. Even though she was – and still is – able to live with Maori and *Pakeha*, her perspective has changed.

Despite primarily belonging to Maori culture, her connection to the *Pakeha* world is re-established when she meets Graeme. Yet, in spite of their love for each other, Ripeka "discovered that in some things there can be no bridge to understanding" (*M* 121). This inability to understand, however, may be compensated by love and tolerance. Graeme is willing to accept Ripeka's culture and finds it much easier than her father finds it to accept his daughter's choice in marriage. It is only at the time of Mutuwhenua when the change in his attitude takes place.

Constituting the book's title, Mutuwhenua is the last night of the lunar cycle, "when the moon is hidden, when the moon goes underground to sleep" (*M* 75) and there is total darkness. The novel describes it as a good time for fishing when the family goes to camp out on the beach and the extended family helps. It is on this important occasion that Graeme is invited to join Ripeka's family in their gathering of food, a sign that he has been accepted as part of the family. Much happens at this time at the beach that Graeme cannot understand, but he does not question or ridicule Ripeka's family, knowing that there may be things he cannot know from his non-Maori perspective. In the evening after the first day's fishing, two of the young men speak disrespectfully about the spirits of the sacred mountains nearby (cf. *M* 62). The next day, the ancestral spirits retaliate with the loss of the fishing, a flooded truck, a half-drowned dog, and uncle Tom's injury. The family knows it is not a coincidence and Graeme, though he is unacquainted with the stories, is respectful of their beliefs.

Of course, Ripeka's relationship with a *Pakeha* is not to everyone's liking as becomes clear very early on. Her grandmother, old and wary of the *Pakeha*, speaks ill of her granddaughter's intention to marry Graeme: "You're as bad as that cousin of yours. Never mind the Maori; he must marry a Pakeha. Both of you just want your children to have fair skin because you think that's better. You care nothing for your own people." (*M* 3) Her harshness has kept away Ripeka's cousin who lives apart with his own family. It seems that Ripeka's lot will be the same. Her grandmother often reminds her of her roots so that she never forgets where she comes from. Even though she dislikes being with her grandmother because of her opinions, this does not make her turn her back on her family:

> After tea she began to tell me the old photographs, which I already knew, fading on every wall. Telling me who they were and what they were to me. Then she told me of the ones before that, who were not on the walls but whom she had known. Then back before that to the ones she had never known or seen. And her voice that had been slow at the beginning and thoughtful began to chant out the ancient names coming from far back, so I could know them. I was beginning to know them because I had heard them many times before. Beginning to know, yet knowing there was more to understand. (*M* 72)

Instead of alienating her, Ripeka's grandmother's stories keep her close to the family, which ultimately helps her when she leaves her family to live with her husband.

In his article, Cliff Watego points out the thematic similarities between South Pacific writers that are evident in the above excerpt: "[E]ach author [...] emphasizes that the first step in assuring that the qualities of this culture are to be maintained in a future that is already conditioned by past and present attitudes is to re-educate the young in the ways and values of their people. Only then can this generation have a firm appreciation of [...] Maori identity, and gain the spiritual strength and dignity necessary to transcend the critical judgement which unjustly focuses the weight of opinion in favour of the material advantages of white society" (Watego 1984: 493). Particularly Ripeka's grandmother is the one who educates the young, telling them their genealogy and offering advice from her point of view. She represents the traditions and customs as they were of old and she holds on to them because this is the way things have always been, and because the past must be remembered since this is who they are.

Significantly, hinting at her development in the course of the novel, Ripeka shares her grandmother's name. This constitutes a connection to the old ways reminiscent of the Maori spiral pattern that underlies all things, and yet she feels that there is more. She is the first in her family to feel a change coming and it is she who wants "to do something different. [...] Be someone different" (*M* 11). She implies that she wants what lies beyond the boundaries of her Maori life with the family because what she has is not sufficient anymore. Ripeka says she wants a job in the *Pakeha* world, but it is clear that she does not have the intention of forsaking her culture. In fact, one of her favourite trees serves as a symbol of how the past offers strength for the future and expresses how she feels about her heritage. Significantly, this passage is found on the very first page of the novel, illustrating Ripeka's love and understanding of her culture: "I know only that [the tree's] roots are thick and heavy and that they spread wide and deep. Only that its sap flows thickly under the flaking hide and that, without its strength against the wind that licks through the gully there, the others [...] would not have taken root and flourished" (*M* 1–2). Judging from the description, the past is what gives her strength for the future and allows her to find her own place to thrive in the world.

As early as this in the novel, Ripeka knows she will make use of the strength her culture has supplied her with to live her own life. The old ways are not enough anymore and do not seem to apply completely to her situation, but they should not be forgotten. A change has become necessary because the times are different now. Gradually, Ripeka, her father and her grandmother all go through changes that help them come to terms with the situation of a changing cultural identity. As a result, her father, who tries to keep her away from Graeme at first, begins to see the good and the necessity of a multicultural union:

My father, I had begun to realise too, had agreed to my marriage to Graeme because he had brought about a change in himself. He had always, although he did not express it in words, seen our home and the family land as a spiritual sanctuary, a kind of stronghold for all of us. But, then he had begun to hope, if I moved away from there into what he thought of as a Pakeha world, I should find a second sanctuary. [...] I would not, as my father saw it, exchange our old way of life for the new way but would learn to be part of both, as I had already begun trying to be some years before. [...] And he would have been thinking too of the children that Graeme and I would have who would inherit both ways of life. (*M* 121)

This is the central theme of the novel also seen in Ihimaera's later work: the necessity and the process of becoming part of two ways of life. Eventually, there is more than a strict adherence to one tradition alone and an opening up to the new.

Consequently, Ripeka's and Graeme's mixed marriage requires adjustment from both partners and, surprisingly, it is mainly Graeme who has to make compromises and accepts his wife's culture. Grace is the first to write about a mixed marriage from the point of view of a Maori whose culture is the dominant one in the union. The significance of tradition is conveyed throughout the novel by Ripeka's need to retain her traditions. Graeme is the outsider who has to adjust to Maori customs and he easily does so. Unexpectedly, he seems not to have any trouble with this at all. Even if he cannot understand, he accepts. Instead of writing about a *Pakeha* whose Maori wife has to adapt to his world, Grace chooses to turn the situation around and make the descendent of colonisers come to terms with the customs of a minority culture. The power relations have been inverted and the greater strength comes from Ripeka and her Maori side of the relationship.

In her writing, like Ihimaera, Grace has "preserved respect for the basic indigenous value of the individual's relationship to his environment", says Watego.

[She has,] however, taken account of changes forced or hastened by the alien culture that result in the need to relinquish certain aspects of a traditional or familiar way of life in order to comprehend the new influences. The crucial point occurs in the individual's need to accommodate himself to the idea and nature of change at the inter-society and/or the intra-community levels. Even when that has been done,

though, formidable problems remain in interpreting the direction of change, whether
it represents progress or regress, how the individual pictures his involvement within
the process, and how the individual finds his way towards self-enlightened content-
ment. (Watego 1984: 489)

Despite all these difficulties, Ripeka's strength and her will to find content-
ment is evident in the way she stands her ground against her father and
grandmother. She has always been the one wanting change, doing what she
believes is right for herself. At the same time, she is strong enough to keep
her cultural heritage without betraying it and manages the difficult task of
combining Maori and *Pakeha* life. Early on in her marriage she realises that
she cannot break with Maori traditions, and her spiritual health only begins
to improve once her family helps her in times of need and enhances the
Maori influence that she misses. Despite having all necessary material wealth
in her *Pakeha* home, the separation from her *whanau* makes it impossible
for her to be happy and healthy. The removal from her culture has a negative physical effect on her that can only be remedied by an incorporation
of Maori spirituality into her new and unfamiliar surroundings.

After her first child is born, she makes an important decision that
would be difficult for *Pakeha* to understand: she leaves her child to be
brought up by her parents. This is not unusual in Maori tradition where
children may often be brought up by grandparents and other relatives. The
relationship between child and grandparents is based on the traditional
tikanga protection, love and reciprocity. According to Ka'ai's article on *The
Whale Rider*'s film version, Maori parents are traditionally responsible for
the child's physical well-being while education, spiritual, and emotional
support was provided by the grandparents instead. Such a relationship is,
says Ka'ai, reflected in the fan-shaped flax bush:

> Each blade of this plant is used as an analogy for the *whānau*. The *rito* (centre shoot)
> is the "child", protected on either side by its "parents", and the outer blades are the
> "extended family" (Higgins nd: ii). If the *rito* is removed, the plant will die. There-
> fore, the role of the *whānau* is to ensure the protection of the *rito* and the child,
> which will ensure the survival of the plant and the *whānau, hapū* and *iwi. Mokopuna*
> [grandchildren] who are raised by their grandparents form a strong bond that cannot
> be penetrated. Furthermore, *mokopuna* who are raised by their grandparents are easy

to identify as they behave in a particular way as a consequence of being given access to tribal knowledge well ahead of their chronological years. (Ka'ai 2005: 7)

Ripeka wants her child to benefit from this tradition, but since she and Graeme no longer live with her *whanau*, it is a significant step to take. The reader does not see Graeme's reaction, but Ripeka is certain that she has done the right thing and that he will accept her decision in the same way that his love enabled him to accept her culture before. Where it would normally have been expected of the Maori wife to adapt to her husband's culture, Grace instead strongly supports the preservation of Maori traditions and customs in a *Pakeha* environment.

Rona and Ripeka: Myth and the Female Perspective

Grace's fiction depicts life in both the nuclear and extended family. In *Mutuwhenua* it is the nuclear family rather than the tribal family of her second novel *Potiki* that she makes the focus of the story. This allows her to exemplify the influences on Ripeka that cause the spiritual tension in herself, threatening to break her. "Selfhood," Isernhagen explains in this context, "is centred, for Grace, in spiritual awareness rather than in social action or interaction, and the self appears in the work [...] as a field where forces from without come together, disruptively or creatively, rather than a point in a network of relationships" (Isernhagen 1984: 191). Ripeka's spiritual balance is disturbed by her move away from home more because of her removal from her Maori culture rather than an increased *Pakeha* influence. The lack of one familiar force impoverishes her well-being so much so that it needs to be replenished. Her family is very much aware of this circumstance and seems to have expected the negative effects of city life, knowing what needs to be done.

Mutuwhenua has much in common with many other South Pacific novels, as Watego points out:

All these novels deal in some way with the individual's finding the best possible reconciliation between himself and society. Partial fulfilment of this quest presents a danger to the individual himself, for society is in a constant state of flux, and for the individual to remain at a level of insight that takes into account only causes or results of such changes isolates that person to one area of human experience. From the point of view of the indigenous novelist, avoiding this quicksand of thought and opinion and accommodating himself to perpetual change is absolutely necessary. Indeed this condition is the most difficult for the individual to sustain, since it prefigures a predicament that required him to sustain a cultural identity (which is based on subsistence) yet adhere to a tradition of change (based on progress). (*ibid.* 495)

Ripeka, then, is not a character who only watches the changes around her despite Isernhagen's impression that Grace's characters are "fundamentally passive" (Isernhagen 1984: 192). As demonstrated in her desire to do something and be someone else, she is the one who actively seeks change. At the same time, the extent of her activity is restricted by her strong wish to preserve her heritage in the form she is familiar with. That is why Ripeka is a less active character than, for instance, Ihimaera's Tama, who is not as bound by his cultural heritage from the start but only develops a new bond gradually. The reason Grace's characters succeed in accommodating two different ways of life is their openness to both and the acceptance of change. Ripeka, her father and her grandmother are all happiest once change is no longer resisted and all aspects of culture and community – even beyond their local boundaries – have been combined harmoniously. Therefore, the characters in *Mutuwhenua* are restless and dissatisfied as long as there is no conformity between social and individual values (cf. Watego 1984: 494). The social values are usually *Pakeha* values that clash with the individual Maori ones that are of greater importance to the characters. In her marriage, Ripeka's public life is that of a *Pakeha* even though her individual values remain Maori, and it is this discrepancy that brings about her illness. Only her indigenous traditions can restore her back to health.

At the centre of Ripeka's well-being lie the beliefs and traditions of her heritage, their legends and myths. Some of the stories are told by the characters themselves and woven into the plot, such as family genealogy, the sacredness of the mountains, and the myth of Rona. *Mutuwhenua* does not appear as mythical in itself as *Potiki*, but the myth of the woman on the moon is an implicit myth and one that proves to be significant for the understanding of the protagonist. Generally, in her fiction, "Grace internalizes and psychologizes the mythical pattern making it the basis of an entirely personal perspective upon reality," Isernhagen observes. "For her narrator-protagonist the mythical figure becomes a correlate of her state of mind and of her character; as a historical being she takes part in a myth that remains unchangingly the same through time" (Isernhagen 1984: 192).

Keeping this in mind, Rona represents Ripeka in three ways. Firstly, she is taken from the home she knew and transplanted to a strange place where she is alone and the only one of her kind. She has been literally uprooted so that Ripeka and Rona are faced with the same plight. Secondly, even though Ripeka is in an unaccustomed place now, she still carries her culture with her, represented by Rona's ngaio tree and calabashes. Unlike Rona, Ripeka has chosen her new place voluntarily and has fought for the chance to live with Graeme, and, like Rona, she carries with her the traditions, customs and knowledge her culture has supplied her with. The myth of Rona as controller of the tides and menstruation has now been turned into a metaphor for change and the cultural dilemma Ripeka faces, and her role as the woman on whom the future of her people depends. Also, what could be viewed as a negative story of uprooting, is slowly turned into a story of positive bicultural incorporation and foregrounds the strength of women. Rona is the woman on the moon who governs fertility, giving her great power over her people's survival. As a result, Ripeka is featured as a mother who will produce the new generation to grow up within both Maori and *Pakeha* culture.

When he speaks of Grace's fiction in general, Isernhagen observes that

> her use of myth is connected with a spirit view of the world. Behind the everyday, as it is particularly experienced by women, there appears, again and again, a spiritual reality which is so overwhelmingly powerful that it can only be accepted in a gesture of submission. Myth, then, still has that quality of immediate evidence and objective validity that makes it the constituent force behind reality; it is ignored only at one's peril and violated with devastating results. [...] There is no need, therefore, to effect any kind of transformation of the myth; its recovery is, in a very simple sense, a return. (Isernhagen 1984: 191)

His conclusions apply even more to Grace's second novel *Potiki* because the myth of Rona in *Mutuwhenua* is used in a subtler way for the protagonist's underlying characterisation while *Potiki* contains clearly mythologised characters. In *Mutuwhenua*, the myth itself is powerful, but less so than the whole of Maori culture and tradition that the author focuses on. It is in short passages throughout the novel that the myths' power is shown as, say, in the section where the family goes fishing and the young men mock the spirits. Furthermore, in several cases Ripeka feels the need to tell Graeme of the *mere*, the greenstone artefact she once found as a child, but she is unable to put its significance into words. The *mere* is part of the past and a mighty heirloom belonging to the spirits buried in the hills, by which great cultural significance is attached to it. The incident stays in her memory and is of such great importance to her that she knows it is the one thing that expresses who she really is at heart as the key to her being. The myths serve as a reminder that Ripeka is and always will be part of her cultural community in spite of whatever changes life requires of her.

Unlike the myths of Western cultures, the ones that Grace incorporates in *Mutuwhenua* and later novels primarily concern themselves with female strength and the role of woman as creator and nourisher of life. This way, the female opposes any patriarchal hierarchies promoted by *Pakeha* myths, especially the Western world's most significant grand narrative of the omnipotence of a male God. Historically, says Leeming,

> [t]he role of the goddess deteriorates with the invasions of so-called Indo-Europeans or Aryans into the Near and Middle East, the Indian subcontinent, and Europe during the Bronze Age (c. 3500–1000 BCE). These invaders were warriors whose primary deities were almost certainly war gods associated with the sky rather than the earth, with conquest rather than nurturing, with light rather than mystery, and with stern fatherhood rather than loving motherhood. The ancient pre-Aryan goddesses had taken their power from the earth rather than from the heavens. (Leeming 2002: 80)

Despite Maori traditionally being a warrior people, the earth mother Papatuanuku retains her importance as one of the two principal creators. In fact, she is referenced more frequently in Maori writing than the Sky Father due to the importance of land, working with the land, nourishment, and the definition of home. Then again, there are myths of gods wanting to conquer goddesses, such as Maui's attempt to enter Hinenuitepo's vagina in order to pluck out her heart. Even here, however, the power of woman equals man's and Hinenuitepo crushes Maui, thereby bringing death into the world. The proverb "Men make heirs, but death carries them off" expresses the powerful position of women in the Maori belief system that prevents them from becoming objects "of conquest and reproductive and sexual [vehicle] to be owned" (*ibid*: 83).

Her preference for the woman's perspective and position in the community characterises Grace's work throughout the years. She replaces the male creator of dominant religions with Maori goddesses and other ancestresses who prove to be as strong as or even more powerful than male deities. The same approach is evident in *Cousins* and Ihimaera's *The Whale Rider*. Even *Potiki*, though one of the central characters is male, emphasises the necessity of women as providers of spiritual, intellectual and physical nourishment in its cast of characters, and the essential nature of the earth both as home and nourisher of its people. Thus, Grace's approach reflects Maori culture in its belief in a joint creation by the First Parents, which denies the notion of an exclusively male or exclusively female supreme being and offers a feminine perspective less common in many Western cultures. Finally, such an interpretation of Maori life foregrounds the need for Ripeka to retain her cultural heritage since it is her only hope to lead a wholesome life. As a young Maori woman, she is meant to follow in the footsteps of her ancestresses who are strong women, nourishers and protectors of their people.

Myth and Memory as Implicit Cultural Knowledge
Mutuwhenua advocates the adherence to one's cultural heritage particularly in difficult times. Assuming that even though a life shared between two cultures is possible, the individual will eventually have to choose between one or the other. In the novel, the choice is clear since Ripeka's Maori roots are the only thing that helps her recover and be truly happy. The memories of her grandmother's stories and the knowledge passed on to her in her young life keep her steeped within Maori tradition despite her early attempts to break from home. Although her grandmother is available as a specialist in Maori culture and tradition – the kind of specialist necessary for memory to be passed on between generations –, a part of Ripeka is connected to the Maori past in a way that has not been influenced by her. To take an example, she recognises the significance of the *mere* when she finds it as a young girl, which becomes an essential part of her identity.

The myths contained within the narrative form a defining set of memories that not only determine Maori identity on the whole but Ripeka's identity as an individual both within and without her *whanau*. It is assumed that cultural identity is based on the memories of ancestors and the land, but the actual problem the protagonist encounters emerges from the choice between two possible lives in different cultures despite her cultural knowledge. Unlike *Tangi*'s Tama, she is fully aware of her heritage and the customs and expectations deriving from it. She is not ignorant of her roots – on the contrary –, but the promise of a different life in the *Pakeha* world is too tempting. Its attraction is presented as inevitable within the novel, forcing the protagonist to find ways of living between cultures. Grace's approach therefore differs from Ihimaera's, who assumes that the missing basic knowledge and awareness of *maoritanga* is the reason for problems of identity. Grace, on the other hand, assumes that the knowledge is there, but foreign influence is inevitable and therefore requires strategies which will help the individual cope. For the most part, she relies on the individual's ability to make the right decisions. However, it becomes clear to Ripeka that she cannot escape from her depression by herself and needs her family's help. The family, then, is the source of support and guidance when all else fails. The novel assumes that, despite all good efforts and knowledge, the individual alone is unable to lead a wholesome life without the help of the Maori community.

This need for inclusion within a greater group of the same heritage explains the preference of ancestral myths in *Mutuwhenua*. Rona, the spirits in the hills, and the photos of ancestors in Ripeka's grandmother's house express the significance of mythical and historical genealogy for cultural and individual identity. The future depends on how the past is remembered and adapted in the present so that one's roots can be maintained while the future leads into a new direction with new influences. While Ripeka may feel that the old stories are a hindrance for the life she wants to lead when she is young, they become her source of happiness when she is older.

The protagonist becomes a subjective point of intersection (cf. Erll 2005: 108ff.) in whom two possible identities – Maori and *Pakeha* – touch and present Ripeka's options. The first option is for her to remain entirely within her familiar environment as her family wishes her to. The second option is the one that appeals to Ripeka most – leaving her family in order to live and work in the city. Another option is the one she only comes to realise towards the end – a firm adherence to her heritage within a *Pakeha* environment. In the latter case, memory plays a central role in maintaining the connection to her past with her *whanau* and it is this collection of memories that makes her personal happiness possible in the first place.

Finally, the distinct ways in which myth and memory are used in *Tangi* and *Mutuwhenua* express the writers' different approaches to the question of Maori identity even in this first phase of the Maori novel. While Ihimaera's first novel is filled with myths and the repetition of the central stories in order to encourage the remembrance of the old tales, Grace's book in comparison seems to mention them in passing. In *Mutuwhenua*, the myths and memories are tied more strongly to the main characters than in *Tangi*, which contrasts with Ihimaera's didactic narrative. Due to his increased mention of Maori myths and references to Maori origin, Ihimaera's novel is a repository of memory containing the most important stories that determine Tama's identity. Grace, in contrast, subtly focuses on particular memories that underlie Ripeka's character without drawing more attention to them than necessary. In doing so, she devotes greater attention to the present situation where memories alone would only confine Ripeka to an unchanging past. *Mutuwhenua* therefore presents myth and memory as implicit cultural knowledge that underlies the protagonist's life and is ever-present but need not be mentioned explicitly. Grace assumes this knowledge in her characters whereby the narrative focuses on the issues they encounter and the options that lead towards their resolution.

3.1.3 Preliminary Conclusion

The first Maori novels in English bear a heavy burden: they present a culture on the brink of extinction by the *Pakeha* who dominate New Zealand society and are the cause for the problems besetting Maori people. The books create an awareness of this foreign culture that is, in fact, indigenous and not foreign at all; but it is a life that is unknown for the most part. At the same time, those Maori who are estranged from their people might find a way to relate to their heritage again and discover parallels to their lives in the literature of their own people. Ultimately, by calling attention to this cultural group, there can be power. The novel, and literature in general, is the first step towards change.

In an article about Blackfeet narrative, Donal Carbaugh explains that, "[i]f we want to grasp some of the meanings people claim about themselves, their world, its objects and people, then we stand to benefit from treating narrative texts as cultural and communicative resources. We thus hear in them deeply organized symbolic statements being crafted to address the contingencies of everyday living, meeting life's challenges in revealing ways and thus engendering the courage to go on" (Carbaugh 2001: 123). The first phase novels contain such symbolic statements in their depiction of Maori life both within the indigenous community and outside it, and in the manner in which the afflicted characters learn to cope with their situation. The use of myth and mythic patterns in the narrative makes the novels the cultural and communicative resources Carbaugh speaks of. Of course, this applies to the novels of the following two phases too, but the observation is particularly crucial for the first novels and the reasons for their emergence in the 1970s when writers could not expect their entire readership to be familiar with Maori life.

The first phase novels in particular are "engendering the courage to go on" (*ibid.*) and uphold the Maori way of life. Like Carbaugh's analysis of Blackfeet texts, Maori novels are treated "as a deeply complex and cultural form which itself uses mythic and dramatic features to honour the relevance of a sacred past to life in a troublesome present" (*ibid.* 107). Ihimaera's and Grace's first novels both refer to a mythic past that gives meaning to the characters' current situation and offers solutions to their problems. At the same time, these features go beyond the narrative as such and reach into the reader's world. As a result, the first novels almost resemble initiation myths in the way they guide readers into the Maori world, and introduce them to traditional practices and knowledge. Though the readers must not suffer the same struggles as the characters, they are led along parallel paths in the reading process to observe an initiation into Maori culture that becomes their own. *Tangi* and *Mutuwhenua* are the introduction to a new type of fiction and a new view into an old indigenous understanding of the world. At the same time, the novels contrast a pre-contact ideal of Maori life with the post-contact difficulties encountered in the 1970s, delineating the space between the two in which Maori must find a balance.

Tangi offers a solution that encourages a return to Maori tradition by allowing the protagonist to recognise the importance of his culture. The end of the novel suggests that Tama will return home instead of remaining in the *Pakeha* city. *Mutuwhenua*, in contrast, does not condemn *Pakeha* influence to the same degree. Instead, Grace allows her main character to live in two worlds that can be combined to a certain extent. The spiritual focus, however, remains firmly rooted in Maori customs. The myths the writers incorporate within the narrative are relevant for the characters' lives in that they show the degree to which both Tama and Ripeka remain connected to their heritage and the Maori worldview regardless of how far removed the characters are geographically or emotionally. At the same time, the myths function as narrative patterns that determine how the characters' lives proceed. This is especially apparent in *Mutuwhenua* where the myth of Rona underlies Ripeka's development from girl to woman that reflects Rona as controller of menstruation, and her move from the Maori community to the city, which mirrors Rona's abduction to the moon. In Tama's case the influence of myth is less obvious since he has cut himself off from his *whanau* to live like a *Pakeha*. Nevertheless, he still sees the world through Maori eyes, as becomes clear whenever he sees his father's spirit. The underlying myth in *Tangi* is the role of the First Parents who are reflected in Tama's own parents and his role as their son.

By drawing parallels between the Maori belief system and the events depicted in the novels, these texts "provide links to the past through traditional actions and morals, [...] the dramatic features provide historical links to contemporary events and worlds" (*ibid.* 120). *Mutuwhenua* therefore presents a new interpretation of the myth of Rona in a contemporary setting. The traditional belief of looking back towards the future is exemplified in Grace's novel in the connections between mythical past and Ripeka's present. Ihimaera's *Tangi* may not follow the underlying myth of the First Parents quite as closely, but the repeated references suffice to function as an underlying feature. If readers are familiar with the myth, it is easy to see the implicit similarities between their children's struggle to be free and Tama's own efforts to escape the close hold of his *whanau*.

Mutuwhenua, in contrast to *Tangi*, provides all the information needed to recognise the parallels between the underlying myth by including a short summary of the myth of Rona in the glossary. Therefore, previous knowledge is unnecessary. Ihimaera, however, only provides the basics. On the one hand, this is due to the expected Maori readership that would be familiar with the creation myth to a certain degree and would not require further explanation. On the other, withholding details may lead readers to find the information elsewhere, thereby encouraging them to look into further aspects of Maori culture. Both novels, nonetheless, include vague references to other myths and beliefs that remain unexplained, such as the sacredness of certain landmarks and geographic features which are significant cultural memories that add to the connection between myth and novel.

The cultural memories found in both novels comprise recollections of ancestors in the form of genealogies, myths, origins (of the individual and the natural world), the practice of rituals and customs, and the Maori language. The notion that myth is history and therefore always part of present and future is expressed by the natural way in which it enters into the characters' thoughts. Like historical fact, the myths are a natural part of their way of thinking and perceiving the world. The natural world is often described in mythic terms, referring to the ancient gods or ancestral spirits that inhabit certain landmarks. Therefore, myth according to Maori belief is history and thus part of cultural memory. The future depends on how the past is remembered in the present and how the belief system is upheld today. For this reason, Tama's father and Ripeka's grandmother teach them their ancestral history, imprinting a Maori identity on them that they will never forget. Armed with this knowledge, both are able to walk backwards into the future to base their lives on fundamental Maori knowledge.

Tangi and *Mutuwhenua* both consist of layers of memory, but to a different extent. While Grace's novel adds memories to the description of Ripeka's present situation, *Tangi* consists entirely of a layering of memories and shifts in chronology. Moving between childhood, myth and the present, Ihimaera's narrative imitates how memory works. Triggered by certain words or events, the action changes and the readership finds itself in another set of Tama's memories. In contrast, Ripeka's story is focused on the present and her way of coping with the situation. Flashbacks are kept to a minimum. Due to Grace's focus on the present, the spiral pattern evident in Ihimaera's novel is less apparent. Grace follows the pattern in the repetition of Ripeka's and her grandmother's name that symbolises the connection of past and present, the myth of Rona, and the similar plight of the protagonist's cousin that hints at repeated remaining difficulties. *Tangi*, in comparison, reflects the spiral in its layering of memories, the steady shifts in time, the move away from and return to the protagonist's home, and the emphasis that an ending is simultaneously a beginning. The cultural memories in both novels, especially as portrayed by the spiral pattern in *Tangi* and the references to myths and family history in *Mutuwhenua*, emphasise the characters' positioning in a field of cultural tension between past and present as well as *Pakeha* and Maori environments.

The novels express the need for change that has become inevitable in the tension between cultures. While the family expects that the tradition is upheld, the protagonists simultaneously find themselves in another culture that seems to be diametrically opposed to their heritage. It must be pointed out that *Mutuwhenua* incorporates a far more positive portrayal of the *Pakeha* in the characterisation of Ripeka's husband. Ihimaera's view of the *Pakeha* is rather negative in his first novel, but a change towards a distinguished and positive view is evident in his later rewriting of the novel as a prequel in *The Rope of Man*. In 1973, however, the *Pakeha* and the city are inappropriate for the Maori, according to *Tangi*. Given the influence and inevitability of contact with *Pakeha*, changes to Maori life are necessary.

Such changes have already taken place as illustrated by the unconventional painting of Rongopai (*T* 116) that combines both traditional indigenous and *Pakeha* designs, signifying the move of different cultures towards each other. Both novels of the first phase recognise the changes that confront the characters, and each chooses a different approach to this circumstance. While Tama's response is to choose between either his Maori heritage or life in a *Pakeha* environment, Ripeka seeks to find ways to combine both aspects in her life. The different approaches suggest a variety of possibilities to deal with cultural difference. At the same time, they are also evidence of the early stages of identity construction in Maori fiction that become more concrete and gradually more alike in later phases. The difference between the two novels' approaches to Maori identity demonstrates that there is no agreed approach to the subject as yet.

As it happens, Grace's *Mutuwhenua* advocates change more than Ihimaera's *Tangi*. This is an interesting observation since it is Ihimaera's stance that becomes more inclusive with time, finally culminating in the confident multicultural features of *The Rope of Man* in 2005 while Grace remains focused on Maori characters and their traditions mostly apart from the *Pakeha*. In her fiction, *Pakeha* influence is portrayed minimally and only where necessary. The Maori community tends to be depicted as a self-sufficient group set apart from the rest of New Zealand society. *Mutuwhenua*, despite being the first of her novels, is more generous in its characterisation of the *Pakeha* than Ihimaera's or Grace's own later novels.

Nonetheless, both authors' focus remains the search for identity at a time of change that results "in the need to relinquish certain aspects of a traditional or familiar way of life in order to comprehend the new influences" (Watego 1984: 489). Despite different approaches, each novel similarly stresses the need of cultural memory for characters to maintain their Maori heritage. The particular memories that have been selected – myths, family history, supernatural occurrences based on Maori beliefs etc. – strengthen the bond between the individual and the native community while helping to construct and maintain an individual and cultural identity at the same time. Memories, therefore, are needed to create a balanced and healthy self-image.

In *Tangi*, cultural memory has a social function that differentiates it from *Mutuwhenua*. The myths and legends encountered in Ihimaera's novel serve to connect the protagonist with his *whanau* and its customs and traditions. The central *tangi* ceremony itself reinforces the social function in its importance within the community. As a result, memories promote the individual's situation within a greater context. While *Mutuwhenua* does the same, its main emphasis lies on memory's spiritual function. Since Ripeka is well integrated within her cultural group, it is her emotional side that requires strengthening. Consequently, her health improves only once her family uses traditional spiritual cures that allow her to find a balance between Maori and *Pakeha* ways of life. Once again, the first phase novels approach different aspects of Maori identity construction with the use of specific cultural memories.

Ultimately, though the novels differ in their approaches to Maori identity, both use myth and memory to strengthen the bond between individual and cultural heritage. The myths referred to in the texts remain as the basis of a common Maori origin that enables the characters to walk backwards into the future with an eye on the knowledge gained from the past. The emphasis lies on Maori roots, with the realisation that change and *Pakeha* influence are inevitable and that a way must be found to uphold one's heritage while adapting to new situations. In this context, the memories of myths, tradition, and family history function as an anchor to Maori culture, and the novels' protagonists become the centre of change and intersection with non-Maori influences. While *Tangi* and *Mutuwhenua* are repositories of memory due to the richness of myths, traditions, and Maori beliefs, the intrusion of the *Pakeha* is featured as an unavoidable, but only mildly threatening influence if the individual retains a stable relationship with his or her culture. Therefore, the writers' main concern in the first phase of the Maori novel is the transfer and protection of cultural knowledge that will enable a future in a predominantly *Pakeha* society.

3.2 *Te Poupou*: The Walls – Occupying the New Maori Space

In the mid-1980s, after a decade of depictions of an idyllic Maori rural life away from the *Pakeha*, angry fiction emerged. A retreat onto the scarce tribal land was no longer sufficient enough to preserve the native culture as Western influence intruded even there. Re-educating the reader remains a crucial feature in the novels of this time, but a new element appears that writers realised was lacking before: active resistance and revolution. The novels from the 1980s and 1990s are characterised by an overt political view of the Maori people's situation and describe acts of aggressive or subtle resistance. However, even the subtle depictions do not shy away from political issues, as we see in Grace's *Potiki*. On the other end of the spectrum we find Duff's shockingly violent *Once Were Warriors*, which reflects reality in a way as yet unknown in previous novels. The wide range allows for a variety of novels that deal with the situation in a number of ways. The settings change and, in some cases, move away from rural New Zealand to the urban arena instead.

The aim of re-educating the reader that was the focus during the first phase of the Maori novel still remains, but it is supplemented by the necessary resistance in writing. By resisting, writers address current agendas, and their insistence may be explained by Achebe's assessment of similar developments in African politics:

> They [African Personality, African Democracy, negritude etc.] are all props we have fashioned at different times to help us get on our feet again. Once we are up we shan't need any of them any more. But for the moment it is in the nature of things that we may need to counter racism with what Jean-Paul Sartre has called an anti-racism, to announce not just that we are as good as the next man but that we are much better.
>
> The writer cannot expect to be excused from the task of re-education and regeneration that must be done. In fact he should march right in front. (Achebe 175c: 45)

Maori writers, too, need to create such props that will help them find a strong foothold with which to confront and address their issues so they may be heard. A certain vehemence enters the novel at this point that was missing before and which had forced writers like Ihimaera to pause and think about the kind of Maori life they wanted to depict. Like Achebe, many decided to "march right in front" because they, as well-known writers, have the publicity and the chance to make a change.

Potiki offers an examination of *Pakeha* politics and Maori resistance as well as an in-depth study of mythical influences in characterisation. Being the most political novel and one that rewrites history from an indigenous point of view, *The Matriarch* is indispensable. Finally, his book *The Whale Rider* concludes the analysis. Compared to *The Matriarch*, this novel is less aggressive, but it inhabits a special place in the second phase as a novel written both for children and adults while discussing important matters of cultural survival.

Of all three phases, the second is the most varied as writers branch out from the originally pastoral settings. For this reason, the novels in this section have been chosen to represent the given variety instead of containing the angriest novels only. As a result, *The Whale Rider* is included despite its focus on Maori history and mythology without the inclusion of *Pakeha*. There is the relatedness of politics and survival in *Potiki*, the urgent need for action in *The Matriarch*, and the mythic resonance of *The Whale Rider* – all of which hint at the variety of the Maori novel of the mid-1980s.

3.2.1 Patricia Grace's Potiki (1986)

Judging from her previous subtle prose, Grace's second novel is surprisingly political while far more steeped in myth than *Mutuwhenua* at the same time. On the one hand, it is full of references to myths and, on the other, the story itself is mythic in its form and content. Events are woven into the mythic strands of the story, connecting politics and history. Grace's writing is less dense than Ihimaera's *Tangi* and may be easier to follow while expressing the same sentiments that Ihimaera's work conveys. This is also illustrated by the descriptions of the *tangi* in both authors' works: while Ihimaera employs condensed poetic language in *Tangi*, Grace's descriptions appear freer and more direct. The significance of the event is made clear both ways, though in different styles.

As opposed to Ihimaera's practice, Grace allows the story to be told from multiple perspectives. While Ihimaera tends to explore topics from a central character's point of view, Grace lets her novel be told by a number of people, imitating the tradition of oral storytelling. Each chapter consists of the name of the person who either tells the story or whom that particular section is about. There are only two first person narrators, however: Roimata, (the mother, but not birth mother) and her son Toko, the *potiki* (last child) of the novel's title. *Potiki* is metafictional in its way of foregrounding the process of oral storytelling, which consists of the retelling of stories by all members of the community and even the dead, hence the varying perspectives. There are passages that appear to be told not by one particular person, but by an omniscient communal voice such as in the case of the prologue in particular or the chapters not written in the first person. These parts of the story represent the result of retelling, and are the current understanding of the story which is not exempt from change in the future. None of these stories are final versions since the process of storytelling is an ongoing one, as emphasised throughout the novel.

"*Potiki* is set out like a whaikorero, a piece of oratory, and a formal piece of oratory has a format to it," the author herself describes the structure in an interview. "It will often have at its beginning a chant, tauparapara it's called, something that brings the attention towards the speaker. And then we have the greetings. Then will come the body or main part of the speech and at the end there will often be 'Ka huri' to turn over to another next speaker or the next storyteller to tell his/her story" (Calleja 2003: 114). So, harking back to Maori formal oratory, the prologue begins with a ritual opening or incantation that leads to the mythic story of the carver, told by the omniscient communal voice. This is the most obviously mythic story, though one should say legend since it is set in the not too distant past of the tribe and it is an historical event within the context of the story. The passage recalls the important and sacred profession of the carver in his community as a preserver of history – and thus of stories – and it tells part of his life's tale in the fashion of a prophecy. This prophecy of the missing and yet to be carved figure in his final work forms the novel's background. Since the carver is an esteemed figure in Maori culture and regarded as a storyteller who derives his inspiration directly from the spirit world, the mythic style employed for this prologue is not at all unusual.

The prologue utilises a number of mythic patterns such as the gifted carver whose talent holds special significance in the community and offers him insight into the future that is unavailable to others. As suggested, it is a gift that is believed to be inherent in his sacred profession. He foretells the coming of a person important for the tribe's future and makes a space for his carved figure. It will not be carved by him, so his last work will remain unfinished until the prophecy comes true. Fully aware of the consequences, the carver commits a forbidden act by carving a figure from living memory and giving breath to the wood, violating the sacredness of the carver profession. Finally, the story ends with his death, the just punishment for his actions. As in all myths, there is no doubt as to the reasons or reality of events, and this is the point at which the novel begins.

Set in a time years after the events described in the prologue, Roimata's chapter is an introduction to family relations and the situation of the
whanau (*P* 15–16). This is reminiscent of the recitation of one's genealogy
or the calling upon ancestors that follow the *tauparapara* of a speech in
Maori tradition, situating the participants. We are also told of their lives
and as much of their history as is necessary to set the scene. The strength
of family ties and the general and unbreakable sense of belonging to this
community pervade the narrative. At this stage, there is no change in the
lives of the *whanau* and things are as they have always been.

Soon the village's routine is disturbed by an unexpected birth that bears
strong resemblance to biblical myth but is enhanced by Maori mythology.
The young mother, significantly named Mary, is a mentally and physically
challenged girl who never reveals the father. There is a suspect, but the
family never comes to the conclusion the omniscient communal voice
implies: that the father is the carving that absorbed the carver's breath a
long time ago, and, possibly, the carver himself through his work of art.
Similar to biblical Mary's Immaculate Conception, the girl conceives from
a spirit she calls "loving-man" (*P* 21), the name she gave the carving. This
is the beginning of another mythical story of the *whanau*, the story of a
fatherless disfigured Christ born of a disfigured Mary, who will be the
tribe's salvation when their stories begin to change.

Similar to the Christian saviour, Toko is the prophet doomed to an
early death. Due to his deformity, his body deteriorates while his mind
remains sharp. In the chapters bearing his name, he tells his own story in
mythical terms similar to the ones found in the prologue. He learns of his
special knowledge about the future, and the reader senses that what Toko
speaks of is laden with significance that is yet to be understood. Toko himself
cannot clearly understand what the things he foresees mean at first, but he
need not emphasise their importance and the fact that his convictions are
true even if he is unable to explain them: "And what I have known ever since
then is that my knowing, my own knowingness, is different. It is a before,
and a now, and an after knowing, and not like the knowing that other people
have" (*P* 52). The reader is expected to accept this in the way Toko and his
family readily believe. To the *whanau* he is a *taniwha* (cf. *P* 67), traditionally
a water spirit and also guardian of his people. Significantly, like a *taniwha*,

he is born in the sea. This role is also made clear by the placenta lost in the water at his birth and cannot be buried as it should be. Toko's placenta, however, is never found even though the villagers dive to find it.

Mary tries to drown her son after birth, but his sister Tangimoana saves him. It is almost like a purification, a baptism in seawater that also reinforces Toko's identification with Christ, and it is an initiation into his special knowingness which puts him in line with prophets. His grandmother saves him from what he calls his second drowning – reminiscent of the Second Coming of Christ – by clearing his mouth and nose so he can breathe: "Soon my Granny Tamihana came with all her gifts. She blew all wrong things away to clear and free me, and rubbed the bubbles up to save me from my second drowning. She gave me magic from her ear, and gave a name from when she was a girl" (*P* 42). His choice of words clarifies the ritual character of his coming into the world. Roimata then adds another Maori component by giving him a greenstone ornament, a *taonga* or treasure and heirloom that invests him with his qualities and which he carries with him all his life.

Apart from the biblical references, Toko's story is a variation of the prototypical hero myth (cf. Leeming 2002: 117ff.). The circumstances of his conception and supposed virgin birth are elements of the hero myth as is his presence at a time of great need for his tribe. Shortly after his birth, he is threatened by the first "'guardian at the gate' of the status quo", someone "who cannot tolerate the presence of a force for new understanding" (Leeming 2003: 120), when his own mother attempts to drown him. Like the hero child, Toko needs to prove himself first, in which he succeeds with his predictions.

Unlike what may be expected from such a myth, however, this hero is physically broken, which ties him to his tribal land. Thus he cannot physically depart on a quest for adventure in an unknown world from which he may return with special knowledge to benefit his people. Nonetheless, Toko is already in possession of such knowledge without needing to leave, and this skill is left unexplained but for the circumstances of his birth and his ensuing recognition as *taniwha*.

The novel is flanked by a mythical prologue and ending, which reflect the structure of the traditional hero myth. While the former sets the stage for his origin, the latter depicts his resurrection. Having died for his people as the hero myth demands (Leeming 2003: 122), Toko is not, however, resurrected in the flesh. Instead, he appears as a spirit who takes part in the telling of his own story after death. Despite the slight alterations, *Potiki* is a prototypical hero myth. Grace has added her own variations, which result in a Maori interpretation of the hero myth, harking back to Christian myths at the same time. The structural division into threes reflects the Christian trinity in the constellation of characters, the Maori art of *kowhaiwhai* (depicting a fern pattern in three colours [cf. Panny 2006]) as it is imitated by the narrators' turns to speak, and the hero myth's structure of birth, quest and death/resurrection. This combination of influences illustrates the variability of myth and its susceptibility to change. At the same time, it also reflects the change that Toko prophesies for his people.

Taking a closer look at the novel, Toko's personal history – like all mythic narratives – consists of things he knows and things he has heard. The line, "I do not remember that, but I've been told" (*P* 48) is often found in his own telling. No story has only one source of reference, as the final chapter entitled "The stories" shows. The stories are collected and told by many, woven together to a complete story of legend and myth. For the Maori in *Potiki*, lives are stories because they cannot know about their past or their present without them. The telling and preservation of stories becomes an important and necessary task in the community: "We could not afford books so we made our own. In this way we were able to find ourselves in books. It is rare for us to find ourselves in books, but in our own books we were able to find and define our lives" (*P* 104). This passage contains a metafictional element in the villagers' need to make their own books so as to find a place in them. They must write themselves into existence the way Maori authors have written themselves into society's awareness. The authority of the written word guarantees attention and it is an important beginning for the making and maintaining of identity, both for a people amongst themselves and in relation to others.

The Maori community is depicted as self-reliant and independent. More than once, Roimata mentions that everything of importance is in this village with the family:

"Everything we need is here. We learn what we need and want to learn, and all of it is here," I said to Hemi, but he had always known it. We needed just to live our lives, seek out our stories and share them with each other.

So I didn't become a teacher [...]. I became instead a teller of stories, a listener to stories, a writer and a reader of stories, an encanter, a collector and a maker of stories. But I only shared in this. What really happened was that we all became all of these things – tellers, listeners, readers, writers, teachers and learners together. (*P* 38–9)

Identities are created and upheld through the narration of stories in the *whanau*. Significantly, the teacher becomes a storyteller just like everyone else. There is no single authority to force an interpretation upon the people and decide what is right or wrong. All versions of the story are equally valid and important and the teacher's version is not better or more correct than the pupil's.

Roimata realises that the stories that have been told in the past and are still told now are related to her own life and important for her and her people today. These are stories that tell of Maori life in general and serve as a reminder of who they are and who they have been. "It was a new discovery to find that these stories were, after all, about our own lives," she says, "were not distant, that there was no past or future, that all time is a now-time, centred in the being. It was a new realisation that the centred being in this now-time simply reaches out in any direction towards the outer circles, these outer circles being named 'past' and 'future' only for our convenience. [...] These are the things I came to realise as we told and retold our own-centre stories" (*ibid.* 39). As in Ihimaera's novels, the spiral plays an important part in Grace's story. The family's stories influence their lives today, connecting the *whanau* to the time and the world of their ancestors. Since everything has its own position on the spiral, time is irrelevant and everything from the past also influences the present and the future. The only time of consequence is the now with its relations to past and future.

This definition of time as open and influenced by all things positioned on the spiral complements the understanding of stories as tales always in a process of retelling, augmentation and change. In this respect, *Potiki* resembles the South American *testimonio*, as described by Doris Bachmann-Medick in her introduction to new concepts of world literature

(1996). The novel resembles this foreign genre in its setting within a collective community in which the tribe's stories are told and retold. Their
history is interspersed with proverbs, anecdotes, myths and legends that
emphasise the importance of oral storytelling within the community (cf.
Bachmann-Medick 1998: 270). According to her definition of the genre,
Potiki's focus on orality is a form of resistance with which Grace opposes
the predominance of Western written genres. Grace, like Ihimaera, chooses
this particular approach in her novel, but unlike him she brings the issue
to the fore in her explicit references to storytelling and particularly in
Roimata's metafictional musings.

Especially the final chapter "The stories" illustrates the significance
of orality within the tribal community and how history consists of a
range of tales told by a number of people. After the family has told all
the versions of Toko's life, each coloured by the teller's perspective, Grace
writes: "But the telling was not complete. As the people slept there was one
more story to be told, a story not of a beginning or an end, but marking
only a position on the spiral" (*ibid.* 180). Since this is Toko's own version
that is missing at this point and it will most likely never be heard by any
living person now that he is dead, the story remains unfinished, varied and
ever changing. The fact that Toko's own version does find its way into the
novel is, however, at one with the Maori belief in the continuing presence
of the spirit of the dead as previously encountered in *Tangi* in which
Ihimaera emphasised the spiral nature of time. Grace does the same:
"End is always beginning. Death is life" (*ibid.* 58). In the same way, death
is not the end of storytelling, but the beginning of more stories and new
versions of the old.

Changing Stories: Tribal Life and the Need for Action

Apart from the novel's concern with the telling of stories, it is also about
the changing of tales through an as yet unknown enemy that Toko foretells.
Soon, it becomes apparent that the enemy is *Pakeha* influence: "Things
were stirring, to the extent of people fighting to hold onto a language that
was in danger of being lost, and to the extent of people struggling to regain
land that had gone from them years before" (*ibid.* 60). The past lives – the
stories – change as politics intrudes. Grace tells the story of a community

that is threatened by extinction and tries to preserve its culture to counter this effect.

The first changes in the native community begin with the children. Not all are educated at home and those who are fit for *Pakeha* education are sent to school or university. Education is important, especially the kind that will enable the younger people to live in a changing world. It is no longer necessary to choose between two types of education, the traditional or the foreign European kind. There is, now, a combination of Maori and *Pakeha* learning available to children that will prove useful. In Hemi's day it was more difficult: "In his day they had been expected to hide things, to pretend they weren't what they were. It was funny how people saw each other. Funny how you came to see yourself in the mould that others put you in, and how you began not to believe in yourself" (*ibid*. 65).

The children are stronger now and willing to stand up for their heritage. Reuben is one of those young Maori who are unwilling to let themselves be led to believe they are worthless. He is strong and rebellious and has decided that school does not teach him what he needs to know, and that wherever you look Maori are seen as less than *Pakeha*. He argues with his parents who want him to finish his education. "Aren't I something already? Aren't I?" he asks. "That's all I learn at school – that I'm not somebody, that my ancestors were rubbish and so I'm rubbish too. That's all I learn from the newspapers, that I'm nobody, or I'm bad and I belong in jail. You're telling me that now too" (*ibid*. 74). Eventually, Reuben goes on to university to study law, which finally enables him to fight against the *Pakeha*. By choosing this education, he has learned the *Pakeha* tools to resist them with their own means.

Beside Grace's concern with storytelling, her novel combines myth with politics. The theme of a return to the land of one's birth also to be found in *The Whale Rider* enters into this novel and is related to the general theme of staying on ancestral land. It becomes a central motif in *Potiki*: the connection between people and the land is the basis for the character's political ambition. The seizure of Maori land and the indigenous people's resistance are the change that Toko foretells. In this manner, the *Pakeha* is woven into the villagers' stories, announcing what Roimata suspects: that "[o]ur lives, our stories had changed" (*ibid*. 138). It seems that Toko is the one with whom all changes begin and an awareness of danger comes into the villagers' lives. Even though he is a rather passive character in that his actions are restricted due to his deformity, his birth is the catalyst for the novel's events. Mainly, he is an observer because of his physical defect. When comparing *the bone people* and *Potiki*, Silvia Mergenthal points out that Toko is indeed *the bone people's* Simon's counterpart (Mergenthal 2002: 139f.). Like Simon, his origin is unclear and both emerge from the sea. They suffer from physical defects and can both be viewed as "prototypes of The New Man [...] in eutopian society" (*ibid.*: 139; see also Oxley 1990: 420f.). Both novels wish to create eutopia, a positive utopia in their fiction and succeed in different ways. In *Potiki*, all characters are already set in their ways and need only do away with and ignore any *Pakeha* interference that comes their way. They are within a strong community from the start and are therefore not in any conflict amongst themselves. Their eutopia exists from the beginning and it is what they know and try to preserve. In the novel, Grace calls for preservation because all they want and need has always been with them.

The basis of the eutopian state is the range of indigenous values and customs as discussed in connection with *tikanga*. Maori values underlie all dealings among Maori and with people such as Dollarman (in fact named Mr. Dolman) who negotiates with them over land. Since *manaakitanga* (hospitality and looking after people) must be maintained "no matter what the circumstances might be" (Mead 2003: 29), Toko's *whanau* are hospitable even though Dollarman is an unwanted guest. Here, resistance is quiet and peaceful due to the *whanau's* adherence to and preservation of their traditions, but the reader is confronted with other types of resistance too.

Apart from the peaceful resistance witnessed in connection with Dollarman's visit and the general preference for teaching children at home until they are fit to be educated elsewhere, there are instances of aggressive resistance once *Pakeha* encroach on the land. It is one of the young ones, Toko's sister Tangimoana, who takes action into her own hands and destroys machines to stop them. There is also Reuben's approach in which he looks at problems from a lawyer's perspective and is in the position to take legal action if necessary. These three types of resistance result in three types of Maori identity, a phenomenon later also encountered in Grace's *Cousins*.

In *Potiki*, two types of identity are overtly political while one, though implicitly so, remains rooted within tribal life within the *whanau*. The resistance that entails destruction is generally unwelcome, which does not keep the perpetrator from putting her plans into action, however. Tangimoana represents the angry young Maori who act on their own, spontaneously and without long-term plans. In contrast, Reuben's approach is slow and tedious. With his knowledge of the legal paths open to him, his life consists of negotiations that may not appear to lead anywhere at first. He represents the Maori politician who speaks on behalf of his people and therefore has longer-lasting influence than Tangimoana. The final type of Maori identity encountered in *Potiki* is a community-based self-image that is firmly rooted in indigenous customs and traditions and need not be directed outside the community. This is an identity that, like in the novels of the first phase, focuses on being Maori and living according to long-held beliefs. Even though the world outside the community cannot be ignored, it has no direct part in the construction – or rather upholding – of this particular identity. The outside world's indirect influence consists of the need it creates within the Maori community to continue focusing on Maori customs and values. It is this third identity that focuses most strongly on memories – the myths, legends, rituals and beliefs that have defined Maoriness since the beginning. Anchored in the past, this type of identity distinguishes itself from the other two who react to outside influence and comes from within the Maori community, but is geared toward the outside in order to represent traditional Maori life.

The need for action and distinct identities in the novel follows the five stages of memory as observed by Rigney in that elements of each identity have to be selected and converged. The characters therefore choose between the elements of their Maori heritage that they are familiar with, resulting in one of the three types of identity the reader encounters in the course of the novel. The elements are based on the memories as passed on within the *whanau* by elders, teachers, parents and others; hence the importance of being "a teller of stories, a listener to stories" (*P* 39). The act of selecting existing elements and forming them into something new by rearranging, enhancing and reducing parts of them imitates the process of remembrance at the same time as it reflects the process of identity construction. The resulting types of identity are models found in all selected novels, such as Grace's *Cousins*, which allows an even more detailed analysis of the main characters and the types of identities they represent. In these texts we are faced with the fighter, the politician, the mother, and the seeker, the elder, to mention the most common ones – all of which become archetypal Maori characters due to their recurring appearance, elemental significance, and origin in indigenous beliefs and traditions.

Being so firmly rooted in Maori culture almost inevitably restricts non-Maori understanding of certain nuances within the text. Given that the novel is written in English, readers unfamiliar with the culture may not encounter obvious problems with the narrative, but subtleties such as Toko's *taniwha* status, the relations between members of the *whanau*, and the underlying significance of land negotiations remain hidden. Any exclusion of non-Maori readers could either be deliberate or coincidental and originates within the subject matter of the narrative.

Return or Refusal? The Exclusion of the Pakeha

There are moments in the novel when the author leaves the non-Maori reader in the dark. *Potiki* harbours a way of thinking between its lines that is unlikely to be recognised by readers unfamiliar with the culture. These instances include, for example, the sacredness of the carving profession, which is, however, hinted at in the prologue's style. Less obvious is the significance of Toko's lost placenta or the meaning of the greenstone ornament which are not elaborated, but which are so imbedded in Maori life that native readers understand the significance. Such references are lost to non-Maori readers and exclude them from a full understanding of the novel and Maori culture.

The most obvious refusal to include the non-Maori readership is the novel's ending (*P* 184–5), which is entirely in Maori and offers no translation. It is a resistance of English as a language that erases difference by assuming that the native tongue is translatable at will (cf. Bachmann-Medick 1996: 274). At the same time, however, this ending in a foreign tongue is also an inclusion. Readers who are unacquainted with the language will have difficulty understanding the final paragraph despite the use of dictionaries. Given that the ending of narratives is a crucial part of any story, readers may feel deprived of the final message, possibly the heart of the story. This circumstance, however, should not be regarded as negative. Instead, it is proof of the intricacies of Maori culture. There are things that cannot be understood and require a different mindset which non-Maori readers are less likely to have. Grace retreats into *te reo* and her culture entirely by the end of the novel in much the same way her characters do by living self-sufficient lives apart from *Pakeha* society. She clearly demonstrates that there are things we cannot understand and perhaps should not understand because they are uniquely Maori. We cannot expect to have a full grasp of anything Maori without growing up in this culture, and all we can do is try to understand and learn as much about it as we can, but also understand that there are limits we cannot overcome. We are expected to accept difference without judgement like Graeme does in *Mutuwhenua*. There are areas that are meant only for the members of a community or culture, but not for others. This coincides with the Maori concept of *tapu* that demands that details of tribal life be kept within the tribe and must not be made known to strangers. Furthermore, by excluding non-Maori readers, Grace makes them feel how Maori feel in the *Pakeha* world from which they have been excluded in turn. Yet perhaps the choice of an ending in *te reo* should be viewed less as a refusal than a return to Maori roots. The emphasis lies on the latter, which automatically marginalises those who cannot speak the language. This is an inevitable side-effect of the return to Maori culture.

Simultaneously, the very ending is an invitation to be included in this foreign culture. The last words, "*Ka huri*" (*P* 185) – spread the word – are commonly used at the end of speeches to hand over to the next speaker. As Calleja (Calleja 2003: 114) points out in conversation with Grace, it is a handing over to the reader who is then responsible for what comes after and how the story is treated.

3.2.2 *Witi Ihimaera's The Matriarch (1986)*

One of Ihimaera's most ambitious novels, *The Matriarch* (*Mat*) reads like a comprehensive book of Maori history. In it, the narrators present their family history, which begins long before their time in the days of their mythic and legendary ancestors and includes a history of politics and religion. At the same time, the accounts function as a guide for the present that gives the characters a sense of their heritage and provides the tools for their actions. In fact, the novel consists of a number of stories told by Tamatea and his grandmother Artemis (or Riripeti), the Matriarch of the Mahana clan, that lead to stories within stories, some of which are expanded by eyewitness accounts, speeches and other reflections. About half of the novel consists of the Matriarch teaching young Tamatea about his history. These sections consist of memories that describe his education, ancestors, and privileged status in the tribe as her successor. While these memories form one storyline, the other takes place in the present and depicts the struggles within the family that make it necessary for Tamatea to prove his rightful status as heir. At the same time, the storyline also describes his struggle to protect ancestral land from being seized by the *Pakeha*.

As mentioned previously, *The Matriarch* is considered Ihimaera's most political novel due to the focus on Maori struggles, retribution and the slow progress of the righting of wrongs both past and present. This view, however, needs to be relativised as *The Uncle's Story* and *The Rope of Man* in the third phase of the Maori novel are at least equally as political as this work. Nevertheless, *The Matriarch* marks a significant change in Maori fiction at a time that begins to resolve Maori grievances in accordance with the Treaty of Waitangi, and which is generally a time of protest. As a result of that time, the demand for greater *Pakeha* awareness of *maoritanga* also influences the fiction, and the general feeling of unrest in the Maori community is evident here.

Unlike any previous novel, *The Matriarch* is a work of historiographic metafiction, as defined by Linda Hutcheon (1988a and 1988b) and partly adopted by Colavincenzo (2003). In it, "theoretical self-awareness of history and fiction as human constructs (historio*graphic meta*fiction) is made the grounds for its rethinking and reworking of the forms and contents of the past" (Hutcheon 1988b: 5). While "demythologizing historical practice" (Colavincenzo 2003: xiv), Ihimaera's novel at the same time mythologises historical events to promote a Maori view of history and an indigenous form of historiography. By writing a historical novel, Ihimaera confronts pre-existing controlling authorities with an alternative. Since "it is the story of the victors that usually gets told" (Hutcheon 1988a: 72), Maori history has been marginalised until it has only remained in the stories passed on among Maori among generations while being located, for the most part, outside of any standard historical records. In line with Hutcheon's definition, *The Matriarch* is a "critical revisiting of history" (Hutcheon 1988b: xii) that is never a "nostalgic 'return'" (*ibid.* 4) despite the clear bond between the protagonists and their ancestors, and the ongoing retelling of their lives. We will see how Ihimaera and his fictional characters rewrite or retell history as part of a greater Maori resistance that will secure a few additional pages in the book of a nation's history.

"Fix the history in your memory": History as a Tool for Battle

By beginning the novel with a prologue relating the Matriarch's account of Creation, Ihimaera positions indigenous history as the primary source of knowledge for Maori that is to be used as the basis from which any action originates. The book itself does so and recounts Tamatea's history that begins "many thousands of years before you were born in Waituhi" (*Mat* 108). This requires a constant retelling of the past, which is an arrangement the novel itself follows in the familiar spiral pattern, moving back and forth between the storylines, times and events that are revisited when necessary in the telling. As Agathe Thornton (1989) observes in her analysis of traditional oral stories, the constant return to elements of a story are typical of Maori oral storytelling tradition. As we discussed, the storyteller may start his tale with the "beginning and end of it in order to satisfy at once the desire of his audience to know *what* they are going to hear about. Then he elaborates 'appositionally', as we shall call it, on the detail of *how* all this came about" (Thornton 1985: 156–7). *The Matriarch* follows a similar pattern by returning repeatedly to events mentioned previously in the novel in order to supply further details that become relevant for the novel's progress. For this reason, the reader is brought back to the Matriarch's attendance at a *marae* that refuses to show her the respect she requires. As this is a central event that characterises Artemis as the Matriarch and a woman of supernatural powers, Ihimaera supplies the reader with information of the event in instalments, interspersed with eyewitness accounts that give both rational and supernatural explanations for the occurrences.

In addition to these events, the book contains the Creation myth and other tales of mythic ancestors such as Maui or Hinenuitepo, and leads to the stories of the Matriarch's legendary ancestors Te Kooti and Wi Pere to whom the author each allots a chapter. Eventually, the tales lead to the narrators themselves, demonstrating that their lives consist of stories of old that give them a strong sense of origin and identity. For this reason, the Matriarch instructs her grandson to "[f]ix the history in your memory" (*Mat* 231), so that he may not only know who he is, but also what he is capable of. In fact, the lessons go beyond a mere instilling of Maori identity and extend into the future, showing both her foresight and the knowledge that the battle between Maori and *Pakeha* is not over yet: "This is why you must learn the whakapapa and the links between the tribes," she says, "for, on day, you too might need to call upon your knowledge to secure your goal" (*Mat* 308).

Inevitably, since the practice of storytelling dominates all historical accounts, there is no guarantee for accuracy, as Tamatea admits in the metafictional passage that begins the novel:

> It was Uncle Alexis who started it all – this imaginative reconstruction of the woman who wore pearls in her hair, the matriarch who ruled the Mahana family for three generations. [...] Father Blain said that all families are somewhat like jungles. So it is with mine, but I have made it even more of a jungle by mingling fiction with fact, like saprophytic vines twining the trunks of already dead trees. I think the Matriarch herself would have approved of this. After all, she was the one who turned my own life into fiction from fact. (*Mat* 1)

This excerpt characterises the entire narrative in its attempts to recreate history through personal memories and myths. Fact and fiction mingle until it is impossible to tell them apart. In the spirit of historiographic metafiction, the Matriarch tells the neglected Maori story so that it may be known and become part of her grandson's own memory. "All truth is fiction really," as a journalist explains, "for the teller tells it as he sees it, and it might be different from some other teller. This is why histories often vary, depending on whether you are the conqueror or not" (*Mat* 403). Being the conquered, the stories are essential within the novel to position the characters and Maori as a whole as significant strong characters who maintain, reclaim and establish their power by recognising their ancestors, particularly the influential Te Kooti and Wi Pere.

The conjunction of fact and fiction is woven through the entire novel not only by constant retelling, but also by the inclusion of eyewitness reports, transcribed speeches, letters and other records. However, deciphering the truth is not the purpose here as the unreliability of eyewitnesses proves. On the contrary, the novel encourages the blending of truth and fiction throughout the story. Despite intimating reliability, the information is fictionalised as much as the Matriarch's own life. She is larger than life, both in her own time and after her death. Tellingly named after the Greek goddess Artemis, she is a hunter who never relents and fights for what is hers. At the same time, she knows how to stage her appearance to greatest effect and is known for wearing pearls and a black veil that she uses to set herself apart from others and to command respect. "The matriarch, my grandmother," Tamatea describes her, "the woman who wore pearls in her hair, is at the second step of the poutama. Hers is a blinding presence, imperious and commanding, bidding me forever forward to battle with the world of the Pakeha" (*Mat* 207).

Since both storylines are set in times of political unrest, the Matriarch's retelling of history supplies Tamatea with the tools to confront the *Pakeha*. Significantly, she herself is part *Pakeha*, which has helped her become the respected figure she is. As a descendant of the rebel leader and prophet Te Kooti and the statesman Wi Pere, she is a ruthless fighter and negotiator. Due to her knowledge of history and her personal experience, she has the instinct that lets her know how and when to act because "[t]hat's what you've got to have if you want to win. The killer instinct." (*Mat* 16). There is no doubt as to her readiness to confront and fight those who are in her way, be they Maori or *Pakeha*. Her grandson's lessons are geared towards the same goal as she asks him to remember and "[a]lways fight, never give up. Your mana will help you. Fight fair if you can. But if you must, use whatever devices are at hand. Remember" (*Mat* 31). Here, she stresses the importance of remembering that justifies the lessons in Maori history from the very beginnings in *Te Kore*, the nothing and non-nothing, till her own time.

The lessons, though mainly consisting of the telling of stories, also comprise a few lessons in fighting and her insistence on a *Pakeha* education.

The latter is particularly important: Tamatea has to be familiar with the *Pakeha*'s language and ways of thinking. "You must grasp the tools of the Pakeha and understand them" Artemis tells him. "Particularly, you must understand the words of the white man, not only what he says but what he really means. [...] We must be alert, grandson, for the Pakeha shark. And we have to fight him in his courts, even his Parliament, if it is necessary" (*Mat* 230).[2] As a result, she requests in her will that Tamatea study law in order to "understand how the law had been manipulated" (*Mat* 381) by the *Pakeha*. This harks back to *Potiki*, in which studying law is seen as the most successful way to oppose more land seizures. The Matriarch shares this sentiment though she is fiercer in her expression. In order "to fight the Pakeha you must learn to be like him. You must become a Pakeha, think like him, act like him and, when you know you are in his image then turn your knowledge to his destruction" (*Mat* 427).

The aggressiveness evident in her words derives from her knowledge of past struggles. She teaches Tamatea about them particularly in the two chapters devoted to her ancestors, pointing out the necessity of their actions in their time and today. Remembering Te Kooti's last words, *"Mine enemies will never see me again; but their children's children will"* (*Mat* 196), Artemis knows that the struggle between the races is not yet at an end and that Tamatea will be in need of appropriate teaching. Each of her tales contains a lesson, but it is not all about violence and holding grudges. Instead, he "will learn in the listening why you have to hate and, then, why you must learn to forgive" (*Mat* 133). With this line the Matriarch shows her awareness of a need for change in the dealings with *Pakeha*. While previous generations fought bloody battles, the time is now ripe for a different approach, which is why Tamatea is meant to study law. Te Kooti's rebellion is no longer suitable; instead, it is a time for people such as Wi Pere, who is "symbolic of this ideal of mediation" (*Mat* 311) between the races. Like him, Maori are now required to "confront the Pakeha from within" (*Mat*

2 These and relating lines are again a justification of Maori writing in English and the much-criticised use of Western frameworks. Ihimaera therefore implies the effectiveness of using Western tools to subvert their power by applying them in a Maori context.

312) and do "works of peace and not of war" (*Mat* 171). After the battles
of previous generations, forgiveness is the only way now since the wrongs
committed by Maori and *Pakeha* alike cannot be righted anymore and a
grudge only leads to more war.

Resisting Pakeha Notions of History and Identity
During the lessons and Tamatea's own research, the extent of cruelty during
the Maori and *Pakeha* wars becomes evident, at the same time showing
that neither group was innocent. However, *Pakeha* are blamed directly
for many deaths. "The killing of innocents, Pakeha. The blood is on your
hands" (*Mat* 174), says an unspecified narrator that could be either the
Matriarch or Tamatea, possibly even a third unnamed narrator. Even before
this accusation, the same narrator blames *Pakeha* for deliberately deceiving
the natives: "For most assuredly *you*, Pakeha, began taking the land from us
as you were signing your worthless Treaty. *You*, Pakeha, began taking away
our culture. You said at the time that we were now one people, *he iwi kotahi
tatou*. What you really meant was that we now belonged to *you*. That was
why we went to war" (*Mat* 73–4). These lines clearly place the blame. Due
to such passages, the rebels' actions in Maori history are presented not as
unchallenged attacks, but as *utu*, retribution for the wrongs committed first
by *Pakeha*. The horrors of war perpetrated by Maori rebels are described
in all their cruelty. These events are presented as excerpts from historical
records relying on eyewitness accounts. As official records of the rebellion,
they are devoid of emotion and relate the events objectively: "5.45 a.m. Tom
Goldsmith was riding past Trooper Mann's house. He saw the raiders in
the distance. They were tossing the body of a baby in the air, catching it
on their bayonets, and tossing it up again." (*Mat* 169).

This is only one example of pages of such records included in the
novel, contrasting starkly with the single detailed report of Maori deaths
at the hands of their captors. In it, the language is full of emotion and far
more poetic than the plain account above: "The shots ring out. The sound
is shocking, echoing and echoing across the valley. The prisoners jerk and
dance to the obscene song of the bullets, and the blood sprays and gouts
from bodies and limbs and heads ripped through by the lethal lead. Then

they begin to fall, pitching over the side of the cliff, 120 men, women and children, crowding the air in the long slow dive into death" (*Mat* 178).

The memories of the war obviously consist of what has been set in official records and what is remembered by individuals. The difference between the accounts in the novel demonstrates that the official *Pakeha* accounts record *Pakeha* deaths at the hand of the rebels. There is, in contrast, no mention of any Maori deaths. Instead, those are only available in Maori memory, most likely passed on orally without having been set down in writing, hence the rather elaborate account above. The imbalanced representation of events calls for Maori memory to fill in the blanks, and this is what *The Matriarch* offers in Artemis' lessons. As a work of historiographic metafiction, the novel therefore rewrites the official history of the war and tells the Maori story that has been ignored. As a result, the rewritten version relies heavily on oral accounts, legends and myths for which there may not be sufficient proof. In *The Matriarch*, the proof may be mainly fictionalised in the telling of stories, but it is believed by the narrators and thus also by the reader. To create the impression of reliability, Ihimaera adds records such as Wi Pere's speeches in parliament to the story. There is no doubt that the speeches were given, yet whether they have been reproduced accurately is unclear. Ihimaera has been criticised for failing to acknowledge some of his sources. In his newspaper article "Matriarch Passages Copied – Historian" in the *Dominion Sunday Times* (1989), Andrew Johnston makes that point as well. As a result, *The Matriarch* is a mosaic of true and fictional passages. In any case, Wi Pere's speeches as included in the text reflect the passion and outspokenness attributed to him (cf. Kohere 1951).

Evidently, *The Matriarch* is a historical novel which tells an alternative story that confronts official *Pakeha*-centric records. It is a necessary step to displace the outsider's discourse and bring the inside Maori view to the fore in order to articulate a new and more accurate national identity (cf. Romaine 2004). For this reason, it is important that any critical voices in the novel are Maori as well, guaranteeing that the inside view is retained. Sir Apirana Ngata, who defeated Wi Pere in parliament, for example, voices his unfavourable opinion of Te Kooti even though the Matriarch's stories turn the rebel leader and prophet into a hero. "Te Kooti," he says, "is the last and greatest representative of the worst side of the Maori character – its subtlety, cunning and treachery; its cruelty and love of bloodshed; and its immorality and fanaticism. His character had no relieving trait [...]" (*Mat* 196). Unlike *Pakeha* records, the Maori voices in the novel present both sides of his character, which is representative of the novel's general aim to supply the other side of the story.

Therefore, the reader encounters two versions of every story in *The Matriarch*: there are surreal occurrences like Artemis' transformation into a giant spider or the sudden spider attack at a meeting (cf. *Mat* 348ff.) that have both a rational and a supernatural explanation. Furthermore, there is the contrasting juxtaposition of two influential Maori figures, represented by Te Kooti and Wi Pere. Also, Ihimaera utilises the image of the chessboard in the novel with its white and black background that again emphasises the existence of two contrasting stories and illustrates how any action is followed by a reaction. At the same time, the chessboard is an image of manipulation that clarifies how one person's move influences another's. Therefore, the game is utilised as a visual demonstration of action and reaction as well as the existence of multiple stories.

Resisting Western notions of nationhood and identity, Ihimaera's historical novel insists that "that they [Maori], and they only, should determine the Maori destiny" (*Mat* 322) without *Pakeha* interference. If the *Pakeha* remain dominant, Tamatea fears, his culture will not survive. The *Pakeha* attempt to have Maori people "establish a civilisation like unto that of the Pakeha [...] [but] there is an inequality here, a basic obscenity. The Pakeha do not want the Maori to be equal" (*Mat* 50). So both Tamatea and the Matriarch object to any Western ideas of identity and need to find their own Maori-based methods to retain and promote their marginalised culture.

One such method, as mentioned earlier, is to fight the *Pakeha* with his own weapons by becoming like him and attaining the same knowledge he has. Most importantly, there must be a secure Maori base from which to begin, which is why the Matriarch's lessons are essential to Tamatea's education in his own culture. Yet Maori must be "takers of life" and not let themselves be undermined. "We don't wait to be offered life," is Tamatea's family's approach. "We *take* it. So, as a result, we've taken every opportunity that has come our way, and in that sense

we've all achieved things and made successes out of our lives" (*Mat* 87).
Compared to previous novels of the first and second phase, *The Matriarch's* and *Potiki's* approach to fight the *Pakeha* with his own weapons is
new and radical in fiction at this time. While other novels up to this point
promoted a return to Maori roots, Grace and Ihimaera now suggest confronting *Pakeha* with their own tools. Like Grace, Ihimaera gives examples
of people who have already taken the path that combines indigenous and
European education. Most notably, the Matriarch's own life – spent in New
Zealand and Italy – reflects how influences from both cultures might be
helpful in becoming a powerful authoritative figure.

Furthermore, there is mention of other relatives who have managed
to lead their lives in both cultures without losing their Maori heritage
and who were "in that taniwha line of fearless women" (*Mat* 25). They
are respected women who have been able to find their place between two
cultures. They know how to use every device at hand to attain their goals,
just like Artemis turns her own life into a myth even in her own lifetime.
Tamatea's research after her death indicates how interwoven fact and fiction
are when it comes to her past. What is certain is that she was a respected
and impressive person who set herself apart with her garb, her occasional
use of Italian, her passion, and dramatic actions that left people wonder-
ing if they had really witnessed what they saw. The reports of the incidents
range from people who believe in the supernatural to those who think they
were just tricks. Such ambiguity threads itself through all of Artemis' life
and solidifies her elusive mythic character.

Mythification as Alternative Historiography

This and similar processes of mythification are another tool to reclaim
Maori identity and a Maori-based notion of history and nationhood. It
is in line with the ongoing traditional telling of stories as demonstrated
in the novel's structure itself and in the account of Maori history since
Creation. Despite the rational explanations given for any unusual occurrences, the supernatural, mythic explanations remain equally valid in the
text. This is a particularity found in all of Ihimaera's work that supports
his philosophy, most evident in the later novels *The Uncle's Story* and *The
Rope of Man*, of a nation in which many cultures can co-exist by embracing

not only their own culture, but also elements of other cultures that have shaped Aotearoa New Zealand. While *Pakeha* culture is characterised as rational and scientific, Maori culture is spiritual. Therefore, the juxtaposition of rational and supernatural explanations in *The Matriarch* offers a first glimpse of Ihimaera's philosophy.

The indigenous view of history is part of his philosophy and requires a change from traditionally Western historiography. As historiographic metafiction, as understood by Colavincenzo (2003), the novel rewrites over 150 years of official history since the arrival of the *Pakeha* and illustrates an alternative to conventional historiography. *The Matriarch*'s key features of the fictionalisation of facts create an ambiguity within the text. Here, truth is regarded as inseparable from fiction, eventually presenting a view of Maori history that differs from accepted official accounts. Mythification therefore becomes the new historiography that not only tells the untold story, but does so in indigenous terms by introducing characteristic Maori features into the telling itself.

Moreover, the history may contain pre-existing myths that "are used as a basis for telling all or part of the story", as Colavincenzo (2003: 99) states. The characters then become "simulacra of a particular figure in a particular myth," he continues, even if only by an extended reference. Such is the case in the Matriarch's account of Te Kooti, who is likened very clearly to Moses (*Mat* 133ff.) when she recounts the Song of Te Kooti for her grandson:

> E mokopuna [grandson], and the song of Te Kooti sings to us of the agony of the war for as he had promised, so it came to pass that in the month of November 1868 the prophet came down from Puketapu Mountain and fell upon the cohorts of Pharaoh, Pakeha and Maori. And as Pharaoh had done unto the prophet, so did the Prophet do unto Pharao. And just as God had done unto the Egyptians when they would not let His people go, by sending death to the first born of the Egyptians during the time of Moses, so did the prophet do so to the Pakeha because he would not let the Maori nation go. (*Mat* 152)

Here, biblical language and parallels between Te Kooti's and Moses' time serve to establish the rebel leader as a prophet. He becomes the Moses of his own people, who demands from the *Pakeha* that he let his people go so he may lead them on the long journey to the Promised Land.

What is more, by combining both legends, Ihimaera comments on past and contemporary injustices. Therefore, the situation of the Maori characters are "granted a new status that exceeds that of fiction or history – he or she attains mythic status" (Colavincenzo 2003: 99), as does the entire Maori resistance. Since Te Kooti has been a legendary character even before his inclusion in fiction, his story is already tinged with myth even if it is not a myth in itself. As a result, the myths and legends surrounding him are part of his history that feed into *The Matriarch*. "In this way," Colavincenzo notes, "history tips over into and mixes with myth, gaining – or, perhaps more accurately, retaining – that mythic element which has little place in standard history. Fiction is used in order to 'keep the myth alive'" (*ibid.* 100). It is apparent in Tamatea's research that his grandmother's life is a similar amalgam of truth and myth that recreates Te Kooti's legendary status. The tales told by those who knew his grandmother are sometimes contradicting when it comes to telling truth from fiction, only adding to the mythic air that surrounds her. The inexplicable events that characterise her life are attributed to an ancient power she may hold or are rationalised, depending on the witness. As a descendant of Te Kooti she incorporates the legendary, mythic status he has whereas Wi Pere's blood represents the rational, realistic aspect of her character.

In addition to matters of characterisation, Ihimaera's novel goes well beyond using myth to characterise his protagonists and introduces, as Julia Calvert (2006) observes, the myth of Te Kooti's diamond to make his strongest political claim in connection with land ownership. Though the diamond's origin is unclear, it is said that the precious stone "is not only an image of hidden wealth, or power to be recovered in 'the days to come'. It recreates the quintessential image for the Maori world, Te Ao Marama, the world of light and knowledge, and it specifically asserts through its biblical reference the salvation of the people in the 'days to come'" (Binney 1987: 20, quoted in Calvert 2006). Calvert concludes that the diamond is a symbol of land, knowledge, and solidarity among Maori people. This interpretation therefore adds to *The Matriarch*'s store of mythic references and at the same time includes Artemis and Tamatea in the ongoing myth of Te Kooti's diamond: at one point, the Matriarch "*uncovered the diamond of Te Kooti*" (*Mat* 293) during Tamatea's lessons, which is the only time it

is referred to explicitly in the entire novel. During the moment of revelation, Tamatea becomes aware of his relations to the land, which is – like
the Song of Te Kooti – related in biblical terms. The diamond's revelation
takes place on a mountaintop, creating another parallel to the story of
Moses (Exodus 33: 20–3).

By placing the story of Te Kooti's diamond in a contemporary context
within the novel, *The Matriarch* carries a message that reveals prominent
cultural and political issues. As a symbol of Maori relationship with the
land, the mention of the diamond in the text solidifies Tamatea's preservation of his ancestral land. Losing the land to the *Pakeha* who will not
treat it as respectfully as they should, Tamatea is bent on protecting it not
only to keep the land within the family, but to preserve Maori life. In the
course of the novel, Tamatea's memories of a visit to Venice reflect his fear
of losing an authentic native life:

> In many respects, though, Venezia Vecchia, as the central city is called, is not at all
> beautiful. The houses and palazzi around the working class areas of Canareggio behind
> the station and castello around the derelict Arsenale are boarded up or crumbling
> away, their foundations succumbing to the slow slap of the sea. The city is only beaut-
> eous where the turisti congregate and, there, it has a ruined beauty of the kind which
> dares us to imagine how it once looked. [...] Ah yes, Venice is a mistress of deception
> for she asks us to substitute our objectivity with melancholia and, once in the grasps
> of that most romantic of senses, only then can the possession begin. (*Mat* 432)

In this passage, deteriorating Venice is symbolic of the Maori fate. The
mythic land of Aotearoa New Zealand is threatened by *Pakeha* notions of
progress that do not coincide with indigenous ideas. The tribal land is the
only place in which the mythic can still exist, which is another reason for
him to protect the land from the *Pakeha*. If the Western ideas of progress
persist, Maori culture will die and with this kind of progress, "Pakeha disease had reaped a rich Maori harvest" (*Mat* 440).

Having been shown Te Kooti's diamond, Tamatea will fight for the
land like Te Kooti and Wi Pere did, situating himself in the long political
protest against land seizure. He finds himself in their tradition, which gives
him historical, mythical and even divine authority to proceed with Maori
protest. Such authority contrasts Western supremacy and opposes standard

historiography. As a result, mythification becomes a valid means by which Maori history is told and remembered. At the same time, myth is empowering and drives Maori action by encouraging people to look into the past for justification of deeds in the present. While this has already been done in novels of the first phase, the emphasis now shifts from looking into the past solely as a reminder of one's origins to utilising one's knowledge of the past in order to be active in political protest. More than any other novel at this point, *The Matriarch* takes the needed step away from a pastoral depiction of Maori life so as to confront the *Pakeha* with his past transgressions and the Maori protest that is the only way to redress those wrongs. The novel, despite the accounts of bloodshed, emphasises that what is needed today are "works of peace and not of war", which is why the Matriarch repeats that her lessons are meant to teach Tamatea "how to hate and then how to forgive" (*Mat* 171). The hate will be a reminder of committed wrongs, but he must forgive to break out of the spiral of violence.

Remembering in Order to Forgive

The accounts of violence and counter violence Ihimaera depicts in his novel centre on *Pakeha* greed for land and their illicit seizing of it. The ruthlessness with which the Land Wars were fought came from both groups involved, but the Matriarch makes clear that it is "you, *Pakeha*" (*Mat* 73) who began. Tamatea's lessons of forgiveness shall break the spiral of violence and make him resort to peaceful but determined action instead.

Consequently, the lessons consist of selected tales from the past, mainly of her two most prominent ancestors, that Artemis recounts from memory. She chooses them to illustrate the two ways Maori have tried to resist *Pakeha* interference in indigenous matters. At the same time, their different approaches demonstrate the change in dealing with injustice: while Te Kooti answers violence with more of the same, Wi Pere's method is a peaceful and relentless stance in parliament. Their actions develop with time, ensuring that Tamatea will in turn continue their struggle peacefully. His aim will be reconciliation and redress instead of more war, as the Matriarch proposes.

Therefore, she chooses the memory of these particular ancestors as a model for future action and protest in the traditional mode of oral storytelling. As opposed to the suggested return to one's Maori heritage that was the focus of previous novels, *The Matriarch* leaves this aspect aside and assumes the characters to be firmly grounded in their *maoritanga*. The text concentrates on the possibilities of resistance learned from Maori history. At the same time, the novel takes care not to promote the re-enactment of past deeds, but exemplifies the need to adapt and improve the form of protest to suit the requirements of the present. For this reason, Te Kooti's early violent approach is no longer acceptable today and is substituted by Wi Pere's work in politics instead. In this respect, *The Matriarch*, even though it consists of tales from the past, is directed towards the future much more than the novels of the first phase.

What Artemis' stories boil down to is the necessity to forgive past bloodshed in order to allow for a fruitful reconciliation and discussion. Her memories are needed for this reason and she, as the elder, is an important figure in ensuring that these memories are preserved. She passes them on to Tamatea as a child, who in turn becomes a significant figure in his tribe (cf. *Mat* 402). Thus the two of them can be considered specialists of cultural memory who, on the one hand, know their history and, on the other, are able to appropriate this knowledge for future use.

Rather than solely forming the basis of a common origin, the memories and myths function as a catalyst for action. The Matriarch, for the same reason, turns her own life into myth so as to demonstrate her *mana* and the power she has and uses to fight on behalf of her people. She is a woman of action, as is evident in her unusual and varied life, and myths and memories are what drive her. Like her, all protagonists in Ihimaera's novel are depicted as people of action with a goal they seek to achieve with the strength and knowledge they gain from their heritage. Te Kooti, Wi Pere, Artemis and Tamatea illustrate part of the Maori line that is fearless and empowered by their culture. Even those who do not shed blood and find other means to fight are warriors of their own kind. While Maori draw a significant part of their cultural identity from the past, *The Matriarch* also encourages change and development to help give Maori the power and respect they have been denied. While remembrance is important in order to forgive and break out of the spiral of fruitless violence, memories supply significant lessons for personal, cultural and national development.

3.2.3 *Witi Ihimaera's The Whale Rider (1987)*

Based on Ihimaera's novel from 1987, the internationally acclaimed motion picture *Whale Rider* (2002) won several awards, including an Academy Award Nomination. Through the medium of film, the story of the young girl Kahu (also known as Paikea), descendant of the legendary whale rider Paikea, reached audiences world-wide. The subsequent publication of a film-tie-in version of the novel found a new readership that could now be introduced to Maori culture through "a modern retelling of a Maori legend" (Mottesheard 2005: 1). Ishimaera, also a writer of children's books, wrote *The Whale Rider* for children and adults and is the only novel featured here for that audience. Thus, the readership differs from that of other works, acquainting younger readers with fundamental Maori stories and convictions.

The shortest novel discussed here, *The Whale Rider* combines a number of characteristics of Maori writing in a clear and focused manner. Thus the new readership is immediately confronted with the essence of Maori literature with this book. It addresses contemporary issues such as the generation gap, culture clash, identity, and changing traditions. The novel contains aspects of Maori culture and politics that are found in Ihimaera's general body of work as well as Grace's writing. Among these is the bond between the land and the people, and the importance of an unbroken line of descent emphasised in the mere recounting of ancestors, the search for an heir, and the prestige and honour that comes with one's relation to mythical and legendary ancestors. Inevitably, certain customs and rituals are important elements of the storytelling and novel-writing process, finding explicit mention in the text as ceremonies of respect and everyday tasks (cf. *WR* 41). Such tasks of daily life in fiction involve allusions to Maori mythology, and *The Whale Rider* is no exception. The text addresses the story of Paikea, the First Parents and their offspring, Hinenuitepo, myths related to the sea and the creatures it harbours, and thoughts on the oneness of all things. These topics are depicted in a style previously encountered in Ihimaera's writing, using lyrical prose and traditional oral storytelling devices.

As early as in the title, the myth that underlies the story is revealed: the tale of Kahutia Te Rangi, also known as Paikea, the whale rider and founder of the tribe in Whangara. Set in the village, this is the story of eight-year-old Kahu and her efforts to make her grandfather Koro love her and accept her as the new leader of the tribe. Since the chief has always been male, Koro does not intend to break with this tradition. It is up to the determined girl to prove that she is a worthy heir because she is, after all, a descendant of Paikea and next in line to be chief.

A Great Emptiness, a Yearning: A Mythical Setting
The text is divided into four sections according to the seasons, flanked by a prologue and an epilogue. This gives the impression of a harmonious, organic division that develops naturally and indicates the balanced relationship between man and nature. The impression is strengthened by the prologue, which is presented in the style of an oral tale. The opening line "In the old days, in the years that have gone before us, the land and sea felt a great emptiness, a yearning" (*WR* 3) is reminiscent of the Western fairy tale's ritual beginning "Once upon a time". The reader immediately becomes aware of the Maori voice that speaks to us. Furthermore, this formula creates the impression of the story actually being told, not written, with a storyteller relating the tale from memory. Like an oral story, the prologue speaks of well-known events that the Maori people have heard many times before, but this time it is a new variation of the myth. So we are guided into the story to see the coming of Paikea on a whale from the point of view of the sea instead of reading a straightforward account of the myth. It is not only a story of the people, but also of the land and the sea. The narrator remains, but he tells the story by focussing on the sea's perspective: "The sea, too, teemed with fish, but they also seemed to be waiting. [...] Suddenly, looking up at the surface, the fish began to see the dark bellies of the canoes from the east. The sea flashed continuously with flying fish, leaping high to look beyond the horizon and to be the first to announce the coming [...]" (*WR* 4). Even the land is joyous at Paikea's coming and the arrival of the tribe that will follow him, beginning "the seeding" (*ibid.*).

The prologue is an energetic beginning, told swiftly to evoke the feeling of yearning, gladness, and expectation in the reader that land and sea feel themselves. Everything is alive and waiting; nature and even objects such as Paikea's spear (*WR* 6) have a life of their own and are focused on the seeding. The narrator uses repetition, and often begins sentences with "and" or "then" to express motion and the action's uninterrupted flow. In barely five pages, the story is told, setting the stage for the current-day tale of Paikea's descendants. The strength of the Maori and richness of their cultural heritage have all been set down on the page in this short prologue, its momentum sweeping the reader into the present day setting with a blessing: "*Hui e, haumi e, taiki e.* Let it be done" (*WR* 7).

Nonetheless, although the novel is dominated by the mythical atmosphere created by the memory of Paikea, it still leaves space for the mention of the work that must be done in order to guarantee the survival of this culture. With the myth as the underlying story, a number of current Maori issues are addressed and, unsurprisingly, it is Koro and his eldest son who are involved in politics to ensure their tribe's survival. They attend Maori Council meetings, open Maori schools so that their knowledge is passed on, and their customs and traditions remain alive. Despite the seeming difference between this – in Western eyes – realistic aspect of the story and the mythical resonance pervading the book, they are firmly connected. *The Whale Rider* is a story of survival that can only be achieved by political involvement, education, remembering and honouring the past. As Ihimaera will also emphasise in *The Uncle's Story*, customs may need to adapt to the new times and old traditions may have to be altered. This is what Koro refuses to do – in his obsession to find an heir, he ignores Kahu completely since only the first male descendants have been chiefs until now and a woman seemingly has no place among them.

This claim, however, is undermined from the beginning: Nanny Flowers, Koro's wife, is clearly the stronger and more outspoken person in the relationship. Her strength, derived from her line of the family, causes her to oppose her husband repeatedly. Her claim that "I'm his chief" (*WR* 16) and similar statements in humorously described sections make it clear that women are indeed leaders as much as men, weakening Koro's repeated allegation that Kahu is "of no use to me" (*WR* 114). After all, it is Nanny Flowers who names the child after their ancestor, giving her a man's name. Thus Kahu receives the strength of a man and it is evident that she will play an important role in the events to come. She will do so just like Nanny Flowers' ancestress Muriwai who said, "I shall make myself a man" to take charge when needed. The memory of the past becomes the catalyst for action as it often does in Maori fiction; here it allows characters to keep "stepping out of line" (*WR* 19) when traditions become a hindrance rather than help. Apparently, to deviate from tradition to a certain extent is the only way to be powerful.

Curiously, despite their stepping out of line, it is merely a deviation from one tradition while remaining in another. It may not be customary for women to be chiefs in Koro's tribe, but it is indeed possible for women to take charge as in Nanny Flower's *iwi*. The characters are faced with the differences between tribes that cause tension between the married couple, and have important consequences for their people's future. Therefore, *The Whale Rider* does not address difference between two seemingly opposed cultures as we see in *Mutuwhenua*; instead, it depicts the tension between two tribes and their respective customs.

"Stepping out of line": Deviating from Linear Narrative
As is customary in oral storytelling, *The Whale Rider* is told from multiple perspectives. The main body is told by Kahu's uncle Rawiri in the first person as someone who witnessed the events and relates them to the reader. He tells his story from memory, indicating that "[t]hat was eight years ago" (*WR* 32) or giving Kahu's age whenever he comes to a new episode. In doing so, not only is Kahu's importance for the story pointed out, but also the relevance of all past events for the future as they influence the present. Consequently, there is a sense of continuity throughout the tale that is in accordance with Maori understanding of time.

Regularly, Rawiri's tale is introduced by the observations of an omniscient unnamed narrator at the beginning of each chapter and towards the end of the novel. This voice is the communal voice relating the coming of the whales led by Paikea's ancient whale. There is one instant, the beginning of the third section of the novel entitled "Autumn", in which the voice directly addresses Paikea, bringing out the very stylised form of the sections narrated by the communal voice and stressing the characteristics of oral storytelling. Ultimately, Rawiri's and the communal voice's articulation of present events and the inclusion of the whale's memories of the past inevitably hark back to the process of passing stories on from one generation to another, giving a view of history that consists of multiple perspectives. Important aspects are repeated by different narrators – the epilogue to the novel tells part of Paikea's coming, the ancient whale remembers his master and their journey, and finally Rawiri tells the story (*WR* 30–2) by recounting his niece's descent from Paikea. Further impressions of the age-old tradition of storytelling are created by the very stylised nature of the narrative that relates Paikea's story, the coming of the whales whose arrival proves to be a final test for the tribe, and the anthropomorphised whales who communicate in more than just song. Each new chapter begins with the naming of the whales' location, giving first the English and then the Maori name. Additionally, the mythic quality is enhanced by the use of descriptive names such as "Pathway of the Sun" (*WR* 11), "The Navel of the Universe" (*WR* 27), "Place of the Gods" (*WR* 57), and "Well of the World" (*WR* 96). The story appears as if it has been told for many generations, resulting in a polished tale that has been enhanced, perfected, and constructed for effect.

In accordance with Maori belief, the whales have a consciousness that is reflected in these sections especially by the ancient whale's remembrance of "the golden human who became his master" (*WR* 11) and the path they travelled that must now be travelled again. To recreate the communication between humans and whales that is part of the belief that there was communion between humans and all of nature in ancient days, the whales are given speech as the story progresses. While the whales seem to communicate solely through song at first, they are depicted as speaking Maori and English. This way, their relatedness to the Maori people is emphasised again. It must be pointed out that this is not the same language that humans speak: the encounters between the two species manage to uphold the claim of mutual understanding, but the whales are not given actual human speech in these cases. Their speaking Maori towards the end of the novel indicates the oneness (*WR* 31) that was said to exist among all creatures in the past and which formed the link between the rational and the irrational: "Whenever asked, the whale would attend the call, as long as the mariner possessed the necessary authority and knew the way of talking to whales. But as the world aged and man grew away from his godliness, he began to lose the power of speech with whales, the power of *interlock*. So it was that the knowledge of whales speaking was given only to a few. One of these was our ancestor Paikea" (*WR* 40). Sections such as these firmly ground the story within Maori tradition. Like the indigenous name that follows the first line of the whale-related sections of each chapter, the whales speaking *te reo* is a means that sets the story apart from others and gives it a distinctly Maori nature. Using these storytelling techniques, the knowledge and beliefs of the mythic past and present are retained within the novel and introduced to a broad readership.

Once again, as in previous novels, the spiral appears in this story. It is echoed in the whale's tattoo that marks him as Paikea's whale, but a spiral pattern can also be detected in the narrative's move from omniscient narrator to Rawiri and back, which is very clearly structured and maintained till the end. Regular points of arrival and departure are marked by the repeated blessing "Haumi e, hui e, taiki e. Let it be done" that also marks the ending. What is more, the story consists of memories, moving the narrative from one set of recollections to another. Rawiri's memory of events is periodically replaced by the whale's, shaping the story by using alternating points of view. Still, theirs are not the only memories encountered in the novel.

"The oneness that the world once had": One Story from a Multiple of Memories

Beside Rawiri and the whale, Koro and Nanny Flowers are further characters who remember events they experienced themselves or learned about. While the whale and Rawiri both tell the tale of Paikea and Kahu from their respective perspectives, Koro imparts sacred knowledge in his lessons only to other men "because men were sacred" (*WR* 35). This knowledge includes Maori history, customs, and personal memories of the tests he had to undergo in order to become chief. His people jokingly name him "Super Maori" (*WR* 38) due to his involvement in the Maori rights struggle, but it is an apt name given to such a very tradition-minded character. Nobody

is more Maori than Koro; he is the embodiment of his culture's values
and beliefs. In contrast to him, Nanny Flowers functions as a reminder
of the other strand of Maori tradition that he does not share, in which
women are powerful when they have to be, going back to the story of her
ancestress. The fact that she and Koro manage to remain married – despite
her constant threats of divorce – while their views on the role of women
differs greatly is a sign of hope for the development of the Maori future.
Even though differences remain, this is a step towards the oneness that
existed before man was removed from godliness. Moreover, there would
be no future and the line would end if these two characters were not married – evidently, it is necessary to bring together differences to secure a
future and to make it possible in the first place. Koro and Nanny Flower's
heartfelt reunion at the end of the novel proves the chance for harmonic
unity despite difference.

Nanny Flowers' motto, "the rules are made to be broken" (*WR* 41),
applies to the novel to a certain extent,[3] but mainly to the way traditions
and beliefs should be treated when they turn into obstacles in a time that
requires their re-evaluation. Before change can take place, however, there
must be memory: given the significance of storytelling in Whangara, the
tribe's stories are present in the people's minds. To keep the knowledge
alive, Koro gives his lessons and begins to open schools to preserve the old
stories, values and customs they impart. As an elder, he possesses knowledge
that must be passed on before his death.

As a result, it is the memory of the past that allows an interpretation of
present events and the recognition of Kahu as the whale rider. Once again,
memory is used in the present to make sense of current developments, and
it reveals the truth about mysteries such as the stranding of the two hun-
dred whales, and especially the ancient one in Whangara. Koro recognises
the whale as a sign and the final test that will seal the fate of his tribe: "[...]
the earlier stranding of whales was merely a prelude to the awesome event

---

3   Despite the Maori subject matter, this novel is far more Western in its form than
    Tangi, for instance. Even the spiral pattern that structures the story is clearer and
    closer to Western fiction than we have seen in other works. Rules of writing have
    not been broken here despite having been expanded to include Maori topics. This,
    however, has already been done in other fiction before *The Whale Rider.*

that followed, an event that had all the cataclysmic power and grandeur of a Second Coming" (*WR* 108). Ultimately, the ancient whale must be saved to ensure survival, for "[i]f it lives, we live. If it dies, we die" (*WR* 117). If the first coming of Paikea and the whale was the first seeding that populated the land, then the return is the second seeding that will ensure the tribe's growth and prosperity.

To achieve this, however, all must work together and the oneness of days of old has to be recreated. It is now that Koro realises that the women are of use to him and that they are needed to help where the men have failed; "it is time for the women to act the men" (*WR* 121) and save the whale, and thus the tribe. The strength of Nanny Flowers' ancestress is needed, and yet Kahu's true gift remains unrecognised until it is almost too late.

Oddly, despite the tribe priding itself on its origin and the obvious signs, the fact that Kahu is given the same gift as Paikea is not realised for a long time. Rawiri observes her speaking to orcas when she is merely two years old (*WR* 45), and though he thinks it strange and remarkable, it is only in the retrospective telling of this story that he understands what she did. This is the case several times throughout the story, mainly whenever Kahu is heard imitating whale song or grieving for them. Especially the day she sneaks into the *marae* during the boys' lessons during which Koro tells the story of how the priest trained him is the most obvious sign:

> "[...] Finally, near the end of my training, he took me into his hut. He put out his foot and, pointing to the big toe, said, 'Bite.' It was part of the ritual to transfer his powers to me. So I did, and—"
> Suddenly Koro Apirana broke off. A look of disbelief spread over his face. Trembling, he peered under the table, and so did we. Kahu was there. [...] Koro Apirana's toes must have looked juicy to her, because there she was, biting on his big toe [...]. (*WR* 36)

The fact that a useless girl whom he had forbidden to attend the lessons would defile the sacredness of the act makes him blind for the gravity of this moment. Again, it is only in retrospect that Rawiri and others understand that the chief's power was transferred to Kahu at that point.

Apart from their function as interpretive tools, memories also function as a bond between individuals and their home, tribe, and culture. This becomes clear during Rawiri's stays abroad during which he meets other Maori in Australia and later feels drawn back to New Zealand while in Papua New Guinea. The cousin he meets in Australia has changed and lives a secret life because it does not conform to their former life among their own people. Their memories always remain close to their heart; they are not ashamed of who they have become, dressing inappropriately or living as transvestites, but keeping their new lifestyle secret allows them to keep the tribe's respect. In their quest for personal freedom and a better life, "they had opted for the base metal and not the gold" (*WR* 62), a life that is only second best to the one among their people.

Unlike these expatriates, Rawiri eventually returns after a few years of travel because he realises that he can only lead a satisfying and whole life in Whangara. Being removed from the tribe's traditional way of life, there is something missing and he yearns to return just like the land yearned for Paikea's coming. The theme of returns is woven throughout the novel, evident in the whale's return to the place he visited many generations before, and Kahu's return to live where her birth cord was buried in Whangara. All these returns, even Nanny Flowers' threats of divorce and regular reconciliation, imitate the course of memory and its winding from one fragment to another. Nonetheless, the journeys the characters undergo, be they figurative or literal, are necessary so as to come to an understanding of oneself. Porourangi's preparation for chieftainship, Koro's unsuccessful search for a male heir, the gradual discovery of Kahu's skills – they all give an account of who they are as Maori. Traditions, myths, and memories prove to be the bonds that connect the individual with the rest of the tribe, giving them a closeness that cannot even be broken by physical distance.

A further memory-related feature of *The Whale Rider* is the importance of tests that is first related by Koro in accounts of his training. Rawiri's travels are another test as is the stranding of the whales. Not only are they tests of knowledge, but of Maori strength. It becomes clear in the course of the novel that storytelling and the acquisition of cultural knowledge that go hand in hand are the means by which Maori will either live or die. To not understand the signs or have knowledge of myths and legends would be the end of the tribe because the connection to cultural roots has been broken. Memory therefore fulfils a vital function through which appropriate action is made possible in the first place. For instance, Koro only knows how to approach the final test because of the knowledge of his tribe's origin and the significance of the whales as harbingers of new life (and possibly death).

Converging Memories: The Way Towards New Interpretations
Koro exemplifies a biased selectivity of memories in the way he treats Kahu. While his memories of the tribe's origin is clear to him and he as chief knows all the stories and traditions, he is inflexible and intolerant when faced with female leadership. When his first-born refuses to be chief, he searches for a male successor instead of searching for the most appropriate leader, regardless of gender. He should consider stories such as those of his wife's ancestress, but since she originates from another tribe, he refuses to do so. In his tribe, he insists, men lead because "men were sacred" (*WR* 35). The grandparents' opposing views on the matter prove the flexibility of memory and the openness to change. Furthermore, they show how constructed memories used to make decisions actually are and how the purpose behind a decision is determined by memories that are chosen to justify it. Since Koro wants to uphold the tradition of a male chief, he ignores the influence of other stories that could become a hindrance. Therefore, he considers Nanny Flowers' ancestress to be insignificant. Reinforced by the successive line of male heirs, the memory of the first male leader prevails, making it impossible for a woman to become chief unless she can prove her legitimacy. As a result, it takes more than humanly possible for Kahu to prove herself. Once she is acknowledged as Paikea's descendant and future chieftainess, opposing memories as represented by her grandparents' beliefs are likely to converge. Her grandparents' final reunion hints at this merging of cultural memories. Perhaps the ancestress's tale will feature more prominently now as one of the stories of the tribe's origins.

The myths encountered in the novel explain the tribe's beginning and promote an image of people bound to the sea due to Paikea's first seeding of the land. This image is later expanded by Nanny Flowers' ancestress, offering a new perspective. The grandparents feature as specialists who have this knowledge and are needed to pass it on. The old idea of tribal origin and the people's strength deriving from it cannot remain unchanged, and is subject to new influences.

The novel further illustrates change that needs to take place if the tribe is to survive. Ihimaera hints at the problems that may ensue if we hold fast to the old ways too inflexibly. Of course he does not advocate a turning away from tradition – on the contrary, the novel is a plea for open-mindedness and tolerance and the ability to adjust to the needs of the day. Change is necessary for survival, and this is reflected in the different stories told by Kahu's grandparents that need to be accepted equally. The openness for change and new interpretations of the past in myth and memory is depicted even more clearly in Ihimaera's *The Uncle's Story*, but its subtle beginnings can already be found here.

By offering a variety of memories within the story, *The Whale Rider* contains elements of change. The tale itself is partly told in a mythic fashion, being flanked by the whales' journey towards land. The novel itself is neither a myth nor is it meant to be perceived as such; instead, it combines myth and fictional reality to reflect the Maori belief system and the rigidity of inappropriate customs. This fictional model of remembrance – the way in which myths have bearing on everyday life and how adaptability is necessary for survival – is transferable into reality. Again, their necessity is clearer in some of Ihimaera's later novels, but the urgent need for change already comes to the fore. In the greater context of Maori cultural identity, the novel offers a first possibility for an expanded new interpretation of identity. Whereas *Tangi* merely suggested a return to the roots, the characters in this novel have to take a more active role that goes beyond simply holding on to traditions as they were of old.

In contrast, Grace's *Potiki* portrays a tribe steeped in its traditions without the need for change in beliefs. The changes that are important for survival lie in politics and protest rather than an adjustment of traditions. Grace sets out from a different perspective than Ihimaera in that the harmony among the tribe remains unthreatened and consequently has no need for change. While Ihimaera's novel is set within one tribe without any intrusion from others, Grace's story includes *Pakeha* interference. This may explain the greater importance of strong tribal unity in the struggle against opposition than we find in *The Whale Rider*'s problems within the tribal community. The second phase of the Maori novel therefore offers a greater variety of approaches to questions of identity, memory and survival than the first, promising increasing diversity for the third phase.

3.2.4 Preliminary Conclusion

The second phase of the Maori novel is characterised by a new confidence acquired gradually in the course of the first. The early novels can be said to test the waters, and their significance lies in their presentation of Maori life, traditional beliefs and customs. There is an explicit need for a return to this indigenous culture that is the only safe haven in a nation dominated by *Pakeha*. About a decade later, while novels still encourage the return to Maori roots, a new focus enters the fiction. The retreat back into Maori culture was a move inward, away from the *Pakeha* and therefore away from society. The second phase then begins to counter this move. One must remember that this is an in-between state that represents neither the early steps into *Pakeha* awareness nor the bold step into another culture as depicted in the third phase. At this point during the second phase, the need for action is emphasised. Its necessity springs from the continuing social and economic disadvantages suffered by Maori, which led to increased protests in the 1980s.

Inevitably, each writer has a different approach by which to express social injustice and offer solutions. Grace combines Maori and Christian imagery to express the depth of the native culture and introduces the idea that, in order to beat the *Pakeha*, Maori must fight them with *Pakeha* weapons. This is an idea taken up in Ihimaera's *The Matriarch* and applies to most of his later novels too. What connects the novels of this phase is the characters' critical stance, which expresses dissatisfaction with *Pakeha* notions of progress or points to issues within the Maori community itself that could lead to Maori extinction.

Marking a significant change from the first-phase novels, the texts here depict a Maori identity that is mostly secure. *Potiki*, *The Matriarch*, and *The*

Whale Rider abound with characters secure in their individual and cultural identity, which allows them to focus on the preservation of Maori culture. This time, however, protecting it goes beyond the mere preservation within the cultural community. *Potiki* and *The Matriarch* in particular describe how important it is to remember stories and myths circulating within the tribe, but they and all other novels also stress the need to apply the knowledge gained from the stories to guard against the *Pakeha* and confront them. As such, the importance of storytelling is repeated in all novels of this phase, exemplifying the need for them as guides in the present.

Between themselves, the novels incorporate mainly Christian and Maori myths that parallel the storylines of the novels such as *Potiki*, which includes protagonists resonating with Christian and Maori myths. *The Whale Rider* draws explicit links between Paikea, the mythic ancestor, and Paikea, the female protagonist whose lives are intertwined in the village's history. Finally, as a historical novel, *The Matriarch* retells Maori history from the early mythic beginnings to the present and compares the lives of Te Kooti, Wi Pere, the Matriarch and Tamatea, which are all extensions of each other. Given this emphasis on myths, it is clear that they remain a significant factor of Maori identity, establishing a lasting strong connection with the protagonists' cultural heritage. Their memories of ancestors and past events continue to guide them in their actions today despite the awareness of inevitable changes.

Such a change is, for instance, the need to be acquainted with those methods that give the *Pakeha* such power. Grace and Ihimaera both mention the importance of studying law to "turn your knowledge to [the *Pakeha*'s] destruction" (*Mat* 427) and understand how the law has been manipulated to his advantage. At the same time, this new approach presents a more determined and empowering form of resistance that requires determination, strength, and the will for confrontation. However, even in this political phase of Maori writing, some novels still prefer to explore Maori issues from within instead of explicitly confronting the *Pakeha*. *The Whale Rider* differs from other texts of the same phase in its focus on the Maori community and its understanding of itself. *Pakeha* influence exists only outside the village and is mentioned only briefly in the narrative of Rawiri's travels. The community is self-contained in the same way as described in the first phase. The first texts, nonetheless, lack the critical view with which Ihimaera now depicts Maori village life. As a result, *The Whale Rider* offers a variety of characters and the problems amid the community, which differentiates it from the first phase in which it was presented as harmonious and intact. Instead, Ihimaera now offers a complex depiction of indigenous life with its own problems independent of any *Pakeha* influence.

Besides the preference to explore Maori life and its problems in the contained settings of the community or within close relations, the novels can also extend towards an explicit resistance of the *Pakeha*. This outward movement to confront the *Pakeha* contrasts with the first phase's novels that mainly encouraged a return to the Maori community. During the first phase, the *Pakeha* therefore remained unchallenged for the most part. Consequently, *Potiki* and *The Matriarch* both allow their characters to take a stand against authority in their attempts to preserve Maori land, the most important concern at this stage in Maori history. A sense of place is crucial in these novels – in fact, it always has been, but the increased political motivation in writing now brings it to the fore. Since the land is connected with Maori history, myth and even language, indigenous writers often address the Land Wars, land theft and customs connected with certain places that emphasise man's relationship with it. It is described as "an extension of one's own being" (Ashcroft *et al.* 2002: 179). What is more, the focus on land also functions as a point of contrast, as Ashcroft *et al.* observe:

> A sense of displacement, of the lack of fit between language and place, may be experienced by those who possess English as a mother tongue or by those who speak it as a second language. In both cases, there appears to be a lack of fit between the place described in English and the place actually experienced by the colonized subject. This comes about firstly because the words developed to describe place originated in an alien European environment, and secondly because many of the words used by the colonizers described "empty space" or "empty time", and so had thrown off any connection to a particular locale. Place can thus be a constant trope of difference in post-colonial writing, a continual reminder of colonial ambivalence, of the separation yet continual mixing of the colonizer and colonized. (*ibid.*)

Given this interpretation of place in ethnic fiction, Maori writers' description of land goes beyond the merely personal and extends into cultural and political dimensions. Such a development is further exemplified in the rewriting of myths which "underpin the commonly held belief that Maori autonomy and spiritual survival is possible only through establishing the 'right' relationship with the land, most significantly by regaining physical and spiritual possession of what has been lost through neglect or conquest [...]" (Wilson 1998: 274).

As we have seen, Grace and Ihimaera both depict attempts to prevent land confiscation and ways in which this has been done in the past. Ihimaera in particular uses the Land Wars as a backdrop for events in *The Matriarch*. While *Potiki*'s characters try to protect the land through sabotage, protest and legal action, *The Matriarch* offers a history of violence that is gradually substituted with protest and legal approaches. Evidently, both writers consider the tools of the *Pakeha* used in an indigenous context best suited for resistance.

Despite the new focus on active resistance, myth and memory remain to form an indispensable foundation of all aspects of Maori life. They are the past, present and future of each tribe and not only supply history, but also guidance for problems today. This becomes particularly evident in the way historic people and events shape characters and their actions in the present: the tribe's future in *The Whale Rider* depends on Paikea's recognition as the descendant of their mythic ancestor, and Wi Pere's work in parliament becomes the precedent for any future resistance of *Pakeha* dominance in *The Matriarch*. Apart from offering thematic parallels the authors use techniques that continue to hark back to traditional oral storytelling by employing the well-known spiral structure introduced in the first phase of the Maori novel. In addition, the narrative consists of repeated returns to points in the story that need further elaboration at a different moment after beginning and outcome of the described event have already been told (cf. Thornton 1985). Notably, the novels themselves have a mythic resonance that derives from the deviation from linear narrative, implicit and explicit references to stories, the inclusion of the supernatural in fictional reality, repetition, metaphor, quotation, and the use of *te reo* ranging from individual words to long passages. Still, it must be pointed out that none of the novels claim to be myths in their own right. They use myth and memory and may even imitate them as far as themes and characters are concerned, but they remain distinct narratives of their own, though rich with the influence of old stories.

Therefore, myth and memory remain as important in the second phase as they were in the first. Nevertheless, while the first-phase novels mainly served to teach Maori and *Pakeha* alike about *maoritanga*, the emphasis of the second-phase novels lies on empowering Maori to take action. Secure in their heritage and cultural identity at this point due to their familiarity with cultural intricacies, preservation through political involvement now poses the new challenge. Consequently, most novels of this phase contain a juxtaposition of traditional Maori approaches and a purposeful involvement with *Pakeha* procedures like the study of law for Maori purposes. The texts express the realisation that, in order to survive, it is impossible to avoid implementing *Pakeha* tools and learning to use them in *Pakeha* ways. Shunning this foreign influence will only lead to the extinction of Maori culture; therefore, preserving the indigenous culture requires a degree of openness towards familiarity with *Pakeha* methods.

As a result, apart from being an in-between phase from a chronological perspective, the second phase is also an in-between one with regard to topics. Situated between a group of novels intent on introducing the Maori perspective and another encouraging the acceptance of difference and the incorporation of more than one culture within an individual, the novels of the second phase contain aspects of both. The focus on the Maori community as in *Potiki* and *The Whale Rider* reflects the first phase's emphasis on the same. In contrast, The *Matriarch* has a wider ranging cast of characters who suggest an openness towards the foreign that will come to the fore at a later stage. At the same time, the diversity contained within the second phase illustrates not only its in-betweenness, but also the variety of the Maori experience. This two-sidedness – an inward-looking life within the Maori community and an outward-looking life ready to utilise *Pakeha* methods – best characterises the second-phase novel and the development of the Maori novel in general.

3.3 *Te Tahu*: The Roof – Moving Towards Home

After two decades of Maori novels, the issues dealt with earlier still remain in the third phase. The struggle of people within two cultures, though eased since the earlier phases, has not been resolved to satisfaction. Slow progress and an ignorance of indigenous culture still prevent an appropriate handling of Maori affairs, but there is an awareness of problems and required changes. Moreover, Maori now begin to see themselves in a global context, which leads to an expanding range of themes going beyond the confines of the Maori community.

What sets this third phase apart from the previous ones is that it shows the beginning expansion of topic and setting. No longer restricted to the rural–urban dichotomy within New Zealand, some novels step beyond borders and are set abroad to depict expatriate or in-transit characters moving between home and foreign places. Once again, it is Ihimaera's work that takes the first step into this new direction. There is still the search for a cultural identity, particularly when Maori characters find themselves abroad like Tom does in *The Rope of Man*, and even now it is made clear that one's true home will always be Aotearoa New Zealand. Deeply rooted in this country, it is time, however, to cast an eye beyond national boundaries to see oneself in a global context.

Quite naturally, the wider view brings new challenges: characters return changed from abroad, and even those who remained home to see gradual changes in society view events from a new perspective that casts a different light on Maori customs. New issues are introduced, as in Ihimaera's novel *The Uncle's Story* that is the first to deal with homosexuality within the Maori community, bringing an intolerance to the fore that is not only found within *Pakeha* society this time. Except for Duff's *Once Were Warriors*, criticism is rarely directed towards the Maori people themselves. Even his novel attributes part of the blame to the *Pakeha*, but Ihimaera's *The Uncle's Story* mainly refrains from this. His focus remains on the Maori people and their beliefs that are the actual cause for this intolerance.

Finally, the novel of the third phase may still be viewed as a combination of Western genre and indigenous storytelling due to the inclusion of

Maori myths, the structural parallels to oral storytelling, native understanding of time, and the similarities to indigenous art as suggested by Panny (2006). It is inappropriate to consider the novel an exclusively Western genre: it has been used and expanded in form, language and theme by indigenous writers, so they can no longer be excluded as developers of the genre. The variety of options in storytelling unfolded by these indigenous novelists is complemented by the plurality of options for Maori identity construction.

What is most striking about the third phase novels is their striving towards a comprehensive and yet far more complex and expanding characterisation of Maori in the early twenty-first century that takes into account their social, national and even global significance. Apart from merely writing the Maori story from the inside, indigenous writers have gradually gone further and freed their characters from geographical, spiritual and economic confines. The third phase offers some examples of the new confident and successful Maori, whereby success may not coincide with the *Pakeha* understanding of it and takes on a clearly indigenous interpretation instead.

3.3.1 Patricia Grace's Cousins (1992)

More so than *Mutuwhenua*, *Cousins* is a story about exile and return. While the earlier novel follows one character's move from *whanau* to city with a partial return to the family, *Cousins* depicts the lives of cousins Mata, Missy and Makareta, raised under different circumstances. Mata is far removed from her culture and her family, brought up in an orphanage. Lacking love and being inexperienced in life, she never quite manages to cope with everyday life and needs to be guided. In contrast to her, Missy enjoys the love of her family despite their poverty, and Makareta has the privilege of a good education and a pleasant life because she was chosen for an arranged marriage long ago.

In effect, their lives are initiations into three different aspects of Maori culture seen from different angles. Introduced as the lost character from the beginning of the novel, Mata's story is an introduction to her heritage with a gradual return to family. Hers is a complete initiation into a culture that is unknown to her due to her upbringing in a *Pakeha* environment. Unlike her, Makareta is fully integrated into her *whanau* and has been educated both in the Maori and *Pakeha* way. Thus, she has knowledge that she can impart in order to improve the situation of her people, and she does so by becoming politically active as she grows up. Her early privileged years guide Makareta towards the role of teacher and fighter for her people. Missy, too, takes on a special role that moves her beyond the life she lived before. Until the day of Makareta's wedding, the reader has the impression that Missy has always come second and that her role is not as important as Makareta's. Yet, when Makareta refuses to be married and Missy offers to take her place, it becomes clear that she has always had strength and was prepared for this moment all along. Ultimately, the cousins represent three kinds of Maori: the lost/seeker, the leader/activist, and the procreator/mother.

In this novel, Grace's focus on woman as a central figure in Maori culture is clearer than in her previous work. Men play a minor role while the cousins' strength and position within the community is emphasised. Represented as archetypal characters, they personify the range of roles women play while pointing out the importance of each. Even though seeker, activist and mother differ greatly from one another, together they form the Maori woman in all her diversity.

Seeker, Activist, Mother – Reflections on Reality, Politics, and Myth

While each cousin is ascribed a particular role, she is also moved into a corresponding realm that she inhabits. Mata inhabits the realm of harsh reality in which she is cut off from her roots and unable to live fully. Consequently, she neither feels at home among *Pakeha* nor Maori, sensing repeatedly that "[o]ther people knew things that she didn't, there was a secret to it" (*C* 89), that "[t]here was a secret to it that she knew nothing of" (*C* 90). This feeling characterises her only holiday with her family as a child when she lives among Maori people for the first time. Even here, like in the orphanage, she feels like a stranger because the place she should belong in is "a place where there were people like her, but she wasn't like them" (*C* 95), and they speak in a strange language that changes them altogether: "Sonny's aunty and uncle sat down at their table and began

talking to Ada and Daisy in low voices in the language she couldn't understand. And she noticed that as Ada spoke she began to move her head and
eyes and hands in a way that she hadn't seen her do before. Her stern face
changed as though it had melted and all the hard lines had been modelled
away" (*C* 88). This passage not only indicates that there is another life
beyond the one Mata knows, but also that hers might change if she was
offered the chance to learn the Maori ways. Unlike her two cousins, she is
unfamiliar with native traditions and is lost between the two worlds she
is forced to live in but can only participate in marginally. For most of the
novel, she has limited access to either and is confused since she is unable
to find the right approach.

    As a result, Mata seeks inclusion as much as she is able to. She wants
to be loved the same as her cousins. At one point, after she finds a marble
buried in the soil, she manages to feel a little more included: "They'd all
liked her when she gave Manny the marble. Keita had bought her a coat
and given her a photo, and Aunty Gloria? Well, Aunty Gloria had cuddled
her and talked to her and loved her, and told her she was their girl with her
own name, belonging to them" (*C* 56). In contrast to the ones she knows
from the orphanage, she begins to see that she is like these people she visits
here. She has a name, Mata Pairama, not May Palmer or even May Parker as
she is called in the orphanage because no one cares for her Maori name.

    Further ties to the family are strewn throughout Mata's chapters and
hint that she may yet be integrated. The marble she finds represents this
strange Maori world. The fact that it has to be unearthed first reflects her
search for the hidden part of her heritage. Furthermore, it signifies Mata's
connection to the land, emphasising this is where she belongs. Makareta
tells her the marble is "[f]rom the old house" (*C* 50), something that has
been there for a long time, not forgotten but remembered. Mata feels "as
if she had stolen something from them" (*ibid.*) because it is part of who
they are. It is at this moment that she begins to seek an understanding of
who she is by wanting to be part of this new world she has visited. The
marble is a symbol of that world, "a new little world right there inside
the marble" (*C* 48), whose many-coloured ribbons mirror the spiral that
weaves itself through life.

Once again, as in novels such as *Tangi*, the exposure to Maori culture marks a turning point in the character's life. It is never a shock as such, but it is a strange encounter that makes an impression strong enough to create a yearning for it. Mata feels she wants to be loved like the other Maori children in the family, but her upbringing in the orphanage makes it too difficult for her to open up during her holiday. Thus, she remains in the care of other less well-meaning people even as a grown-up. Similar to Ihimaera's first novel, the real change takes place at a *tangi*. Since it is a very emotional occasion that is characterised by strict rituals, Mata begins to feel as if she were part of something. At last, when she and other members of the family are welcomed to the *marae*, she realised, "[s]omething was happening to me. Something" (*C* 254). After so many years of loneliness, Mata finds that she is wanted and that she belongs somewhere with people who do not try to take control over her life. Through traditions and ceremonies that evoke links to the cultural past as at the *tangi*, new ways into the future are opened for the lost individual. This serves as an example of the inter-relatedness not only of people, but of past, present and future as understood in the Maori belief system.

Furthermore, Mata's being part of the family is made evident not only in the fact that her relatives have always wanted to bring her home. Her connection to the family is emphasised and literally made visible in the last section of the novel in which she appears to share Makareta's gift. At Makareta's *tangi*, she sees the spirits of her ancestors like her deceased cousin used to. The "shadow people" (*C* 255) are present even beyond death as Maori believe, and Mata knows they are there now too. Finally, she is not merely outwardly a part of the family anymore; instead, she now has a spiritual connection to her family that she lacked before. This bond will always remain now that it has been established, and Mata is certain of it herself even after she can no longer see the spirits: "They seemed to be there even though I couldn't see them anymore, but I knew I would see them again" (*C* 256). Ending with this line, Grace emphasises the significance of the moment and marks the end of Mata's lonely ordeal. Having come out of the void, she is "here", not "nowhere" (cf. *C* 14), and the seeker has come to the end of her long journey.

In contrast, Makareta's own journey is one of emancipation and a move from the bosom of her family out into the world. Since her marriage was arranged "for the people" (*C* 229) many years earlier, she has special status in her family and enjoys the comforts and privileges few have. Her education is the best: she has extensive knowledge of her own culture and is sent to boarding school once she is old enough. Living both in rural and urban places, she learns to lead a double life because of the different, sometimes incompatible cultures: "So it was a double life, as my life always has been in the city, but it became less difficult as I understood it more. It's an absorbing and interesting life as long as you are certain, and as long as you keep hold of who you know you are" (*C* 204). Through Makareta's own voice, Grace makes a point that can be found in all Maori novels discussed here, not least in Grace's own *Mutuwhenua* – you have to know who you are and remember your heritage in order to live in places where other cultures dominate.

The resulting dichotomy of village and city life that Makareta experiences leads her into her role as Maori activist. Thus representing a stereotype of the involved and resisting Maori today, Grace explores her character in depth to give reasons for her choice. The activist is part of the three significant Maori types represented in the novel who seem necessary for a general understanding of the Maori situation today. The reader follows her development in Makareta's letters to her mother. Given her upbringing, she has a different status than most Maori. She is also above most of her boarding school classmates, she writes: "It was rumoured that I was a princess. 'It's because you look stately,' Polly said. 'And because you're Maori and you're top of the class. It's hard for them to understand that, a Maori being top of the class, that's why they have to make you a princess.'" (*C* 204) Here, the common preconception that Maori are less educated than others clashes with Makareta's achievements and the way she carries herself. It is only once she interacts with other children at school that she becomes aware of the perceived difference between herself and others that she did not know before.

Successively, her letters become more like treatises on the situation of her people in a country that is their own, but which is governed by others whom they have to ask for their natural rights: "[I]t is an injustice, an absurdity, for a language and culture to be pleading its worth in the place that is its home" (*C* 210–15). For Maori readers, Makareta's concerns will be close to their own hearts while others will see the validity of her argument: belief systems can be maintained within oneself, as she proves in the way she lives her life in the city, but people's rights – the visible "official" perception of a culture – can only be ascertained with the correct policies. "[T]he disinherited who were the truly poor" (*C* 210), those who are deprived of their rights in their own country, need her. Thus Makareta is the one who attempts to preserve her culture from outside while both Mata and Missy move towards it and remain within it, respectively. Therefore, Makareta's task spans a wider frame by including the conditions outside the tribe's immediate family life. Her view is directed inward as well as outward – towards the centre in which she grew up for many years and to which she will return, and towards the world beyond the family, which is where she wants to make sure "[...] that we as a people survive and have authority over our lives" (*C* 207).

Clearly, there is a tension resulting from the expectation that she will remain in the *whanau* in order to marry and have children, and her choice to use her energy and knowledge to not just preserve her *whanau* but the survival of all Maori. Only the understanding of Maori culture that she has gained in her education at home enables her to go out and fight for it when many others are unable to do so themselves. Like the author, it is Makareta's aim to create an awareness of the persisting injustice that hinders Maori to live as their tradition dictates. "People need to know," she says, "that there has been a massive robbery. There's been treachery, and they, the victims, are receiving the punishment day by day. Losers pay. If they have not fought bravely, or at all, it is because theft has been complete and includes theft of will to fight, theft of will to survive" (*C* 215).

This attribution of blame to the unnamed *Pakeha* clarifies her stance and expresses her devotion to her cause, yet she also admits "no one was blameless" (*C* 208), not even Maori. In fact, the problem lies deeper "where there was no memory, where the void had been defiled by an inrushing of anger and weeping" (*ibid.*). Nonetheless, she has the tools to be a successful

activist due to her education within Maori and *Pakeha* environments. These
tools include the myths and legends that transport Maori customs and
values into her life and the life of her *whanau*: "I had been given knowledge," Makareta writes, "understandings in my childhood that I knew I
must share, yet all the time there were obstacles – because culture is deep.
It is deep. Even the remnants or the memories of it are deep. It is not something that can be adequately explained to those of another culture, but
neither should it need to be explained, I think. It only needs, at the least,
to be allowed, to be let be, to be trusted. But there was, is, fear out there,
for that is difficult to allay and difficult to comprehend" (*C* 209).

Here she points out that the memories, too, are one of the things
that define Maori cultural identity. They contain a depth that shapes her
understanding of her heritage, but it is exactly this depth that is difficult
to convey. Pleading for the right "to be let be, to be trusted", Makareta
simultaneously expresses the impossibility of making people outside the
native community grasp the full meaning of *maoritanga*. Though she can
cope very well with life outside her own community, there is a point where
Maori and *Pakeha* culture are no longer entirely compatible. The reasons
lie in the memories – those aspects of her culture that are beyond explanation and are simply known because they have been transported through
stories and made manifest in customs and values over centuries. Therefore,
from Makareta's point of view, the coexistence of two or more cultural
groups is only possible to a certain extent. Furthermore, apart from the
inability to convey certain aspects of Maori culture, she emphasises that
not everything *should* be understood. This harks back to the concept of
tapu that assigns sacred knowledge that must not be passed to anyone
outside this culture.

Grace, moreover, makes use of the knowledge that runs between the
lines of this story as it does between the obvious aspects of Maori culture
that are visible to all. In her entire oeuvre, she depicts the situation of her
Maori characters truthfully and in detail, and yet there are sections that are
left unexplained or preserve a mythic quality within the text that non-Maori
readers may find difficult to understand. Like Makareta, Grace intimates
that not everything can or should be understood. *Potiki*'s ending, to take
an example, is the most obvious instance that denies a full appreciation of

the tale unless the reader has knowledge of *te reo*. One of the purposes even of fiction is the expression of truth in Maori works. Be it the depiction of their true situation, the true difficulties, the true expressions of cultural identity, the true potential of Maori people and their beliefs – between the lines of fiction, there is a glimpse of truth. Both Makareta and the author take it upon themselves to preserve this truth in their own ways, one as an activist, the other primarily as a writer, because "[t]hey need to know that our truth does not appear on pages of books unless it is there between the lines. Our truths need to be revealed" (*C* 215). In this respect, a meta-fictional dimension enters the novel particularly in Makareta's chapters. Her striving for Maori rights and recognition mirror similar attempts by Maori authors in their fiction and reality. Among others, Ihimaera's *The Uncle's Story* contains autobiographical sections of political interest and resistance. Apparently, the need to record the truth in one's own books to allow an equal representation of Maori experience among the vast body of *Pakeha* literature is an aim the writers pursue, as evidenced by their novels. As Makareta states, their truths have to be revealed, and the authors take it upon themselves to portray the Maori situation as it is. Grace has chosen a realistic, but exemplary portrayal in *Cousins* so that one might say that as an activist and teacher Makareta becomes an archetype of Maori resistance and represents the political aspect of Maori life, thereby complementing Mata and Missy in their own archetypal representations.

Missy's role, finally, emerges more clearly once Makareta refuses to marry and she takes her cousin's place. Not only does Missy thereby uphold the honour of her family, she also preserves it and the culture by taking on the role of procreator. It is the family's concern that "the whakapapa [genealogy] is not upset" (*C* 102). Her purpose is hinted at throughout the novel, both with references to her physical ability to be a mother and to myth. The latter establishes a strong link between past and present, alluding to the preservation of Maori life since the ancient days. Since the mother is arguably the most important figure for the creation of life, Missy's early understated part in the novel is possibly the weightiest as it allows for the continuation of a culture and forms the basis of and reason for political activism. Ultimately, the mother is the central point from which all emerges and to which all is bound. She has connections to the future as the mother of the next generation, and she springs from the line of her ancestors at the same time, thereby personifying a central link within genealogy.

As mother, Missy is undoubtedly the origin of the future, but her unborn twin brother who narrates her story also links her to the past and the spirit world. As mentioned earlier, Grace again incorporates the point of view of an unborn child in *Baby No-Eyes*, which reflects the Maori belief of the lingering presence of the deceased and is an example of the simultaneous existence of the real and the spiritual world. "As Margaret Orbell recognises," says Thornley in her article "Breaking With English", "'the history of the world is the history of ancestors [*tupuna*]' and this history constitutes religious understandings for the Maori. Therefore, according to Maori beliefs, 'human society and the physical world came into existence at the same time. Each is inseparable from the other.'" (Thornley 2004: 64). In keeping with this notion, Missy's twin exists even beyond death and is part of her being.

Furthermore, Missy's relation to other mothers of her line is emphasised by the verses that speak of mothers in Maori mythology beginning each of her chapters. On the one hand, Missy is thereby established as their offspring in genealogy, and on the other, her designation as mother is clarified. Among others, Missy is likened to the goddess Hinenuitepo who brought mortality to man (*C* 155), and once again Rona makes an appearance as the goddess of fertility who controls the tides and the blood (*C* 169). Even though woman is *noa*, profane, she is most powerful at the time of menstruation when her role as procreator is most obvious. In "Myth, Omen, Ghost and Dream", Keri Hulme mentions that "the most *noa* time of all – menstruation – is both dangerous [...] and powerful. You are then at one with, and at the hub of, the turning earth. You are the hinge of the worlds of life and death, the worlds of light and dark [...]" (Hulme 1984: 36). Therefore, Missy's placement within the centre of the novel reflects her importance as mother. She is also descended from Hineahuone, the mother of man (*C* 172) and of her daughter Hinenuitepo. Of course, no genealogy is complete unless it goes back to the First Parents (*C* 193). As a result, the chapter beginnings represent Missy's complete genealogy back to the days of Creation.

Spiralling Towards Light: Structure, Tradition, and Spirituality

As seen in Missy's case in particular, a symbolic and mythical frame contains the stories of the three characters from childhood to adulthood, told by six different voices, which remind Judith Dell Panny (2006) of *whiri*, the Maori art of plaiting. Roughly following this basic spiralling pattern, the three lives move together, overlap, and move apart again as they are narrated by an unnamed third-person narrator, Polly (Makareta's mother), Makareta, Missy, Mata, and finally Missy's unborn twin brother. The multiple perspectives are once again reminiscent of oral storytelling in the way they converge, alternate and move apart repeatedly. What Grace has produced, among other things, is a novel that tells a greater story by bringing together different smaller stories by a number of characters. As a result, the greater story cannot be told fully if its components are incomplete or homogenous. The explicit references to myths before Missy's chapters add an element to the tale that hints at the greater context within which *Cousins* should be seen as a small part of the Maori story.

Furthermore, each of the characters is assigned one section of the novel and a part in its overall structure. Opening with lost and wandering Mata, the book presents her in a mental void with nowhere to go. She represents the figure lost in *Te Kore*, the mythical void that is the place of nothing and non-nothing, a void as well as the origin of life. Considering the creative potential of *Te Kore*, Grace already suggests Mata's rescue and return to her family that we see at the end, as does the marble she finds and gives away because "[g]ifts are meant to be given, and one day returned. It must be her turn, again, to hold the coloured marble" (*C* 218).

Within the world the three inhabit, however, the girls contrast each other in a fashion that reminds Panny of "the Māori art of kōwhaiwhai [fern pattern often depicting a spiral], which features on the rafters of many meetinghouses, using the traditional colours red, white and black" (Panny 2006). Though she does not specify which of the colours might be attributed to which character, the red is echoed in the hint of ginger in Missy's hair. Generally, their hair is a significant symbol within the story since it exemplifies each character's status. Therefore Missy's reddish hair sets her apart as a future mother, echoing the red soil from which the first woman, Hineahuone, was made. Moreover, the hair on her head is not nearly as important as her pubic hair: "Hair there like mama's, fluffy, curly. You squeezed the cloth against your stomach and watched the water run, slicking the little curls then running down your legs. Legs blotched from old sores, ugly. But you had a pretty place between your legs, pretty to touch" (*C* 182). Significantly, Missy's most beautiful parts of the body happen to be the ones that set her apart as a fertile woman created from the soil of Mother Earth.

In contrast to Missy, Mata has been made to feel that her black hair is bad because it is not as straight and easy to handle as that of the other orphans. When her hair is cut off and burned, it is an ignorant violation of her as a Maori since the head is *tapu* and must not be touched. Mata's self-image suffers from this characterisation as the one with bad, springy hair that must be burned. Matron's insensitivity and ignorance of Maori culture lead Mata to *Te Kore*, preventing her from becoming a self-sufficient and confident adult. The lack of respect she is shown results in a lack of self-worth that contrasts starkly with Makareta's perception of herself.

Due to her special status, Makareta is free from the other children's daily tasks at home. "She has a river of hair that falls, touching the backs of her knees. Every strand of it has been touched and cared for" (*C* 131). Her hair is a symbol of her *mana*, her honour and prestige and is therefore attended to by her mother for half an hour a day. This becomes a problem once the girl goes to boarding school and has to do her hair herself, but it is a moment that forces her to take charge. Her hair grants her this realisation, encouraging her to take charge of her own life and eventually leading to her refusal to marry. Panny mentions that "[i]n mythology, hair can hold magical power, forming a link between the human and the spiritual realm" (Panny 2006), which suggests that Makareta herself has powers that others around her do not have. This explains her strength and will as an adult to take life into her own hands and fight prominently for Maori rights. Even as an adult, she cares for her hair and treats it well, and she has "plaits that wound round my head three times" (*C* 203), expressing her *mana*. Her resulting confidence and positive self-image set her apart from her two cousins, especially from bereft and awkward Mata who otherwise physically resembles her (cf. *C* 131).

Apart from the spiralling progression from childhood to adulthood and death within the novel as well as Mata's gradual removal from darkness to light, the book also follows possibilities to their final realisation. Grace arranges the characters' chapters to demonstrate a natural process from darkness to life and to death by opening the novel with lost Mata's section, moving on to descriptions of Missy's representation as procreator, and finally bringing the characters together at Makareta's funeral. While this forms the general larger structure of the text, the cousins' stories and perspectives echo it on a smaller scale in their individual journeys.

In *Mutuwhenua* and *Potiki*, Grace has previously demonstrated that it is possible to combine the spiritual aspects of Maori culture with the rational without compromising the Western reader's attention. We see this in Mata's chapters that begin with allusions to mythical ancestresses but otherwise continue with realistic depictions of her life. Yet there are further instances in which Grace subtly offers both supernatural and rational explanations for events such as Missy's destiny to take Makareta's place in the arranged marriage: at the precise moment she wants "to be the one" (*C* 195), Missy appears to want to do this to uphold her family's honour, but there are also "the flickering eyes of the ancestress" (*ibid.*) that watch. Thus, the reader is offered two explanations for Missy's choice, a rational and a supernatural reason (cf. Panny 2006). If this is accepted, the reader easily embraces the existence of spirits which Makareta – and later her son Michael and also Mata – can see. Due to this particular fusion of the rational and the supernatural, Grace's readers are able to suspend their disbelief like Mata who feels that "[n]othing about that night or morning seemed strange to me at the time" (*C* 248). In fact, Mata is the character who is closest to the uninformed reader owing to her early removal from her own culture. Like Tama in *Tangi*, she (re)learns aspects of her culture in the process, mirroring the reader's own initiation.

In *Cousins*, readers will see that reciprocity and the needs of the family are set above individual needs in all aspects of Maori culture. Hence Missy chooses to save her family's honour and Makareta devotes herself to resistance and the securing of Maori rights. These are goals beyond their personal needs and extend to the family, the tribe, the entire culture, allowing their survival. Grace has thus written a novel which incorporates Maori values in its scope while giving a realistic and believable account of three Maori girls. In an interview, she explains that the crucial elements that define Maori culture are not merely the myths and legends, the language or art, but the values that pervade Grace's fiction and are the basis of all novels featured here (cf. Panny 1997: 4).

The reality of language also contains and conveys aspects of identity and inherent cultural values as has been discussed in connection with previous novels. This is also the case in *Cousins*. What is more, your own language gives you strength and confidence, which is part of the reason why Makareta who knows both Maori and English is more confident than Mata, who is unfamiliar with Maori. The mother tongue is "that security, that sound base [that] allowed me to reach out and know that I could do anything else in the world that I wanted to" (*C* 211). Since Makareta can speak, she has power that Mata lacks in her silence. Moreover, Mata is continually oppressed by the English language and mostly left in the dark by *te reo*. In the orphanage, only English is spoken and everything Maori about her is attributed with negative words: she has bad hair, "bad curls" that need to be burned, she has dirty skin unlike the other orphans who are fair-skinned. Since Maori is forbidden at school and not used in the orphanage, the children associate it with being a bad language. At home, however, this is quite different. Both Maori and English are spoken freely, but English takes on the structure of Maori, becoming infused with the tongue that was meant to be oppressed. "English variants," Panny (2006) explains, "are spoken by Missy's siblings and father, by Mata's elderly aunts and by Missy's friend Tuahine. Bobby and his children typify those brought up hearing distinctive forms of English in Māori households. Māori were never taught 'English as a second language'; they have developed their own idiom." English is just as much a mother tongue as Maori in the text, but the people have made the coloniser's language their own by adapting it to suit their original native tongue, resulting in a hybrid form that is claimed as one's own and wrests power from English as an exclusively Western language. Instead, it has been absorbed into an indigenous context, so that power must be shared.

Still, since the family's English differs from the English used by the orphanage, Mata's relatives are unable to bring her home. In this instance,

English once again takes on the role of the oppressor, obstructing native customs. The family is not consulted as Mata grows up and has to leave the orphanage. Instead, she is appointed a stranger as guardian without her relatives' knowledge instead of being sent home. Her grandmother writes to the orphanage, which yields no satisfactory outcome and leaves Mata in the care of her legal guardian instead. Here, English is used as a weapon and forms a wall between the two cultures that cannot be breached despite the family's efforts. The legal situation further complicates matters, disregarding Maori values that would require Mata to be close to her mother's family instead of the harsh world she inhabits until she is of age.

"Culture is deep": Cultural Memory as Foundation and Guide

The clash of two cultures in *Cousins* is a reality. The events of the novel are stages of "transculturation, a term that describes the ways marginalised groups reinvent and use products and ideologies transmitted by a dominant culture and, in turn, transform the dominant culture" (Thornley 2004: 61). Following the lives of the three cousins over a period of about three decades, the novel depicts the difficult beginnings of the transculturation process. In accordance with the problematic process described in the fiction, Thornley refers to Mary Louise Pratt's notions of transculturalism: "Pratt recognises that within transcultural exchanges there are always different levels of power. By acknowledging the inevitability of conflict in these exchanges, Pratt allows for problems of violence and non-equivalence during the process of transcultural change." (Thornley 2004: 61). Subsequently, the change is coming, but it is a difficult and long process as *Cousins* suggests. A successful sharing of power between cultures within one nation as delineated in Ihimaera's *The Rope of Man* is not yet possible in the 1970s, 1980s, or 1990s in which the cousins' story is set. Instead, the reader follows the three cousins' lives through stages of the transculturation process. Each cousin is subject to it to a different degree: Missy is less affected by it than Mata and Makareta, who are both greatly exposed to two cultures while her place is and has always been within the family. Compared to the others, she is much more shielded from *Pakeha* influence, and the challenges she encounters in her life have nothing to do with a two-fold society, but emerge from Maori traditions and expectations.

We may assume that Makareta and Missy share the same knowledge of their culture since they grew up together despite Makareta's privileges. Yet this knowledge affects them in different ways and determines their individual paths in life in two opposite directions. While Makareta's knowledge, coupled with her familiarity with the *Pakeha* world, encourages her to move outside the safety of her *whanau*, her cousin chooses to stay. Therefore, the tales, traditions and beliefs of their culture allow them to choose their individual ways of life based on their cultural memories.

As an adult, Makareta takes on the role of the specialist who has knowledge and is in the position to impart it. To her, knowledge is memory, a deep and resourceful body of cultural information that establishes identity (cf. *C* 209). In spite of passing on her knowledge, Makareta does not promote a return to tradition as such. She does encourage remembrance of Maori origins, but she looks towards the future so as to strengthen her people and improve their situation. This way, memory serves as a catalyst for change. The resulting focus on the future is reflected in Makareta's chapters, which urge the reader to look towards the possibilities she sees in sharing her knowledge.

In contrast, Missy's chapters are both directed towards the past and the present. The references to her ancestors are an obvious link to the past, but they are important for her standing within the community today. Therefore, she is firmly situated in the present while Mata is struggling with her past and caught in memories of a difficult childhood among people ignorant of her culture. Mata's narrative is also geared towards the past to a greater extent than that of her cousins due the focus on her past, which assigns each of the main characters a different place within time.

As a result, it is impossible to say that the novel is about a return to tradition by virtue of cultural memory as such. Given that each one of the cousins represents a different time – past, present and future – and functions as a particular archetype, their significance rather lies in their function as types of Maori identities. The cousins are points of intersection that suggest a plurality of options for the construction of Maori identity today. For this reason, the novel is not a repository of memories like some of the books from the first two phases. Though *Cousins* certainly contains references to myths, they are minimal and mainly assigned to Missy's character and the archetype she represents, or to Mata's being lost. Therefore, even though myths still tell the story of a common origin, the self-images that are being portrayed in the present are varied and expressions of possible Maori identities. As opposed to other writers, Grace manages to give a more detailed idea of the possibilities for Maori identity and its variety. Instead of suggesting a vague move forward, her characters are intricate examples of what a fulfilling life could be. Unlike *Tangi*, *Cousins* does not stop at the suggestion of change but allows the characters to play out different scenarios and their consequences.

As mentioned, the novel is neither a repository of memory as such nor do myths appear to hinder the construction of identity. The set of memories Makareta refers to as essential parts of the Maori self are the foundation on which the future is built. *Cousins* is not a mythical narrative, but it does imitate memory in its storytelling pattern by moving from one narrator to the other between the three protagonists. While this pattern duplicates the spiral previously encountered in the Maori novel, it also copies the way memory works with its fragmented patterns and the absence of a binding chronology. The novel does proceed chronologically on the whole as it depicts the characters' lives form childhood to old age and death, but it is filled with shifts between the cousins' lives and several flashbacks.

In conclusion, it may be said that memories form the foundation and starting point of identity construction in *Cousins* while the narrative imitates its mode of operation. Following Rigney's five stages of memory, the text chooses the memories that are relevant for each character's development. These are Makareta's experiences at boarding school that are crucial for her politically active role as an adult. For Missy, the memories connected with her ancestresses are the basis of her development and her role as mother whereas Mata's memories of the orphanage and the holiday at home awake her desire to know who she is. All their memories converge to form a range of Maori experiences although Grace has divided them into the three cousins' lives for clarity. By offering three tales in one novel, there is a certain degree of recursivity, particularly since the protagonists' lives intersect at several points. Each intersection has the potential to alter the existing story, adding to the dynamics of the tale. Undoubtedly, Grace's representation of Maori identity may function as a model for remembrance and, most of all, identity construction beyond the fictional world. Transfer and translation between fictional and real world, even between cultures, seems possible especially due to the creative capacity of memory and identity. All in all, as a work of fiction, *Cousins* itself is a model containing three possible modes of identity construction. The activist, the mother and the seeker are three basic identities available not only to the women despite the author's focus on them. Her depiction is universal and contains room for individual variation, making *Cousins* an ideal framework for the possibilities of identity construction.

3.3.2 Witi Ihimaera's The Uncle's Story (2000)

While previous novels concerned themselves with finding a place for Maori people in New Zealand, *The Uncle's Story* goes even further in its plea for tolerance and acceptance. Whereas novels before this time worked towards a better understanding of Maori culture from outside and depicted the difficulties encountered in a bicultural country, Ihimaera now introduces a subject that is controversial within the Maori community itself. In this novel for the new millennium, the taboo of homosexuality is addressed in detail in a plea for the acceptance of gay men and women.

In *The Uncle's Story*, Ihimaera depicts the life of Michael, a young gay man struggling with the traditions that do not allow him to be who he is. Within the patriarchal Maori community that prides itself on its unbroken lineage and the sacredness of the union between man and woman, his lifestyle has no place. It is only his aunt who finally tells him the hushed-up story of his uncle Sam, a Vietnam War hero, who fell in love with Cliff Harper, an American helicopter pilot. Both of their stories, Sam's and Michael's, are intertwined in the course of the narrative, showing the parallels and differences between the treatment of homosexuality in their respective times. Partly autobiographical, the novel is a compelling story with a pressing message: gay Maori must come into their own and find an unimpeachable place not only within society at large, but within the tribal community in particular in which they will be respected.

At the same time, reclaiming the deserved respect is a long process that Ihimaera also traces in the process of storytelling. For this reason, the author addresses and reinvents the traditions and myths of his people to create a place for what he refers to as a new tribe, a group of people who inadvertently challenge the patriarchy simply by being homosexual. Asked about the gay tribe he envisions, Ihimaera explains his revolutionary approach in an interview:

> "It was a challenging thing for me to even think about," he says. "Young gay Maori men and women were escaping the tribal frameworks to become themselves because they had been told: 'If you're gay, you can't be married, you can't have children'. So I was trying to say: 'No. Don't believe in those sorts of frameworks because essentially they're European frameworks. What we have to do is to create a Polynesian framework which allows the possibility of gay men and women having children and maintaining the whakapapa." (Dickson 2005: 2)

At this point, both *Pakeha* and Maori are challenged, but, even more importantly, the novel proves that this new struggle is connected to the issues addressed in Ihimaera's earlier work. Therefore, it comes as no surprise that the inevitable political dimension opened by this topic makes the novel an important narrative in the struggle for Maori sovereignty on the whole.

In the story, at first, Michael is unaware of the connection between his struggle as a gay man and as a Maori. It is only when Roimata points out the double colonisation that gay Maori have been subjected to that he feels the urge to actively encourage the fight for Maori rights, gay or straight. "I only wish, Michael," Roimata says, "that you would see that you've been colonised twice over. First, by the Pakeha. Second by the *gay* Pakeha. [...] The issues of identity and space – of sovereignty, of *tino rangitiratanga* – that our people have been fighting for within Pakeha society are the same issues for gay Maori within Pakeha gay society!" (*US* 125) This moment of recognition sets in motion the course the narrative will take: a political, urgent striving for personal freedom and the right of gay Maori to be identified as people in their own right. As Roimata explains, the homosexual Maori's struggle for recognition is part of the greater fight for indigenous sovereignty that Ihimaera's fiction encourages. Only this time it is a two-pronged approach that confronts *Pakeha* and Maori at the same time and in the same measure – something that has not been done before.

The Uncle's Story is yet another one of Ihimaera's novels with a message that is driven home vehemently, demanding acceptance from what the writer calls "the most homophobic people in the world" (Dickson 2005: 2). Homosexuality goes against their beliefs not only as Christians, but also as Maori because a same-sex union endangers their genealogy. The strength of a people comes from its direct descent from the first ancestors to the present day and the unborn children that are yet to follow in an unbroken lineage. With this in mind, early in the novel, Michael's father explains why his son cannot – indeed must not – be gay: "You have been brought up to have a place in the tribe. People like you are outcasts. They do not belong. If you are a Maori, one of the privileges is that when you die your tribe will honour you by coming for you and bringing you home to be buried. No matter where you are or what you've done – murdered somebody even – they will honour their obligations. [...] What will happen to our *whakapapa*, our genealogy? It will finish with you, Michael. How dare you be so selfish" (*US* 21).

Still, his father's reaction is much milder than the one Sam was made to suffer many years earlier. Sam is whipped and renounced by his father who casts him out of the tribe for this sin of homosexuality. Though he rebels, he cannot change his father's mind because he is too steeped in the traditional interpretations of myths that would condemn same-sex unions. His father, as head of the tribe, is particularly intent on upholding the Maori values that have been passed down through the ages, and he is a determined man of high standing. As the leading patriarch, his father is highly regarded and too strong for Sam to fight. Being such a strong and respected figure, Arapeta personifies age-old traditions and beliefs, which is the reason Sam's struggle is bound to fail. Unlike Michael, who lives in times that are more liberal than his uncle's, Sam's homosexuality condemns him to isolation. Michael, at least, has the assurance of being accepted in society generally, and it is only his family and the tribe that cannot tolerate his lifestyle. This circumstance gives him a different toehold that allows him to launch the revolution of a new Maori tribe he believes is necessary.

The difficulty is related to the fact that Maori people have held fast to unchanging interpretations of customs and traditions for many generations, which is the reason for Sam's misery. Even before he is cast out of the tribe, he torments himself with the knowledge that he will not be forgiven if he gives in to his desires because the stories tell him it would be wrong. The power and honour of men and the sacredness of a union with women is deeply seated within myth and well-known so that, at a moment in which he refuses his potential lover, he cannot help but think of the stories that are the reason for his suffering: "it transgressed the order of the Maori world, it transgressed the *tapu*, sacred, nature of man. The consequences were too fearful to contemplate. [...] You brought *noa* upon yourself, the loss of sacredness, and, without sacredness, you were prone to punishment, dishonour, banishment and death. You also brought this on your partner" (*US* 150). Similarly, thinking of the tale of Tane's creation of Hineahuone, the first woman to come into the world among gods, Sam once again realises why a single-sex union is the basest union of all. Clearly, the myths of old are a hindrance for Sam even more so than for Michael who, though familiar with the same stories, has the advantage of living in a more tolerant society.

Despite their different circumstances, visions of *Te Kore*, the eternal void, torment both characters throughout the novel, resembling the void they feel within themselves. Enhanced by a mortal threat, symbolised by the owl as the messenger of death, the oppressive darkness threatens to overcome Sam in particular. The owl accompanies him not only during the Vietnam War where death is palpable every second, but also on his return home. In his mind, the owl is a recurring omen of the punishment he deserves for his sexual orientation: "He should have known he couldn't spit in the face of the gods and get away with it. He was to be punished, and all those around him were being punished too" (*US* 238). Throughout the novel in passages such as these, Sam is very conscious of the mythic significance of situations. The stories are ever present in his mind, enabling him to apply them to his own life. Unfortunately, it is this memory that causes his inner turmoil and makes him miserable. Torn between his desires and his culture's expectations, Sam is doomed to an unfulfilled life.

Michael, on the other hand, is unwilling to let conventions dictate his life. The same stories that hinder Sam are still known in his own time, but he has found that there are new chances Sam was unaware of. It is possible to live with the old stories in a way that will allow for change and tolerance: instead of discarding the myths altogether, they can be approached from a new angle. As a result, Maori life remains grounded in mythology while enabling the individual to adapt to new needs and requirements.

New Stories for a New Tribe

Beside the central myths of the First Parents, and Tane and the first woman that Ihimaera incorporates in the body of the text, it is particularly the sections of the novel that follow Sam's life at home and in Vietnam that incorporate myth as an everyday part of Maori life. Since Maori are a warrior people, the emphasised mythical connections seem fitting in the context of war. Michael himself is presented as a different kind of warrior in another age who believes that gay people, too, have a right to live in the light like the children of the First Parents (cf. *US* 337). His fight is not in a war between nations, but one that is needed to negotiate a life within a community. The weapons he has are none that kill, but like Sam he is equipped with the richness of his cultural heritage. Unlike his uncle, however, Michael actively opposes the myths that hinder him because they obstruct his struggle for acceptance. While the myths of old were the most powerful weapons in earlier struggles to establish cultural identity, they prove to be the source of the problem in Michael's case. Without weapons, Michael stands his ground and encourages the telling of new stories that will include the new tribe he envisages.

The search for a new mythology also explains why Michael is not the traditional mythical hero that we find in Grace's *Potiki*. He is removed from the prototypical hero and becomes a modern day warrior instead. Unlike Toko, he is not conceived or born under unusual circumstances and he suffers no threat of death. The only comparable instance is his not being accepted as a gay man by his people, which equals a metaphoric death. Nonetheless, Michael has a quest that leads him to the creation of a new tribe with the knowledge he has gained from his uncle's story. It is Sam's tale itself that constitutes Michael's heroic journey into another world – the Vietnam War and his uncle's suffering – teaching him what he has to fight in his own day.

In line with Leeming's observations, Michael is the new mythic hero. "The new mythology," he says,

> does not create conquering heroes but rather seekers after the transpersonal Self of the Gaian world [characteristically nourishing and feminine]. We are either heroes of the new myth or captives of the old. Those who refuse the call, who hang on desperately to the dying gods and myths of past value systems, will continue to endanger the world with their blindness to reality. Those who answer the call will depart from the status quo and join those planetary universalists in a breaking away – as heroes have always done – from the merely individual, the merely local, so as to become truly human. These adventures will confront the guardians at the gates of progress and new understanding – those powers who would protect the nation-state, patriarchal exclusionary religion, and corporate power at all costs. [...] It will be the role of the new hero [...] to lead the way to the formations of belief systems and ways of thinking that will celebrate and be in accordance with the miracle of the ecological universe. (Leeming 2002: 159–60)

Leeming's new mythic hero is on a quest for identity and therefore tied to reality rather than the restricting beliefs of an old order. His quest requires of him to leave the old value system in the way that Michael does by confronting an old Maori way of life. By breaking away from "the merely local" and orienting himself within a greater framework that exceeds the familiar Maori tribes and opposes existing authority within the community, he attempts to pave the way for his new tribe.

As the new hero, Michael is the forerunner of the tribe he envisions, but his courageous approach was unthinkable in Sam's time. Sam's darkness and inner turmoil threaten to consume him as he and the people around him hang on to old mythology, and this becomes the reason why he first rejects his lover. It is a sin to act against the teachings transported by the old myths, causing so much anguish for Sam that he suffers through most of the time of his relationship with Cliff. It is only once he accepts him in their first sexual encounter that the conflict within him is resolved. There is a burst of light at last that dispels the eternal darkness of *Te Kore* he had dreaded before (cf. *US* 241).

At this moment, with rebellion and the courage to make a change comes, perhaps unexpectedly, the light and new hope for the future. *Te Kore* is now also the place where new life begins. Finally, when Sam let's go of his fears and takes the step he had dreaded he is able to feel that what he is doing is good despite his people's beliefs. In doing this, he proves that a courageous move has to be made away from old customs in order to embrace the new that must not be altogether bad just because it is different.

Michael has already discovered this and is at peace with himself. What is more, he goes beyond the wish for his own personal fulfilment. His rebellion, unlike his uncle's, is public and on a much greater scale due to his realisation that new times require a new approach and new ways of thinking in order to restore the all-embracing inclusiveness inherent in Maori culture. This is the point at which the author's own political agenda mingles with his fiction by turning Michael into "a gay Maori Moses" (*US* 32) who wants to lead homosexual Maori towards a tribe of their own: "In a passage based on Ihimaera's own speech delivered at a First Nations conference in Canada," Jane E. Dickson says in a *Times* article, "Michael Mahana calls for the establishment of gay Maori tribe, with children born to gay men and women continuing the line of succession" (Dickson 2005: 2). Apparently, Michael's rite of passage as a gay man is not his coming-out to the family, but his speech at the conference (cf. *US* 311ff.) in which he steps forth as Maori and speaks out for all homosexuals of his culture. This change of focus from Sam's longing to be accepted and understood by his family to Michael's orientation towards a wider frame indicates the general openness that has developed since the previous generation. While Sam's life took place mainly in the *whanau*, Michael's is not restricted in this way. On the contrary, his life is often separate from his family and has thus expanded the framework within which his uncle was trapped. Familiar with the tolerant view of homosexuality within New Zealand society, he gains strength from its knowledge that Sam was denied. Unlike his uncle, Michael gains purchase from his position within New Zealand society, allowing him to challenge conventional Maori beliefs. As a result, he contests old customs as a representative of homosexual native peoples while clearly identifying himself as Maori at the same time. By coming forward at the conference and making his point in traditional Maori oratory, honouring his people's ways with the *karanga* (ceremonial call of welcome), *korero* (speech) and *haka* (dance), Michael claims the two identities that had heretofore been regarded as separate and incompatible: Michael the Maori and Michael the gay man.

Thus, the conference is the perfect setting for the book's ideological message where the characters can aggressively pursue their agenda. Harking back to Roimata's statement that gay issues are part of Maori issues in general, Michael takes the opportunity at the conference to address all First Nations to unite them in the creation of the new gay tribe: "'[...] We have been dispossessed. We have been marginalised. In many places our cultures, yours and mine, have been destroyed. We occupy the borderlands of White society. We live only by the White man's leave within White structures that are White driven and White kept. Our jailers might be kindly, but they are still our jailers. [...] We must disconnect from the White umbilical.'" (*US* 320) To his surprise, his speech is received with great applause and the first change has been made. He is evidently the much-needed leader of his cause, which he proves with his informed speeches and his regard for Maori customs.

As a leader, Michael possesses the skill set and the traditional knowledge to make the change he envisions and lead his new tribe into a different direction. His identification as a member of an indigenous people furthermore allows him to be accepted by other First Nations, who will follow his call for a new tribe. Michael's role is that of chief in keeping with known Maori structures. Once again, he does not separate himself from his heritage, but remains within the traditional framework. Even though Michael advocates a change, it is not a fundamental change of existing Maori customs as such. Instead, they can be used to bring about the needed changes he calls for. As a result, the Maori structures are preserved while the content may be different in order to allow the needed flexibility. To illustrate, the myths that are fundamental to the Maori worldview are part of the structure within which Maori life is made possible in its existing form. The guidelines extracted from the tales delineate how an indigenous life should be led, and a reinterpretation of myths as depicted in *The Uncle's Story* still upholds the existing structures. Evidently, Michael does not intend to break down

Maori tradition. What he offers instead is a variety of approaches to set beliefs by moving within the structures he is familiar with.

It is not, however, only public acceptance that is necessary, but also the private recognition from Michael's family. Thanks to his leadership qualities, Michael achieves this with his conference speech as well. His grandfather, a member of the older generation that was unable to accept homosexuality before, sees him as a Maori warrior – foolishly going to battle without weapons, but brave enough to do so for a cause that makes him vulnerable to attack. The old man's realisation that Michael is a warrior despite being gay is a great triumph. Whether it will be a complete triumph must yet be determined.

As mentioned in earlier analyses, Ihimaera himself has said that the *tangi* is the ritual that best expresses Maori customs and beliefs, and it is only fitting that this occasion should be the moment in which Michael's cause either fails or triumphs. On returning the body of a gay friend, Michael, together with others of his new gay tribe, faces the deceased man's grand-mother, not knowing how they will be received. It is a critical moment, a decisive moment that might prove their defeat:

> Lilly straightened up. She looked at us. I think we probably gave her a bit of a shock. She knew we had brought Waka's body back, but she was trying to figure out some tribal reference point. My goodness, we were like no tribe she had ever seen. Ah well –
>
> Lilly raised her right arm.
>
> "*Haramai ki te ope tane me wahine takatapui –*"
>
> [...]
>
> "Welcome to this *marae*," called Lilly. "Welcome you strange tribe I see before me! Come forward, you tribe of men who love men and women who love women! Welcome, you brave gay tribe, whom none have seen before! Come! Bring your dead who is also our dead –"
>
> Our tribe was born that day. It was born out of a grandmother's compulsion to take her grandchild back to her bosom. Out of a need to accept that a new tribe was coming. That day we signalled, "Make way, we are coming through."
>
> We would not be stopped. (*US* 359)

To their relief, they are received as they had hoped. Nothing stands in their way any longer, and the beginnings of the new tribe have taken root.

In this novel, Ihimaera creates a narrative to permeate and break up the grand narratives that hinder minorities in finding their rightful place in the world. As a result, the characters within the fiction and the author confront those who have enjoyed heretofore unquestioned authority. Michael's realisation that "[t]hey had all denied gay men and women a place in the main narrative of the world – God, his prophets and his followers" (*US* 315), reveals the significance attributed to his cause.

In this context, myths take up an ambivalent position within the novel. On the one hand they are powerful narratives with authority that guide people and are a strong feature of their identity. In *The Uncle's Story*, myth's authority is a hindrance for homosexuals and the reason behind their struggle for acceptance. On the other hand, however, it is clear from the narrative that these myths are also essential and inseparable from any Maori, regardless of their sexual orientation. The fact that references to myths and rituals of old in positive situations outweigh those in negative situations that obstruct the characters suggests that the novel does not intend to condemn myth and tradition. On the contrary, they are important for Maori culture and should remain so while being open for change at the same time.

Retaining the Old within the New

The new tribe requires its own stories. Existing ones will have to be retold, renewed and supplemented. Michael sums this up best in a metafictional section towards the end of the novel:

> I have realised, Uncle Sam, that the telling of our story will bring a location and a history to the world that we build. We who are gay and lesbian must fix the stories with firmness and solder their knots with purpose so that they become part of the narratives – the foundations, walls and roof – all peoples tell about each other. We must speak our stories, we must enact them, we must sing our songs throughout this hostile universe. We must bring a new promise to life and a new music to the impulse of history. (*US* 365)

Even the novel's structure reflects the characters' struggle with the old and the new that must come. The new, here, is the same it has been for all other Maori novels in English that use this Western genre and language to transport indigenous values. Like in his very first novel, Ihimaera combines conventional genre elements with traditional Maori storytelling elements. Once again we encounter the spiral pattern that winds itself through the story and through Sam and Michael's lives. The plot's spiral structure demonstrates their similar circumstances while also allowing for change through Michael's successful struggle. All is connected: both men, though living in different times, know the same problems that come with being gay and steeped in Maori traditions. They are similar in their sexual identity, cultural identity and family resemblance. Due to these parallels, the spiral plot winds around them both, allowing their stories to finally intersect when Michael meets Cliff, bringing past and present together for a moment.

Past and present are further joined in the novel's structure by letting Sam's story be told by Auntie Pat and George, and Michael's by a third-person narrator and himself. Again, the conventions of indigenous and Western storytelling are combined in this novel without obstructing each other by incorporating multiple storytellers within the structure of the novel. As is customary in Maori storytelling, each person takes a turn. Consequently, Auntie Pat relates Sam's suppressed story while the reader follows Michael's tale and is offered a number of smaller stories in the recounted myths, Cliff's own brief perspective towards the end of the novel, and of course Michael's vision of the new tribe. These different narrative strands come together and separate repeatedly throughout the book as parts of each tale are told, superseded by another only to be continued at a later point in the traditional spiral pattern. On the whole, the novel contains retellings of the characters' lives and traditional myths that emphasise the significance of storytelling.

So, harking back to Maori custom, the chapter beginning Sam's story is introduced by a chant that also ends the novel, thus connecting and concluding the tale in the traditional manner and expressing the joining of the outer and inner frameworks, the stories within the story. The continuous cycle of storytelling threads itself throughout the narrative, emphasising its importance among Maori people on the one hand, and its necessity for acceptance on the other: "That night, speaking Uncle Sam's story to

Amiria, singing and crying his story into the dawn, was the First Telling"
(*US* 346). Once the silence has been broken, the story will continue and
become the first of many new stories for the new tribe that will "bind
the outer framework of the world with the inner framework" (*US* 365),
a connection reminiscent of the spiral.

While Michael, George, and Auntie Pat take their turns telling stories
and thus hark back to Maori oral tradition, it becomes evident that the only
way to tell a suppressed story is to bring it to life again in the telling. In *The
Uncle's Story*, this is achieved both orally and in written form. While the
characters tell their tales face to face when Michael asks them to, readers
receive the same information in writing. The multiple voices contained in
the novel tell the same story, but they add new perspectives and new aspects
to the same man's tale that a single-voiced narrative is unable to supply.
Their alternating telling follows the spiral pattern once again, leading us
from the present into the past and back again several times.

The connection between the lives of the past and the present is
strengthened and rendered visible for listener and reader. Moving in time
(past and present), between places (Vietnam and several locations in New
Zealand), cultures and customs (Maori, Western, Vietnamese, the old
and the new), and a number of storytellers, the novel offers an array of
elements that follow the alternating pattern encountered in previous novels.
Despite the geographical and temporal distance between characters and
events related in the text, the age-old tradition of storytelling retains its
significance even now and is established as the beginning and continuation
not only of remembrance, but of change and progress. It is made abundantly
clear that remaining in the past entirely will cause problems. After all, Sam
suffers due to his family's unshakeable beliefs while Michael encourages
the construction of an expanded Maori identity that is more tolerant and
open to variety.

The crucial point is that myth – like memory and identity, as pointed
out by Rigney, Erll, Assmann, Bhabha and others – is open to change
and development, and is therefore a flexible construct. *The Uncle's Story*
explicitly offers new interpretations of crucial myths that are the only way
for homosexual Maori to be accepted within the indigenous community.

The stories are neither renounced nor replaced, but remain the same except for the new perspective that is presented by Sam's experiences. Michael calls for new stories, but these will be tales of people's lives such as Sam's that will eventually turn to legend and possibly myth. These stories will not replace the old myths. Instead, they will be tales that exist alongside the old and be the foundation of the new tribe.

The Uncle's Story is the only novel to suggest such a crucial reinterpretation of existing myths. It coincides with the understanding that Maori memory and identity are flexible constructs that are susceptible to change. Therefore, it stands to reason that myths themselves are anything but rigid stories. Ihimaera takes a daring step towards myth in this novel by suggesting that the old stories are a hindrance for Maori development. As is often the case in his work, he gives an example of the necessary change that would lead Maori into the right direction. The novel is a suggestion, an experiment that may be applicable in reality. The author considers the current situation in New Zealand and creates a possible solution in a fictional setting. His claim, however, is not to change Maori cultural memory, but to augment it with new tales for a new tribe.

Ihimaera's affinity to retelling stories and expanding them from a new point of view with additional knowledge and a changed perspective is evident in the many new versions of his own publications or sequels such as *Whanau II* (2004) – a rewriting of *Whanau* (1974) –, *The Dream Swimmer* (1997) – sequel to *The Matriarch* (1986) – and *The Rope of Man* (2005), which includes a rewriting of *Tangi* and a new sequel. As the following analysis of *The Rope of Man* will illustrate, Ihimaera for the first time presents a world in which the obstacles portrayed in previous novels have been overcome to a degree so that the reader encounters a protagonist who is confident and can identify himself as Maori with all the potential the modern world has to offer. *The Uncle's Story* therefore marks the stage at which Ihimaera's fiction leaves the common ground shared by previous novels – accusing *Pakeha* society alone for the slow integration of the Maori way of life and the lack of traditional knowledge among younger generations of Maori – and enters an optimistic and confident phase of the Maori novel.

3.3.3 Witi Ihimaera's *The Rope of Man* (2005)

In their introduction to the writer, Corballis and Garrett point out something that Ihimaera's readers have often encountered in his work. They
note that "[h]e is an inveterate reviser who often continues to tinker with
his work even after the first *authorised* publication" (Corballis and Garrett
1984: 11). While the revisions may be the result of a perfectionist's drive to
continually improve his opus, one might also say that Ihimaera is walking
backwards into the future by rewriting his novels to suit another time with
other concerns. In the new version of *Tangi* from 2005, Ihimaera's focus
shifts. He no longer needs to introduce Maori culture to his readers because
much has been done in the last thirty years to raise awareness. Now he is
more concerned about how both Maori and *Pakeha* in New Zealand are
related and we no longer witness an exclusively Maori worldview. It is no
longer possible to say a Maori is exclusively Maori, or a *Pakeha* is merely a
descendant of the white settlers, or that neither group has any relevant connections to the other except for sharing the same space. Both have become
joined as different strands of the mythical Rope of Man. Ihimaera promotes
this new development in his country, redefining Maori and *Pakeha* identity
in fiction and reality today.

The new "Tangi" of 2005 is the prequel to an illustration of this new
interdependence and the strength of a joint society of mixed racial backgrounds. Ihimaera makes alterations to his first novel, thus changing the
emphasis. As pointed out, he no longer needs to introduce the reader to
Maori culture because the last three decades have increased awareness of
it and the government launched several projects to promote *te reo* and the
conservation of indigenous customs. Ihimaera uses a language that is now
simpler, less emotional and less condensed. The lyrical language of the original version was closely associated with traditional Maori oral literature, but
now that the author concentrates on the closer relationship between Maori
and *Pakeha*, such poetic diction seems out of place and too exclusively indigenous. As he explains, "Our literature is 'loosening up', relaxing. It is not as
self-conscious or always determinedly artistic" (Ihimaera 2006: 5).

The *Pakeha* world plays a more significant role in the new version
which goes beyond the individual Maori's plight and addresses historical

and political issues more openly within the confines of its narrator's limited perspective. Most of all, it sheds a more benign light on the *Pakeha*. Mr Ralston, Tama's first boss, for instance, is no longer the helpless man the reader of 1973 encountered. He is calm and respectful when he hears of Tama's loss and is no longer clumsy or embarrassed. In fact, Ralston even becomes one of Tama's mentors who opens his eyes to Maori political concerns. Generally, the rewritten version of *Tangi* proves to be a more tolerant version that includes *Pakeha* who are rounded and complex characters as opposed to the simplified depictions previously encountered in the early *Tangi*. The expanded characterisations therefore confirm the changes in New Zealand that have taken place since the 1970s. As a result, instead of retaining the anti-*Pakeha* stance of the original *Tangi*, Ihimaera gives his readers an open-minded new "Tangi" in *The Rope of Man* with elaborate Maori and *Pakeha* characters alike.

In a similar vein, Ihimaera gives equal weight to Maori mythology and (Western understanding of) history, placing them side by side in the narrative – neither has a claim to the ultimate truth. Instead, both are equally important. We now have clearer insight into both aspects when reading about Maori historical events and more detailed Maori myths that explain the indigenous perspective. At the same time, we get a closer look at the negative effects of marginalisation that previously remained unmentioned such as alcoholism in the indigenous communities, physical and sexual abuse. Tama no longer serves as the only focal figure in this new version, thereby giving the narrative a wider perspective. The third person narrator is more prominent than before, taking over from Tama's own narration, which allows us to have a more encompassing view of the situation.

Moreover, Ihimaera introduces a new motif that gives the novel its title and symbolises the intertwined lives of all New Zealanders. Named after *te taura tangata*, the narrative contains not only a new version of his first novel, but also a sequel, "The Return 2005". This Rope of Man has become the writer's metaphor for the joint nature of all New Zealanders regardless of race.[4] It is a myth of the Maori people, which, in his eyes, best

---

4   Recent talks such as "New Zealand Literature: Writing From the Edge of the
      Universe" (2006) and Ihimaera's Fulbright lecture "Witi Ihimaera's New Zealand

expresses the importance of keeping their culture alive. At the same time, the many strands of the rope encourage sharing in the experience of others, which allows *Pakeha* and Maori to live not just alongside each other, but with one another.

Aware of the risk that this rope might break, Ihimaera's contribution to its conservation in literature began in 1973 with *Tangi* and has continued even beyond *The Rope of Man*. Battista notes in his review that "*the rope of man* [*sic*.] successfully communicates the need to realise a sense of belonging and place, one which allows us to appreciate our cultural diversity" (Battista 2006: 120). He particularly refers to the consequences of the traumatic experience which Tama and his mother have to come to grips with. "Tangi" has been slightly changed in places to introduce this new event of which the reader learns in the sequel "The Return" that revolves around a secret between mother and son. Only when she knows she is dying does she call Tama home to reveal the secret of her rape and the resulting unwanted son she gave up for adoption. This son, brought up by *Pakeha* parents, dreams of the Rope of Man though he does not realise its significance until he is reunited with his Maori family and "[t]his time as he swam towards the river, the rope recognised him" (*RM* 313).

Battista further remarks that "[t]here are implications here too for the future in the idea of an adoptive *Pakeha* mother seeking a Maori healing for her son" (Battista 2006: 120). Making the relationship between Maori and *Pakeha* work as the main theme of his novel, Ihimaera combines people of different cultures to demonstrate that both can benefit from one another. Harking back to the rise of a new tribe, Tama realises that there is "a great new tribe of New Zealanders" (*RM* 325) today that focuses on similarities rather than differences. Setting the stage for the rise of the new tribe, Ihimaera begins *The Rope of Man* with a necessary revised version

---

Dreams" (2005) in particular demonstrate the author's personal philosophy in his consistent use of the rope metaphor and the emphasis of the similar origins of all New Zealanders. Both in his fiction and non-fiction, Ihimaera suggests that New Zealanders regardless of race should see themselves as people of one nation with several cultural influences that should be embraced. As a result, *Pakeha* should seek their Maori roots, which they have as New Zealanders, while Maori should not fear to make their way among *Pakeha*.

of *Tangi* that, unlike its original, permits the desired development as portrayed in "The Return 2005". Both parts of the novel will be examined in the following to allow a comparison of original and rewriting while at the same time tracing the changes in Ihimaera's personal philosophy and New Zealand's development since the 1970s.

"Tangi": A Revision

As mentioned earlier, the new "Tangi" uses simpler language that is less poetic and loses much of its density to a more easy-going telling. The narrative is more relaxed since the poetic language has been reduced, which allows the text to flow smoothly. As a consequence, the "emphasis on sentiment, validated by cultural practice, and sentimentality" (Battista 2006: 117) has been reduced, which opens up the original version that was too exclusively Maori. In this manner, Ihimaera enables the new emphasis he gives "Tangi" in 2005. The extended focus on the cultural multiplicity in New Zealand is introduced by Ihimaera's additional passages describing the *Pakeha* world Tama encounters during his time as a journalist in the city. Even though we are presented with a primarily Maori perspective, it is a more encompassing one than in the earlier version, indicating that there are weightier, more political matters of greater scope that affect and exceed the individual dilemma.

The general spiral pattern of the original is retained and expanded on. The story moves naturally back and forth in time and space as a thread or rope weaving its way between memories and the present, different countries and cultures. Passages have been rearranged or added to the existing text for the new emphasis as have new images and hints at the secret to be revealed in "The Return". They are included in "Tangi" to smoothen the transition between the two parts since the original *Tangi* is very much a novel of its time that requires adaptation. The spiral allows readers "to go back into history and then come out again. Back from personal to political [...] [and] out again" (DeLoughrey, forthcoming: 218; cited in Battista 2006: 118). In this manner, Ihimaera does just that, showing the reader how all things are connected and influence the individual's life.

However, saying that the new version no longer has an exclusively Maori perspective does not mean there is less to learn. On the contrary,

"Tangi" offers a deeper insight into Maori history, myth and politics now than it did before. There is still myth in the depicted reality, influencing Tama's view of the world – his parents are still Earth and Sky to him, but now the reader is offered more insight into myths such as the ones of Paikea or the origin of Hinenuitepo. Maui's betrayal by the piwakawa is expanded, there are further details about the messengers of death of which Tama spoke in 1973. There are new passages about Paikea and of the canoe of Death which had not mentioned before. The history of the coming of the Maori is extended and, in this context, Ihimaera introduces a critical, political dimension with the telling of the Maori story up until the Treaty of Waitangi and beyond.

In 2005, for the first time, the problems of the Maori community are expressed more clearly: "Physical and sexual abuse seemed to come with rural living" (*RM* 53), alcohol ruins people and children are exposed to disease. Tama's view is more expansive than in the original now that he has an eye for such things. It is his teacher Mr Grundy, a white man, who actually helps him remember who he is in this *Pakeha* world he has entered. It is also Mr Grundy who awakens Tama's interest in politics and makes him aware of his need to fight for the rights of his people because no one else will. Significantly, he warns him to "never walk away, Master Mahana. Walking away is not an appropriate response. Fight back, young sir" (*RM* 122).

At this crucial moment when Tama intuits his roll in the world, father and son cannot agree on how to deal with the overwhelming *Pakeha* influence. Each has a valid opinion that further complicates any decision: "'Sometimes you have to stand against the wind.' – 'If you do that, you can be uprooted, Dad, and blown away.' – 'Then bend with it, son, and let the wind blow over you.'" (*RM* 125). The older and perhaps wiser man encourages him to be passive, flexible but resilient. The younger man is proactive and seeks his fortune in the unknown. The generational divide and Tama's final independence from his parents are likened to New Zealand's independence from Britain and "the ways in which New Zealand was creating fresh relationships for itself in the world and the roles that young New Zealanders had in making it happen" (*RM* 125). Being cut off from his parents requires Tama to rely on his own resources in much the same way his country has had to make use of its own means in order to rise in power and status in the world. New Zealand has grown and so will Tama, as a Maori not only of Waituhi and not only of a white society, but of Aotearoa New Zealand.

In passages such as these, Ihimaera strengthens his political point of view and lets Tama become a character of greater political interest whereas he was merely a character concerned with personal issues in 1973. The emphasis on politics becomes all the more evident in his work as journalist, particularly in the sequel, and it is global as opposed to regional politics that takes centre stage the further the novel progresses. Such development is a sign of the new orientation that is no longer directed inward, but outward towards all of New Zealand and the world. This is a stark contrast to the restricted regional view readers are offered in the first two phases of the Maori novel that depicted rural Maori life with the inevitable migration to the city.

Yet all things must begin on a small scale, and so does Tama's beginning interest in politics during his apprenticeship. In "Tangi", the author describes the awakening of an awareness of issues that separate indigenous people from succeeding in their own country. Mr Grundy encourages Tama to take pride in his heritage and the things that make him stand out as an individual, especially when he is an *other* among others.

Equality has to manifest itself first because, in truth, there is a great divide between New Zealanders at the time in which "Tangi" is set: "There were Pakeha bosses and Maori workers. There were the Pakeha who had the privileges and the Maori who did not. There were the Pakeha parts of town and the Maori parts of town. Sometimes the barriers were permeable but most times they could not be negotiated" (*RM* 121). In the entire novel, Tama stands on the threshold of a change that is the writer's vision of New Zealand's future. Working to overcome the barriers, Tama is not afraid to put himself outside the comfort zone of his *whanau*. In fact, he demands to be treated and appreciated like any *Pakeha* in a job that few, if any, Maori succeeded in at the time. Eventually, this leads to him becoming a pioneer who explores and expands not only Maori but New Zealand territory by demanding a space for them in the world and putting them on the map. Tama's range of influence has thus expanded from the merely local to the global. Yet moving outward into the world also requires a return.

Consequently, after coming back to his roots to reduce his cultural distance as described in "Tangi", Tama now returns to bridge the geographic distance he has put between himself and his country in his career. The return is, therefore, a natural progression: the spiritual return in "Tangi" is only complete if there is also a spatial return to Tama's home, be it a permanent or intermittent return. As emphasised in *The Whale Rider* and *Potiki*, home is linked to the soil of one's birth and the characters always eventually return to tribal land.

"The Return 2005": The Sequel

In "The Return", Tama does just this. The reader sees him again as a successful anchorman in London who is known throughout New Zealand and beyond thirty-two years later. Structurally and temporarily, the spiral converges across space and time and he receives a phonecall much like the one informing him of his father's death so many years ago, only now he learns that he is called home again because his mother is dying.

We learn that he did not keep his promise. While "Tangi" left the reader with the conviction that Tama would leave the city and return home to take his place as head of family as his father had asked, he stays in the city and pursues his dreams of a career in journalism instead. He breaks with tradition, and this causes strife between him and his older sister in particular. His decision is especially surprising since it goes against all that Ihimaera tried to convey in 1973. However, the writer's philosophy has evolved since then, leading him to rewrite his previous work. Once again, Ihimaera's habit of rewriting his own work is a result of wanting to adapt the narrative to the current Maori situation. While the original *Tangi* was necessary to bring Maori life into focus to draw attention to its gradual extinction, the new version is altered to permit the thematic transition described in *The Rope of Man*. Ihimaera allows the narrative to open up to move away from the restricted local setting. In this manner, the author manages to incorporate his vision of a new New Zealand that has moved on from the obstructing racial division and promotes balanced and tolerant co-existence instead.

In "The Return 2005", as a result of the changed thematic approach, Tama explains that he never intended to return: "All those promises to go back had been made to console my family, to get them over Dad's dying and make them feel safe – but I had never meant them" (*RM* 228). Instead of coming home, he has moved further away, first to the city, then to Australia, and finally to England. His sister Ripeka cannot forgive him for following his "selfish" ambition (*RM* 293) while she stays with the family, unable to have a career. This is the dichotomy of Maori life, the choice that has to be made between the old and the new, the familiar, and the unknown future. It demonstrates that the process of creating identities is still ongoing and has not yet been resolved. Ripeka's strong reaction to Tama's chosen life also proves that the old life with its traditions and customs must be present, if only in the background of Maori life, even when others move on to build lives of their own. This background is important to come back to, not for good but once in a while, in order to remember.

The Maori difficulty of living according to *Pakeha* requirements is something Tama is all too familiar with and Ripeka is unaware of. As other Maori returned to village life and followed a predestined path, he followed his ambition despite his fear that he might still have to succumb to the Maori lot (cf. *RM* 204). To avoid it, he must learn how to combine two cultures: "As for me, I took wobbly steps forward into the Pakeha world and somehow managed to straddle most of it. Some things had to go: like my language, my whanau and tribal relationships, my culture. It didn't seem as if you could have one with the other" (*RM* 203). So he fails to accomplish this task and can only rectify it later, but it becomes clear in the course of "The Return" that he never completely loses the connection to his culture despite his career. There is indeed a way "to take those cultural frameworks where we were going so that our cultures could cross over with us" (*RM* 221). After all, the Rope of Man may be frayed, but it has not been severed completely.

"Prove to me that you are a New Zealander!" Growing Awareness of Identity
Tama's absence from his ancestral land cannot keep him from being aware of his people's situation. It begins at school where Mr Grundy forces his pupils to rethink who they are: "Until it is created, a country doesn't exist, boys! And how is a country created? It has to be named, claimed, possessed. It has to be written into existence, sung about, spoken into existence. People have to fight for this land, boys, be born in it and be buried in its soil and

be cried over. They have to develop their own identity. [...] Prove to me that you are a New Zealander!" (*RM* 213)

Significantly, Grundy asks for proof of New Zealand identity instead of asking Tama to prove that he is Maori. He therefore regards being Maori as one aspect of national identity, which makes a welcome change from the usual racial differentiation. His view of identity is important because it marks a change from the original *Tangi* once again. In 1973 he would have asked what makes Tama Maori, but in 2005 the question is different. Being Maori or *Pakeha* has become a restricting definition of identity, which is why he aims at an interpretation that is distinctly individual and free from constraining racial definitions at the same time. What he wants from his pupils is for all of them to create an identity based on personal history, the way Tama finally does when he stands up and recites his genealogy in the manner of his people. It is Grundy who first opens his eyes to the way into the future to become a new brand of New Zealander, someone "like Sir Edmund Hillary, standing at the top of the highest mountain in the world, not so that we can see him standing there, but showing us where it is" (*RM* 212).

His first job as a journalist-in-training shows him the necessity to be involved in order to learn where he stands. His boss Mr Ralston, who was a rather helpless character in 1973, becomes his advisor and mentor, teaching him to "[n]ever be afraid of becoming the last man standing" (*RM* 233). It is then that Tama crosses "the line from just reporting the news to creating the news, to becoming an activist" (*RM* 231) who is unafraid of addressing political and social issues that are uncomfortable and unjust. In "The Return" Tama becomes a spokesperson for the Maori people, a character who develops from being the focus of an identity crisis within himself to someone who extends the perspective to include all of his people. Once again, Tama is the figure who educates the reader, this time by educating the fictional public.

It is no coincidence that all his mentors throughout his early beginnings are *Pakeha*. This enables Ihimaera to emphasise his point that "indeed, you don't make it by yourself" (*RM* 205) and that New Zealanders are blending together to become something new, "the great *new* tribe of New Zealanders, Maori and Pakeha, [...] the seeds of a modern Raiatea" (*RM*

325). Tama is one of the first of the tribe, a "new young warrior who came into [their] midst looking Maori but with Pakeha skills and manners" (*RM* 221). Here, as in *The Uncle's Story*, Ihimaera continues to introduce his idea of a new tribe that will augment rather than replace the older generation. Like Michael, Tama is described as a new type of warrior with the needed skills that will enable him to be part of the new tribe in a New Zealand that has changed since the last generation. Learning to confidently make their way in the world, the members of the new Maori tribe will be more firmly rooted in New Zealand since their identity goes beyond the limited regional and racial definitions and extends into the personal, national and global perception of themselves. Possibly, the new tribe may even extend to include the *Pakeha*.

Such a philosophy of race relations in New Zealand has at its heart the same idea brought forth by Bachmann-Medick (cf. Bachmann-Medick 1996: 278). The focus is conflict that can be resolved – not by assimilation or homogenisation, but by preserving that which is different and finding productive ways to use difference as a catalyst for healthy co-existence. This requires the relocation and reinterpretation of myths and traditions that Ihimaera introduces in *The Uncle's Story* and *The Rope of Man*. By exposing oneself to that which is different, Maori and *Pakeha* alike are forced to examine aspects of their respective culture that clash with the other. Only in this manner is reinterpretation possible, granting a positive existence in an inevitably hybrid sphere (cf. Bachmann-Medick 1996: 279). By being aware of cultural difference, Ihimaera is also able to emphasise the similarities that exist between New Zealanders of different heritages. This is not yet Bachmann-Medick's reinterpretation, but it is a change of focus that eventually leads to it.

To take an example, the text gives this impression of similarity since the author compares *Pakeha* to Maori and shows that they are not as different from one another as one might think. Both people came to New Zealand where they found a new home, and Ihimaera tries to reconcile these two groups that have often been portrayed as rivals. For the first time, the white settlers' journey is also portrayed as a long and arduous one that deserves to be remembered (cf. *RM* 188). Ihimaera has taken up Belich's (1996) and Jock Phillips' (2003) idea of New Zealanders as the Boat People

who are all immigrants to the country. It is unusual to see the two people's
arrival in Aotearoa New Zealand being presented as equal. Ihimaera also
strips the Maori journey of any mythic features to give the reader a realistic
account instead of retelling the myth of the departure from Hawaiki, as
it has often been told. This new way of narrating complements his intention to reconcile the two sides of the New Zealand story. A calm, rational
style marks *The Rope of Man* that contrasts the emotional style employed
in the original *Tangi*.

A New Mythology

What Ihimaera is creating here is a new version of the New Zealand story.
Such an undertaking requires the introduction of new themes such as
the Rope of Man and the new tribe to illustrate an innovative perspective that distinguishes the new from the old. The events and some of
the problems are similar, but the emphasis has changed, which leads to
the author giving equal weight to Maori and *Pakeha* history. Including
the old mythology, Ihimaera attempts to mythologise his own narrative in
order to create a fundamental story that can become myth. The myths that
were in the foreground in *Tangi* are still important, but they have made
way for a more rational tone in the novel by moving away from excessively
poetic language. Also, "The Return 2005" introduces Tama as a strong
character rivalled only by *The Uncle's Story's* Michael in his determination
and confidence to make a change for himself and others like him. Tama
therefore becomes the ideal figure in a world of change: he has adapted
to the demands of the day, but he has also retained his cultural identity.
What is more, he has been able to prevent becoming the average *Pakeha*,
a fear that was shared by Maori before. True to Bhabha's hybridity, Tama
inhabits the third space in-between cultures that makes him a product of
old and new, with unique views and understanding that differentiate him
from the rest. Not only has Tama incorporated the best of both worlds
within himself – he has also introduced a new philosophy that regards all
New Zealanders as people of similar origins. Reducing the cultural gap
between Maori and *Pakeha* in this manner, the tale has the potential to
become one of the new stories for the new tribe in the same way as Sam's
tale in *The Uncle's Story*.

The telling demonstrates no preference for Maori or *Pakeha* because it expresses their interdependence and the fact that without the other "we are nothing" (*RM* 188). Ihimaera creates a new mythology with the approach evident in previous novels by choosing a blend of Maori and *Pakeha* narrative styles – oral and written – to make his novel more inclusive. This becomes especially clear in his explanation of the traditional Maori spiral and its significance: the purpose of the spiral is to connect generations, keeping individuals connected with ancestors, thereby connecting the past with the present. In scientific terms that express Ihimaera's turn from the poetic and mythic view of things towards a more rational point of view,

> [t]he shape of the double helix [...] is the same shape of the universe as it expands and contracts; it's the shape of infinity, with a unique curve into three-dimensional space. The ratio of the curvature is a constant, a result known as Lancret's theorem.
>
> The double helix is also the shape of the chromosome, the geometric shape of that compact spool of DNA [...] which locates us within the human race and a particular family, identity and nation. [...] [N]obody should underestimate [the helix's] capacity to *bind*. (*RM* 276–7)

This scientific explanation of the double helix expresses the same things that the mythic spiral expresses in other words. Once again, the author demonstrates that, though ways of thinking and expression differ, ultimately, all of life's experiences are shared and merely perceived differently. The mythic language heretofore considered a typically Maori feature is enhanced by science, which was thought to be a primarily *Pakeha* domain up until this point.

Due to the shift from an exclusively Maori viewpoint to an all-inclusive one, the cultural memories that the early novels brought to the fore can now be used more often as an underlying layer instead of a prominent feature in the text. Since the ideal reader will by now be familiar with Maori myths and traditions, they need not be made explicit as much as in the early phases. This circumstance also explains the shift to a more realistic way of storytelling with rational explanations in *The Rope of Man* and especially Michael's chapters in *The Uncle's Story*. Still, myth and memory remain as features in the narratives as elements of storytelling that illustrate the character's actions. Again there is a difference between their use in the early phases and the third in that the old Maori stories used to be necessary to explain indigenous characters' ways of thinking. In the third phase, however, they are more often used to initiate action. Both are related, of course: myth and memory influence thought and may ultimately lead to action. In *The Rope of Man*, they are part of Tama's identity and need not be made too explicit anymore. Instead, the focus lies on his actions that are determined by his position in the third space.

The new mythology Ihimaera creates here fulfils Leeming's demands for a new hero (Leeming 2002: 159ff.) who will free himself of the restrictions of the old order to explore new territory. Tama is the pioneer, the new hero who has gone where Maori have seldom gone before, and he leads the way for others after him. In accordance with Maori beliefs, he walks backwards into the future by remembering his heritage as he progresses professionally and personally. The fact that the focus has shifted from memory to action in the present aimed at the future does not indicate that memory or myth have lost their importance within the culture. Instead, this development should be viewed as the process of identity construction – of which the Maori stories of old still remain the main influence – in a multicultural environment that has become part of the new mythology.

3.3.4 Preliminary Conclusion

Unlike the first novels, those of the third phase are geared towards the future instead of a return to tradition because these old traditions have to be adapted if life in the third space is to succeed. The novels of the twenty-first century are the beginning of a new mythology Grace and Ihimaera approach in individual ways. Grace offers a variety of possible identities in her novel *Cousins* by depicting characters who are representations of three different Maori identities. The heroines of her new mythology can be found in a number of areas: the first is a teacher and leader of people, the second takes on the role of mother and nourisher while the third is the lost seeker who must find herself. Ihimaera's character studies in *The Uncle's Story* and *The Rope of Man* are less varied in this respect, portraying men who are confident and strong from the outset. As heroes of the new

mythology, they seldom show signs of weakness. After a brief struggle at
the beginning, their transition into pioneering heroes seems effortless and
inevitable in comparison to Mata's, Missy's and Makareta's own lives that
were originally meant to lead in other directions. Sam in *The Uncle's Story*
resembles the cousins, especially Mata, in his confusion and unhappiness,
but Michael outshines him as the hero who uses Sam's story to create the
new tribe.

The self-image that is being portrayed in these novels is a pioneering,
determined image of Maori today who can make a change and succeed
in whatever they set their mind to anywhere in the world without losing
their cultural identity. At the same time, as we see in Grace's novel, there
remains a place for traditional roles which are still important influences
in the Maori community. Furthermore, a specialist is still needed to pass
on traditional knowledge. Beside the elders readers have encountered previously, the new teachers are young men and women who can instruct their
peers. Makareta, Michael and Tama are specialists due to their traditional
knowledge and their familiarity with the situation of young Maori today.
Unlike the older generation, they have more credibility because they share
the situation of their peers. The resulting change within Maori hierarchy
is yet another inevitable development in the third phase. Despite younger
men and women taking the place as teachers, the novels retain the respect
attributed to the old order. The focus, however, has been moved from the
old generation to the new that is taking steps into a future that promises
them the opportunity to do everything that was impossible before. Evidently, this phase indicates that these characters have progressed from
marginalised figures to people with the strength and opportunity to make
their way in the world. The struggle for Maori rights and acceptance in a
predominantly *Pakeha* society as depicted in the first and second phases
comes to fruition at last.

While *Cousins* focuses on Maori characters and uses *Pakeha* figures
merely as hindrances in Mata's search for identity, this is mainly due to
the novel's setting throughout the protagonists' lifetime. So the *Pakeha* at
Makareta's boarding school and Mata's orphanage, including her guardian,
are examples of ignorant white people unsympathetic to Maori needs. As
is often the case, Grace's emphasis remains on Maori characters almost to

the exclusion of the *Pakeha* while Ihimaera's characterisation is benign and complex in this third phase. The future envisioned by the writers, therefore, is quite different. *Cousins* presents a Maori future apart from the *Pakeha* that allows for a life that is clearly distinct. Ihimaera's novels, in comparison, promote social interaction and the coexistence with other cultures and a willingness to adapt that *Cousins* addresses only vaguely.

Surprisingly, the innovative approach to Maori myths as a hindrance in today's world as described in *The Uncle's Story* remains unique to this novel. Ihimaera's rewriting of *Tangi* again emphasises the importance of old stories and the customs and beliefs deriving form them without mentioning the need for change. Instead, the innovation in *The Rope of Man* lies not in a new tribe that tells new stories based on the old ones, but in a new tribe that has been formed by the requirements of life in a multicultural world. Both may be viewed as two parts of the same general development as hinted at in *The Uncle's Story* in which Roimata makes Michael aware of the fact that "[t]he issues of identity and space [...] that our people have been fighting for within Pakeha society are the same issues for gay Maori within Pakeha gay society [...]" (*US* 125). Therefore, the emergence of a new tribe in both novels is part of the same development, the same struggle for identity. Yet, surprisingly, one requires the reinterpretation of existing myths and the addition of new stories that may yet become myths while the other makes no mention of reinterpretation. On the contrary, "Tangi" retains the old myths previously included in *Tangi* and even enhances the body of myth by including more.

However, although no new myths are introduced that are meant to be shared by the whole tribe, *The Rope of Man* approaches the topics of cultural identity and personal development by introducing Tama as the ideal Maori character who is spiritually grounded in his cultural heritage and successful in the *Pakeha* world at the same time. The personal successes as described in *Cousins*, *The Uncle's Story*, and *The Rope of Man* present a plurality of options for Maori today. Despite the absence of new myths, the authors do mythologise certain occurrences that express plurality. Grace's depiction of the cousins as archetypal representatives is a mythologisation imitated by Sam's biography in *The Uncle's Story* and Michael's rise as leader. Similarly, Tama is considered a role model in *The Rope of Man* due to his clear identification as Maori and his achievements. Here in particular, Ihimaera works towards a new mythology that will include people of all races for a New Zealand mythology. As a result, he introduces a Maori boy adopted by *Pakeha* parents who ultimately returns to his *whanau*. Ihimaera also repeatedly mentions "a tall curly-haired blond boy with a South African accent" (*RM* 189) who is familiar with Maori customs and yet another unexpected member of the new New Zealand tribe. In both novels, he expresses that New Zealanders, be they Maori or *Pakeha* or of other origin, have "become included with us in singing not our songs but *our* songs, and that rope, well, it's still roaring along carrying us all toward infinity" (*ibid.* 191).

Ultimately, the old fundamental memories remain as the basis of Maori cultural identity, but they are now expanded to include new stories deriving from life in another day and age with new requirements. It is time for a new mythology that Ihimaera takes further than Grace. Her archetypal characters are more established than Ihimaera's new tribes simply because she does not introduce anything new to them. The cousins draw from their cultural heritage and traditional knowledge while finding their place in the scheme of things. The new myths – or, rather, the tales that are meant to become new myths – introduced in Ihimaera's novels yet need to undergo the process of selection, convergence, recursivity, transfer and translation that cultural memory undergoes because they are too new to be elements of cultural memory at this stage. Therefore, the novels of the third phase reflect the process of identity construction and an expected change in cultural memory with the help of new stories that may eventually turn into new myths.

CHAPTER FOUR

He Kupu Whakatepe: Conclusion

Ihimaera and Grace have indeed taken on the task "to complicate and/ or dismantle the reductive formulae" (Said 2003: xxiii) of a multicultural or transcultural life in their own writing. Their range of characters, experiences, themes, and events exemplifies the complexity of a life between two cultures. Yet while their novels confront and undermine *Pakeha* – or generally European – "ideological fiction, metaphysical confrontation, and collective passion" (*ibid.*), they also create Maori versions of these in the process.

The discussed novels share a degree of an ideology that is offered as a necessary alternative to *Pakeha* convictions. By ideological fiction I mean any creative text that systematically furthers a political or other agenda. By this definition, particularly *The Matriarch*, *The Uncle's Story* and *The Rope of Man* promote a Maori ideology that is evident in the characters' speeches, stories and letters that are directed at a fictional audience or readership. In comparison, Grace's work is subtler, but especially her use of archetypal characters in *Cousins* displays an ideological approach in some of her fiction. *Potiki* is similar in its skilful revitalisation of the Maori way of life at a time when *Pakeha* control is almost inevitable. *Tangi*, *Mutuwhenua*, and *The Whale Rider* focus on traditional Maori village life and, while promoting it, include *Pakeha* culture mainly as a marginal influence that can be prevented from penetrating into Maori life if the characters are firmly grounded in their *maoritanga*.

As a result of the focus on Maori experience, *Pakeha* notions of culture, identity, knowledge, and history are replaced or expanded by Maori concepts. Western demands are undermined and pushed towards a marginal position that had heretofore been the place of Maori culture. The authors achieve this repositioning by preferring the indigenous perspective in all aspects. Maori spirituality, customs, ceremonies, rituals, *tikanga*, the importance of storytelling, *whakapapa*, and an alternative Maori-centred historiography counter instances of *Pakeha* authority in the novels. The texts therefore aid the distillation, construction, and preservation of Maori identity in a fictional context that may, as suggested by Erll's thoughts on "iconic enrichment" (2005: 153f.), affect or, ideally, guide action in the reader's reality. In this sense, Maori novels that depict situations reflecting current issues are an experimental playground in which authors can explore a variety of possible solutions to tribal, societal and political problems.

4.1 The Novel as Re-interpreter of the Past and Guide to the Future

What is particularly evident in the discussion of the novels is that myth and memory are essential components of individual and collective Maori identity. They spring from the notion of a Maori approach by "walking backwards into the future" (Ihimaera 1998a: 200), which makes any knowledge of the past a determining factor for the future that awaits them. Consequently, the resulting emphasis on the past expressed by the retelling of myths and personal memories, the recitation of *whakapapa*, and communion with spirits, to name only a few, are inevitably reflected in the novels. The use of myths in particular that Panny (2006) laments had not been examined enough in Maori fiction before and is central to the construction and reconstruction of indigenous identity. With their help, the past is not only retrieved, but also reinterpreted from a modern-day point of view that offers solutions to important issues. On the one hand, therefore, the use of myths in the novels functions as a retrieval of memories of the past that have influenced Maori cultural identity and still have the potential to do so today. On the other hand, however, these myths are re-interpreted according to current needs due to the selection process that memory undergoes (cf. Erll 2005; Rigney 2005).

Therefore, since the memory of past events and people – be they myths, legends, or memories of things in closer temporal proximity – varies depending on the storyteller's perspective and place in time, memory is open to change. Due to the convergence of writing traditions from several cultures that results in a hybrid genre with heretofore unseen approaches to topics, and the continued use of certain traditional elements such as the spiral structure and the variations to existing stories, the novels in question contain reworked myths to suit the context and time in which the novels were written. Evidently, the use of myths is still important in the present day given their continued application in indigenous fiction. Similarly, Leeming insists that "we need myths – those of our individual and cultural past and origins – and a mythical consciousness in the present time, to show us who we are, self-knowledge and identity having to do with intangibles that transcend mere name, parentage and geographical location" (Leeming 2002: 10).

The mythical consciousness that is simulated by Ihimaera's and Grace's novels then serves an important purpose in the construction of identity. Ironically, while Leeming proposes that "name, parentage and geographical location" are transcended by this mythical consciousness, the study has proved that these are some of the most important aspects of identity that the Maori novel attempts to preserve. These elements are crucial due to the significance of maintaining an unbroken line since the first ancestors, demonstrated by the many references to the First Parents throughout the three phases. The novels repeatedly emphasise the significance of lineage and the place of origin, which is then strengthened by myths that address these connections between individual, ancestor and land.

These connections would have remained unnoticed without the study of myth in Maori novels, which is part of Panny's complaint. Furthermore, she notes several aspects that need to be investigated, such as "mythology and its influence on Maori thought; symbolism derived from ancient oral traditions; spiritual and metaphysical beliefs; protocols, cultural values, obligations; and history as perceived by Māori, predating and following colonisation" (Panny 2006). This study is a contribution to the illumination of these elements that pervade Maori writing in English by examining how myths, features of oral storytelling, and *tikanga* influence the texts.

It is by no means an exhaustive analysis and has focused mainly on their influence in selected novels over three decades. Their discussion has further revealed that hybridity, continuity and variation as contributing factors in the development and application of myths reflect how the past and one's relationship to it are viewed at a given time. Likewise, they mirror Maori identity and its gradual development. Thus we have established that the use of myths differs in the three distinguished phases of the novel. What is more, how extensively and in which way myths are used in the texts goes hand in hand with changes in the cast of characters, location, and the depicted relationship with *Pakeha*. As a means of clarification, Table 1 summarises the general development detected during each phase.

As illustrated by Table 1, the continual incorporation of myths through all three phases illustrates the interaction of past, present and future as believed in Maori culture. Even during the third phase, in which the old mythology makes way for a new kind, the myths of the previous phases still have their place. At this point, however, the old mythology is on the verge of being replaced by the new, which encourages a re-evaluation and re-interpretation of the myths that identify the culture from a modern-day point of view. Such a development also coincides with Rigney's (2005) and Erll's (2005) findings relating to the re-interpretation of memory from the individual's or group's current perspective, which is considered a natural and inevitable progression.

As a consequence of the continual re-interpretation of myth and memory, a changing Maori identity is inevitable in the process. Since they inform identity, any changes in the interpretation of myths and legends ultimately lead to an altered or enhanced self-image. Therefore, myth and memory are essential elements of Maori cultural identity. As it finds expression in the novel, the texts portray particular images of the Maori, which change from one phase to another. The first phase therefore consists of novels expressing the need for the native culture to be seen instead of ignored. The second progresses to a determined coming-forward that is perpetuated further in the third. It is the necessary selection of particular myths and memories that helps encourage this development and turns the novel into a medium of collective and cultural memory and identity construction.

Table 1: Diachronic Developments in the Maori Novel

Phase	Cast of characters	Location	Relation to *Pakeha*	Use of myths
First	Maori, with a small cast of marginal *Pakeha* characters	Maori community, usually a temporary move to the *Pakeha*-dominated city	Unsatisfactory; potentially physically and mentally destabilising	Extensive; characters and readers are introduced to concepts of *maoritanga*
Second	Maori, with occasional rounded *Pakeha* characters	Maori community on ancestral land; life in the city depicted as unsuccessful or harmful	Mostly strained and confrontational; focus on struggle for independence from *Pakeha* authority	Extensive; preference for myths that emphasise Maori strength and determination
Third	Mainly Maori, with complex *Pakeha* characters; emergence of new tribe	Ancestral land and the city; settings may extend beyond Aotearoa New Zealand	Sometimes minimal, mostly open, tolerant and inclusive; promoting and practising multicultural relations with firm grounding in primary culture; awareness of common origins in a nation of immigrants	Illustration of Maori destiny; creation of new mythology based on old mythology and new demands

Thus, the first-phase novels contain myths that go back to Creation, the gods and the first Maori in order to create a bond between indigenous readers and their heritage. The second step, realised in the second phase, is a selection of motivating and enabling tales which may result in the rewriting of history as in *The Matriarch*. This new historiography is yet another sign of Maori empowerment and their striving for independence from standard notions of history and progress. Consequently, the myths and memories applied in such a novel contribute to the re-evaluation of approved concepts that are not in line with traditional indigenous beliefs.

Therefore, due to their inclusion of essential myths and the importance of *tikanga*, Maori novels are literary representations of cultural memory and identity. What is significant in their analysis is that myth and the observation of *tikanga* have maintained their importance throughout all three phases. Though they vary depending on the novel's topics, they always remain as central characterising features of the narrative. While forgetting and remembering may be natural developments and the selectivity of remembrance further determines which myths are told in the novels, they never lose their significance. On the contrary, the re-interpretation that arises from this selectivity paves the way for the third phase's ongoing creation of a new mythology. As a result, the novel has shifted from being part of a literature of survival (Heim 1998) to guiding novels of empowerment.

4.2 From a Literature of Survival to Novels of Empowerment and Pioneering

Considering the development of the Maori novel since 1973, it is evident that it goes beyond being merely part of a literature of survival. In fact, the novels of the third phase in particular are more often than not characterised by a set of confident, determined protagonists who are empowered by their culture and the desire to move forward and contribute to New Zealand. With their focus on politics and resistance, the second-phase novels already lead the way towards empowerment, but theirs is an approach that leaves the *Pakeha* an outsider since they deal with matters of Maori survival. Therefore, novels of the third phase like *The Uncle's Story* and *The Rope of Man* are pioneers in leading towards an inclusive, tolerant and multicultural vision of Aotearoa New Zealand. *Cousins*, too, delineates characters who gradually grow into confident women and find their places in the traditional life of their Maori community and in the *Pakeha* world. Grace's protagonists, nonetheless, are still at the beginning of the process while Ihimaera's have easily straddled both cultures and are at home in this in-between space.

What is more, *The Uncle's Story* and *The Rope of Man* encourage the creation of a new mythology that has been suggested by Leeming (2003) in a more general context. In the matter of the Maori novel, the need for a new mythology is most evident in the characters' request for a new tribe. It is at this point that the Maori novel enters new ground, portraying pioneers who take the step towards something entirely new. Moving into this unexplored direction is only possible in Maori literature because it is, as Somerville (cf. 2007: 87) insists, an established literature. The novel has examined the Maori perspective in detail and addressed a number of important issues for more than thirty years. Maori literature, as a result, is nothing new. On the contrary, Ihimaera, Grace, and others have helped establish indigenous literature as a significant contribution to New Zealand literature on the whole, gaining international acclaim. Therefore, being part of an established literature, the Maori novel is in a position to introduce innovation. This development coincides with the fictional characters coming to realise that myths of old, though fundamental and important, do not wholly apply to the new situation with which Maori are faced today. Hence new stories that adequately reflect the new generation must be told. Eventually, these stories will turn into new myths and offer a re-interpretation of the old.

Most importantly, the new tribe stands for the possibility to live in an in-between space where, as Bhabha's concept of the third space proposes, something new will come into being. Those characters who straddle Maori and *Pakeha* culture are not a simple synthesis of the two; instead, they bring together aspects of each culture that are relevant to their lives, evolving into the new tribe with new views. In *Myth: A Biography of Belief*, Leeming elaborates on the changes the new mythology will bring:

> [T]his emerging narrative of interconnectedness as opposed to dominance and exclusivity [...] takes hold, people will necessarily look at politics, nationalism, gender roles, economics, race, moral values, art, education, religion – at everything – in a new way. In light of this new myth, the old religious systems that once stressed the importance of revelation for their own communities may well take on a more planetary, ecological, nurturing, more feminine dimension. (Leeming 2003: 25)

The old religious systems Leeming mentions may well be regarded as *Pakeha* standards in general in the New Zealand context. As the analysis of the third-phase novels has shown, the changes Leeming speaks of are already taking place: both writers counter racial stereotypes as they did before, and their characters take an active part in politics, which eventually changes views of New Zealand as a nation. Gender roles change, as do opinions on sexuality. *Cousins* in particular promotes the nurturing, feminine element in Maori culture while expanding it to include women as active, politically sensitive leaders. Especially *The Uncle's Story* and *The Rope of Man* emphasise the global approach Leeming notes above, which expands the setting beyond local borders and opens up the narrative for it to become an example of multicultural relations.

In effect, the new tribe reflects the "real power" (Royal 2007: 7) that exists within Maori to be as involved in the world as *Pakeha*. The third-phase novel has therefore changed its focus from the education of Maori and *Pakeha* to a pioneering fiction that demonstrates what Maori are capable of today. At the same time, the term *literature of survival* is no longer entirely applicable since survival is not the only important point made in the latest novels. Due to the focus on the relationships between cultures, another central concern besides upholding Maori customs and beliefs is to find ways in which different cultures can co-exist by sharing an awareness of their similarities. The novels of the second phase are part of the literature of survival since they are novels of resistance, and *Cousins*, despite being part of the third phase, continues in this tradition. Still, it is also an empowering novel with characters who realise their strengths and put them to use in a variety of ways. As opposed to Ihimaera's novels,

Grace's continue to concentrate on a distinctly Maori life mainly within the indigenous community.

Evidently, the authors' views of Maori identity differ in the third phase. Grace prefers a cultural identity that springs from tradition with an eye on the past rather than the future in spite of aiming towards the latter. Ihimaera, in comparison, assumes his characters to be firmly grounded in their cultural heritage already so that they can now move forward and approach the future with their knowledge. He therefore trusts that the learning phase with regard to *maoritanga* has been completed so that the world outside the safety of one's own culture is the new challenge.

The literary search for Maori identity in novels has therefore developed from (re)learning basic *tikanga* perpetuated by the myths incorporated in the narratives to the application of Maori knowledge, which finally results in the re-interpretation of old myths and the demand for new ones that are appropriate in the present. In short, the use of carefully selected myths in the Maori novel may be summarised in Table 2.

Table 2: The Diachronic Selectivity of Myths

Phase	Types of myth	Function in Maori novels
First	Basic myths, especially ones explaining Maori origins: First Parents, Great Fleet, Maui myth cycle, etc.	General: Lessons in *maoritanga*, observation of *tikanga* to strengthen Maori identity; *Pakeha* readers are introduced to native concepts; representing neglected indigenous perspectives
Second	Myths and legends of strong, gifted ancestors and warriors: Paikea, Te Kooti, Wi Pere, etc.	Political: challenging Western beliefs, supporting Maori resistance and empowerment; promotion of political agenda; novel as a weapon; history vs History
Third	Re-interpretations of established myths; emergence of new myths and archetypes	Multicultural: introducing global view; Maori as confident people of the world; presenting a variety of choices for Maori identity

Table 2 demonstrates which myths have been selected to complement the authors' chosen topics. More importantly, it is easy to follow the development from a choice of myths that allow a general view of Maori culture to those which become more and more specific with time. Such a progression indicates that the general introduction to Maori culture reached its peak in the 1970s, but was no longer necessary in the second phase. Instead, the following phases were able to be selective in their choice of myths that would support particular, mainly political, topics.

Furthermore, the evident development of functions displayed by the novels from the 1970s onward describes the change of Maori identity. The literary quest for identity offers a variety of solutions that ranges from a traditional, community-centred one that is strictly distinguished from *Pakeha* identity in the first phase to a greater diversity that includes a number of cultural influences in the third. The early novels are marked by the need for distinction and the creation of a clearly Maori self-image. Later, the second phase novels reinforce the difference created by this distinction to enable resisting the *Pakeha*. Eventually, the third-phase novels on the one hand, as Grace's work illustrates, remains Maori-centred while offering a variety of possible indigenous identities as seeker, mother or leader. On the other, Ihimaera's novels demonstrate an opening up of the concept of cultural identity by including the influence of other cultures on Maori identity and *vice versa*. Thus, the search for Maori identity – at least in Ihimaera's work – has evolved to a search for a New Zealand identity on the whole, which could be the final step in a long decolonisation process. Thus, as Phillips (2003) and Royal (2007) request, there is a move away from a rigid self-image to an open, varied cultural identity that adequately represents the nation's diversity and is in favour of multicultural influences.

The latest approach, therefore, is aimed at a peaceful co-existence marked by mutual influence and acceptance without the loss of one's heritage. The first two phases of the Maori novel have contributed to the distinction of indigenous identity, enabling its strengthening. In the following phase, the focus on unification instead of separation is made possible with the help of a secure Maori cultural identity as developed with the help of aspects of cultural memory in novels since the 1970s. Finally, the old and new myths that Ihimaera and Grace have brought back into memory or created so that they may become part of memory in the long run illuminate a number of paths that the search for identity follows in fiction and might, ideally, follow in reality as well. The nature of New Zealand's diversity necessitates a variety of approaches as demonstrated by writers from an indigenous point of view. Whichever future course the Maori novel may take, it is likely to maintain its myths, old and new, for a long time to come and be – as it has always been – a significant part of New Zealand literature.

Ka huri.

Bibliography

Primary Texts

Duff, Alan. 1990. *Once Were Warriors*. Auckland: Tandem Press.

Grace, Patricia. 1986 [Longman Paul, 1978]. *Mutuwhenua: The Moon Sleeps*. Auckland: Penguin.

——1986. *Potiki*. Auckland: Penguin.

——1988. *Electric City and Other Stories*. Auckland: Penguin.

——1992. [Auckland: Penguin, 1992] *Cousins*. Honolulu: University of Hawai'i Press.

——1994. *The Sky People*. Auckland: Penguin.

——1998. *Baby No-Eyes*. Auckland: Penguin.

Hulme, Keri. 1986 [Spiral Collectives, 1983]. *the bone people*. London: Picador.

Ihimaera, Witi. 1973. *Tangi*. Auckland: Heinemann.

——1974. *Whanau*. Auckland: Heinemann.

——1977. *The New Net Goes Fishing*. London: Heinemann.

——1986. *The Matriarch*. Auckland: Heinemann.

——1992–1996. *Te Ao Mārama*. Auckland: Reed.

——1997. *The Dream Swimmer*. Auckland: Penguin.

——2003 [Auckland: Reed, 1987]. *The Whale Rider*. New York, Toronto, London: Harcourt.

——2004. *Whanau II*. Auckland: Reed.

——2005. *The Rope of Man*. Auckland: Reed.

——2005 [Auckland: Penguin, 2000]. *The Uncle's Story*. London: Robson Books.

King, Thomas. 1994 [1993]. *Green Grass, Running Water*. New York: Bantam.

Tuwhare, Hone. 1964. *No Ordinary Sun*. Auckland: Blackwood and Janet Paul.

Secondary Texts

Achebe, Chinua. 1975a. "The African Writer and the English Language." *Morning Yet on Creation Day: Essays.* London, Nairobi: Heinemann. 55–62.
——1975b. "Colonialist Criticism." *Morning Yet on Creation Day: Essays.* London, Nairobi: Heinemann. 3–18.
——1975c. "The Novelist as Teacher." *Morning Yet on Creation Day: Essays.* London, Nairobi: Heinemann. 42–5.
—— 1975d. "Where Angels Fear to Tread." *Morning Yet on Creation Day: Essays.* London, Nairobi: Heinemann. 46–8.
Achilles, Jochen; Birkle, Carmen (eds.). 1998. *(Trans)Formations of Cultural Identity in the English-Speaking World.* Heidelberg: Winter.
Alley, Elizabeth (ed.) 1992a. *In the Same Room. Conversations With New Zealand Writers.* Auckland: Auckland University Press.
——1992b. "Janet Frame/Interviewed by Elizabeth Alley." In: Alley, Elizabeth (ed.), *In the Same Room. Conversations With New Zealand Writers.* Auckland: Auckland University Press. 39–54.
——1992c. "Keri Hulme/Interviewed by Elizabeth Alley." In: Alley, Elizabeth (ed.), *In the Same Room. Conversations With New Zealand Writers.* Auckland: Auckland University Press. 140–56.
Angehrn, Emil. 1985. *Geschichte und Identität.* Berlin, New York: de Gruyter.
Appiah, K. Anthony. 1994. "Identity, Authenticity and Survival: Multicultural Societies and Social Reproduction." In: Taylor, Charles (ed.), *Multiculturalism and the Politics of Recognition.* Princeton, NJ: Princeton University Press. 149–65.
Ashcroft, Bill; Griffiths, Gareth; Tiffin, Helen (eds.). 1989. *The Empire Writes Back. Theory and Practice in Post-Colonial Literatures. (New Accents)* London: Routledge.
——1995. *The Post-Colonial Studies Reader.* London, New York: Routledge.
——1998. *Key Concepts in Post-Colonial Studies.* London, New York: Routledge.
——2002. *Post-colonial Studies: The Key Concepts.* Repr. London, New York: Routledge.
Assmann, Aleida. 1995. "Was sind kulturelle Texte?" In: Poltermann, Andreas (ed.), *Literaturkanon – Medienereignis – kultureller Text. Formen kultureller Kommunikation und Übersetzung.* Berlin: Erich Schmidt. 232–44.
—— 2001. "Three Stabilizers of Memory: Affect – Symbol – Trauma." In: Hebel, Udo (ed.), *Sites of Memory in American Literatures and Cultures.* Heidelberg: Winter. 15–30.

Assmann, Jan. 1988. "Kollektives Gedächtnis und kulturelle Identität." In: Assmann, Jan; Hölscher, Tonio (eds.), *Kultur und Gedächtnis*. Frankfurt a.M.: Suhrkamp. 9–19.

—— 1992. *Das kulturelle Gedächtnis. Schrift, Erinnerung und politische Identität in frühen Hochkulturen*. München: Beck.

—— and Hölscher, Tonio (eds.). 1988. *Kultur und Gedächtnis*. Frankfurt a.M.: Suhrkamp.

Bachmann-Medick, Doris. 1996. "Multikultur oder kulturelle Differenz? Neue Konzepte von Weltliteratur und Übersetzung in postkolonialer Perspektive." Bachmann-Medick, Doris (ed.), *Kultur als Text. Die anthropologische Wende in der Literaturwissenschaft*. Frankfurt a.M.: Fischer. 262–96.

Bakhtin, M. M. 1981. *The Dialogic Imagination: Four Essays*. Trans. Caryl Emerson and Michael Holquist. Austin, TX: University of Texas Press.

Bal, Mieke; Crewer, Jonathan; Spitzer, Leo (eds.). 1999. *Acts of Memory. Cultural Recall in the Present*. Hannover, London: University Press of New England.

Ballara, Angela. 1993. "Pakeha Uses of Takitimutanga: Who Owns Tribal Tradition?" *Stout Centre Review* 3(2): 17–21.

Bargh, Maria (ed.). 2007. *Resistance: An Indigenous Response to Neoliberalism*. Wellington: Huia Publishers.

Barnes, J. A. "Postscript. Structural Amnesia." 1990. In: Barnes, J. A. *Models and Interpretations: Selected Essays*. Cambridge: Cambridge University Press. 52–3.

Barthes, Roland. 1964 [1956]. *Mythen des Alltags*. Frankfurt a.M.: Suhrkamp.

—— 1973 [1957; trans. Anette Lavers, 1972]. *Mythologies*. London: Granada.

Battista, Jon. 2006. "Engaging in Metaphors: A Review of Witi Ihimaera's *the rope of man*. Reed: Auckland, 2005, 325pp. ISBN 9–78079000–894–3." *Graduate Journal of Asia-Pacific Studies* 4(1): 117–21.

Baxter, James K. 1955. *The Fire and the Anvil: Notes on Modern Poetry*. Wellington: New Zealand University Press. 63–4.

Beaugrande, Robert-Alain de, and Wolfgang Dressler. 1981. *Introduction to Text Linguistics*. London, New York: Longman.

Beckmann, Susan. 1981. "Language as Cultural Identity in Achebe, Ihimaera, Laurence and Atwood." *World Literature Written in English* 20(1): 117–34.

Belich, James. 1996. *Making Peoples: A History of the New Zealanders, from Polynesian Settlement to the End of the Nineteenth Century*. Auckland: Penguin.

—— 1997. "Myth, Race and Identity in New Zealand." *The New Zealand Journal of History* 31(1): 9–22.

—— 2007. "Globalization and the Nation." Keynote address to the Concepts of the Nation symposium, September 26, 2007. Wellington.

Berthoff, Warner. 1970. "Fiction, History, Myth: Notes Towards the Discrimination of Narrative Forms." In: Bloomfield, Morton W. (ed.), *The Interpretation of Narrative Theory and Practice.* Cambridge, MA: Harvard University Press. 263–87.

Bhabha, Homi, K. 1984. "Of Mimicry and Man: The Ambivalence of Colonial Discourse." *October* 28: 125–33.

—— 1985. "Signs Taken for Wonders: Questions of Ambivalence and Authority under a Tree Outside Delhi, May 1817." In: Barker, Francis et al. (eds.), *Europe and Its Others*, vol. I. Colchester: University of Essex, 1985. 89–106. Reprint: Critical Enquiry. 12:1: 144–65.

—— 1990. "The Third Space: Interview With Homi Bhabha." In: Rutherford, Jonathan (ed.), *Identity: Community, Culture, Difference.* London: Lawrence & Wishart: 207–21.

—— 1994. *The Location of Culture.* London: Routledge.

Bidney, David. 1966. "Myth, Symbolism and Truth." In: Vickery, John B. (ed.), *Myth and Literature: Contemporary Theory and Practice.* Lincoln, NE: University of Nebraska Press: 3–13.

Biggs, Bruce. 1960. *Maori Marriage: An Essay in Reconstruction.* Wellington, Sydney: Reed.

Binney, Judith. 1987. "Maori Oral Narratives, Pakeha Written Texts." *New Zealand Journal of History* 21(1): 16–28.

Braunias, Steve. (2004). "The Sensualist." In: *The Listener* (Online), No. 3364. (30 Oct.–5 Nov.).

Brenner, Peter. 1999. 1989. "Interkulturelle Hermeneutik. Probleme einer Theorie kulturellen Verstehens." In: Zimmer, Peter (ed.), *Interkulturelle Germanistik: Dialog der Kulturen auf Deutsch.* Frankfurt a.M.: Peter Lang. 35–55.

—— *Kulturanthropologie und Kulturhermeneutik: Grundlagen interkulturellen Verstehens* (Paderborner Universitätsreden 69). Paderborn: Universität Gesamthochschule Paderborn.

Brown, Ruth. 1989. "Maori Spirituality As Pakeha Construct." *Meanjin* 48(2): 252–8.

Bruner, Jerome. 1991. "The Narrative Construction of Reality." In: *Critical Enquiry* 18: 1–21.

Brydon, Diana and Helen Tiffin. 1993. *Decolonising Fictions.* Sydney, Mundelstrup: Dangaroo.

Buckman, Jacqueline. 1996. "Challenging the Conventions of the Künstlerroman: Keri Hulme's *The Bone People.*" *World Literature Written In English* 35(2): 49–63.

Calleja, Paloma Fresno. 2003. "An Interview With Patricia Grace." *Atlantis* 25(1) (June): 109–20.

Calvert, Julia. 2006. "Witi Ihimaera's Use of Nineteenth Century Maori Prophets' Oral Narratives in *The Matriarch and The Dream Swimmer.*" *Kōtare* 6. Wellington: Victoria University of Wellington.
<http://www.nzetc.org/tm/scholarly/tei-Whi06Kota-t1-g1-t2.html#reference-to-_ftn3> accessed June 7, 2010.

Carbaugh, Donal. 2001. "'The people will come to you': Blackfeet Narrative as a Resource for Contemporary Living." In: Brockmeier, Jens; Carbaugh, Donal (eds.), *Narrative and Identity.* (SiN 1). Amsterdam/Philadelphia: John Benjamins Publishing Company. 103–28.

Cassirer, Ernst. 1990 [1944]. *Versuch über den Menschen: Einführung in eine Philosophie der Kultur.* 2nd ed. Frankfurt a.M.: Fischer.

Chapman, Robert. 1973. "Fiction and the Social Pattern: Some Implications of Recent N.Z. Writing." In: Curnow, Wystan (ed.), *Essays on New Zealand Literature.* Auckland: Heinemann. 71–98.

Colavincenzo, Marc. 2003. *"Trading Magic for Fact," Fact for Magic: Myth and Mythologizing in Postmodern Canadian Historical Fiction.* Cross/Cultures 67. Amsterdam/New York: Rodopi.

Corballis, Richard; Garrett, Simon. 1984. *Introducing Witi Ihimaera. (Introducing New Zealand Writers.)* Auckland: Longman.

Coupe, Laurence. 1997. *Myth. (The New Critical Idiom.)* London, New York: Routledge.

Cupitt, Don. 1982. *The World to Come.* London: SCM Press.

Dale, Judith. 1985. *"the bone people*: (Not) Having It Both Ways." *Landfall* 39: 413–28.

—— and Janet Wilson. 1998. "Intertextual Strategies: Reinventing the Myths of Aotearoa in Contemporary New Zealand Fiction." In: Kloss, Wolfgang (ed.), *Across the Lines: Intertextuality and Transcultural Communication in the New Literatures in English.* Atlanta, GA: Rodopi. 271–90.

Davies, Sioned (trans.). 2007. *The Mabinogion.* Oxford: Oxford University Press.

Davis, Denise; Solomon, Māui. 2006. "Moriori." *Te Ara – the Encyclopedia of New Zealand.* Updated December 21, 2006.
<http://www.TeAra.govt.nz/NewZealanders/MaoriNewZealanders/Moriori/en> accessed June 7, 2010.

Day, Paul. 2006. "Mulgan, John Alan Edward 1911 – 1945." *Dictionary of New Zealand Biography.* Updated April 7, 2006.
<http://www.dnzb.govt.nz> accessed June 7, 2010.

Dever, Maryanne. 1989. "Violence as *Lingua Franca*: Keri Hulme's *The Bone People.*" *World Literature Written In English* 29(2) (Autumn): 23–35.

Dhawan. R. K. 1993. "New Zealand Literature Today." In: Dhawan. R.K.; Tonetto, William (eds.), *New Zealand Literature Today*. New Delhi. 12–22.

—— Tonetto, William (eds.). 1993. *New Zealand Literature Today*. New Delhi.

Dickson, E. Jane. 2005. "In the Deep End." (March 19). *Times Online*.
<http://entertainment.timesonline.co.uk/tol/arts_and_entertainment/books/article430721.ece> accessed June 7, 2010.

During, Simon. 1985. "Postmodernism or Postcolonialism?" *Landfall* 34: 373–4.

Erll, Astrid. 2005. *Kollektives Gedächtnis und Erinnerungskulturen. Eine Einführung.* Stuttgart, Weimar: J. B. Metzler.

—— Gymnich, Marion; Nünning, Ansgar (eds.). 2003. *Literatur, Erinnerung, Identität. Theoriekonzeptionen und Fallstudien.* (ELCH) Trier: Wissenschaftlicher Verlag Trier.

Evans, Patrick. 1990. *The Penguin History of New Zealand Literature.* Auckland: Penguin Books (New Zealand) Ltd.

Farrell, Fiona. 1995. "Mixed Marriage." In: Williams, Mark (ed.), *The Source of the Song. New Zealand Writers On Catholicism.* Wellington: Victoria University Press. 40–5.

Feder, Lillian. 1980. "Myth, Poetry, and Critical Theory." In: Strelka, Joseph P. (ed.), *Literary Criticism and Myth. (Yearbook of Comparative Criticism* IX.) University Park and London: Pennsylvania State University Press. 51–71.

Fee, Margery. 1989. "Why C. K. Stead Didn't Like *the bone people*: Who Can Write as Other?" In: Robinson, James (ed.), *Imaginary Journal.*
<http://journal.imaginary.com.au/anzsc/1/fee> accessed March 3, 2008.
[Orig.: *Australian and New Zealand Studies in Canada* Number 1 (Spring): 11–32.]

Finnegan, Ruth. 1976. *Oral Literature in Africa.* London, Nairobi: Oxford University Press.

Fludernik, Monika (ed.). 2003. "Introduction: The Diasporic Imaginary. Postcolonial Reconfigurations in the Context of Multiculturalism." In: Fludernik, Monika (ed.), *Diaspora and Multiculturalism: Common Traditions and New Developments.* Collier, Gordon; Maes-Jelinek, Hena; Davis, Geoffrey (eds.). *Cross/Cultures* 66. Rodopi: Amsterdam, New York. xi–xxxviii.

Fox, Stephen D. 2003. "Keri Hulme's The Bone People: The Problem of Beneficial Child Abuse." *The Journal of Evolutionary Psychology* 24.

Frye, Northrop. 1963. *Fables of Identity: Studies In Poetic Mythology.* New York, Burlingame: Harcourt, Brace & World.

Gaffney, Carmel. 1986. "Making the Net Whole: Design in Keri Hulme's *The Bone People*." *Southerly* 46(3) (September): 293–302.

Goldie, Terry. 1988. "Getting it Right: Images of Indigenous Peoples in Canadian Fiction in the Eighties." *English Studies in Canada* 14: 64–81.

—— 1989. "The Representation of the Indigene." *Fear and Temptation: The Image of the Indigene in Canadian, Australian and New Zealand Literatures.* Kingston: McGill-Queens University Press. In: Ashcroft, Bill; Griffiths, Gareth; Tiffin, Helen (eds.). 1995. *The Post-Colonial Studies Reader.* London, New York: Routledge. 232–6.

Gordon, Raymond G., Jr. (ed.). 2005. *Ethnologue: Languages of the World.* 15th ed. Dallas, TX: SIL International. <http://www.ethnologue.com/> accessed March 3, 2008.

Gore, James M. 2003. "Representations of Non-Indigenous History and Identity in the National Museum of Australia and Museum of New Zealand Te Papa Tongarewa." *The Electronic Journal of Australian and New Zealand History and H-Net.* <http://www.jcu.edu.au/aff/history/articles/gore.htm> accessed June 7, 2010.

Greenblatt, Stephen. 1988. *Shakespearean Negotiations: The Circulation of Social Energy in Renaissance England.* Berkeley: University of California Press.

Grey, George. 1971. *Ngā Mahi ā Ngā Tūpuna.* 4th ed. H. W. Williams (ed.). Wellington: Reed.

Griffiths, Gareth. 1994. "The Myth of Authenticity: Representation, Discourse and Social Practice." In: Tiffin, Chris; Lawson, Alan (eds.), *De-Scribing Empire: Postcolonialism and Textuality.* London: Routledge. 70–85.

Halbwachs, Maurice. 1985 [1925]. *Das Gedächtnis und seine sozialen Bedingungen.* Frankfurt a.M.: Suhrkamp. [Orig.: Les cardres sociaux de la mémoire. Paris: Alcan.]

—— 1991 [1950]. *Das kollektive Gedächtnis.* Frankfurt a.M.: Fischer. [Orig.: La mémoire collective. Paris: Presses universitaires de France.]

Hall, Stuart. 1990. "Cultural Identity and Diaspora." In: Rutherford, Jonathan (ed.), *Identity: Community, Culture, Difference.* London: Lawrence & Wishart: 222–37.

Hanson, Allan. 1989. "The Making of the Maori: Culture Invention and Its Logic." *American Anthropologist.* New Series 91(4) (Dec.). 890–902.

Harrax, S. C.; Amrithanayagam, G. (eds.). *Only Connect: Literary Perspectives East and West.* Adelaide: Centre for Research in the New Literatures in English; Honolulu: East–West Center, 1981.

Haverkamp, Anselm. 1991. "Auswendigkeit. Das Gedächtnis der Rhetorik". In: Haverkamp, Anselm; Lachmann, Renate (eds.), *Gedächtniskunst: Raum – Bild – Schrift. Studien zur Mnemotechnik.* Frankfurt a.M.: Suhrkamp. 25–52.

Hawken, Dinah. 1995. "Breaking the Argument Down: A Conversation With Dinah Hawken." In: Williams, Mark (ed.), *The Source of the Song. New Zealand Writers On Catholicism.* Wellington: Victoria University Press. 78–90.

Heim, Otto. 1998. *Writing Along Broken Lines: Violence and Ethnicity in Contemporary Maori Fiction.* Auckland: Auckland University Press.

Henke, Suzette. 1993. "Keri Hulme's *The Bone People* and *Te Kaihau*: Postmodern Heteroglossia and Pre-textual Play." In: Dhawan, R. K.; Tonetto, William (eds.), New Zealand Literature Today. New Delhi. 135–49.

Hereniko, V. 1993. "An Interview With Albert Wendt." *Manoa* 5(1): 51–9.

Howe, K. R. 2006. "Ideas of Māori origins." *Te Ara – the Encyclopedia of New Zealand,* updated September 26, 2006.
<http://www.TeAra.govt.nz/NewZealanders/MaoriNewZealanders/IdeasOf-MaoriOrigins/en> accessed March 3, 2008.

Huf, Linda. 1983. *A Portrait of the Artist as a Young Woman.* New York: Ungar Publishing Co.

Huggan, Graham. 1989. "Opting Out of the (Critical) Common Market: Creolization and the Post-Colonial Text." *Kunapipi* 11(1): 27–40.

Hulme, Keri. 1981. "Maori: An Introduction to Bicultural Poetry in New Zealand." In: Harrax; Amrithanayagam (eds.), *Only Connect.* Adelaide, South Australia. 299.

——1984. "Myth, Omen, Ghost and Dream." In: Sharad, P. (ed.), *Poetry of the Pacific Region.* Adelaide. 32.

Hutcheon, Linda. 1988a. *The Canadian Postmodern: A Study of Contemporary English-Canadian Fiction.* Toronto: Oxford University Press.

——1988b. *A Poetics of Postmodernism: History, Theory, Fiction.* London and New York: Routledge.

Ihimaera, Witi. 1975. "Why I Write." *World Literature Written in English* 14: 116–19.

——1998a. "And Then There's Us: A Maori Perspective." *Poetica* 50: 195–207.

——1998b. *LIANZA Conference Proceedings.*
<www.lianza.org.nz/conference99/ihimaera.htm> accessed June 1, 2008.

——November 2005. "Witi Ihimaera's New Zealand Dreams." *Fulbright New Zealand.*
<www.fulbright.org.nz/news/releases/051102-nzdreams.html> accessed June 7, 2010.

——June 2006. "New Zealand Literature: Writing From the Edge of the Universe."
<http://home.e07.itscom.net/mfat/speeches/IhimaeraSpeechE170606.pdf, 1–6> accessed June 7, 2010.

——and Don S. Long (eds.). 1982. *Into the World of Light: An Anthology of Maori Writing.* Auckland: Heinemann.

Irwin, Geoff; Walrond, Carl. 2006. "When was New Zealand first settled?" *Te Ara – the Encyclopedia of New Zealand*, updated September 26, 2006. <www.TeAra.govt. nz/NewZealanders/MaoriNewZealanders/WhenWasNewZealandFirstSettled/ en> accessed March 10, 2008.

Iser, Wolfgang. 1991. *Das Fiktive und das Imaginäre: Perspektiven literarischer Anthropologie.* Frankfurt/Main: Suhrkamp.

Isernhagen, Hartwig. 1984. "Witi Ihimaera's Fiction: From Indigenous Myth to Late Modernist City Myth?" *World Literature Written In English* 24(1): 189–200.

Jackson, MacDonald P. 1992. "Kendrick Smithyman/Interviewed by MacDonald P. Jackson." In: Alley, Elizabeth (ed.), *In the Same Room. Conversations With New Zealand Writers.* Auckland: Auckland University Press. 121–39.

Johnston, Andrew. 1989. "Matriarch Passages Copied – Historian." *Dominion Sunday Times*, November 26. 1.

——1994. "Keri Hulme: Of Death and Fishing." *Evening Post.* November 5 (Wellington, New Zealand). <http://andrewjohnston.org/hulme.htm> accessed June 7, 2010.

——1995. "Catholic With a Small c." In: Williams, Mark (ed.), *The Source of the Song. New Zealand Writers On Catholicism.* Wellington: Victoria University Press. 147–54.

Jones, Lawrence. 1987. *Barbed Wire & Mirrors. Essays on New Zealand Prose.* Dunedin: University of Otago Press.

Jussawalla, Feroza. 1992. *Interviews with Writers of the Post-colonial World.* Conducted and edited by Feroza Jussawalla and Reed Way Dazenbrock. Jackson, MI: University of Mississippi Press.

Ka'ai, Tania M. 2005. "*Te Kauae Mārō o Muri-ranga-whenua* (The Jawbone of Muri-ranga-whenua): Globalising Local Indigenous Culture – Māori Leadership, Gender and Cultural Knowledge Transmission as Represented in the Film Whale Rider." *Portal Journal of Multidisciplinary International Studies* 2(2) (July): 1–15.

——and Reilly, M. P. J. 2003. "*Rangatiratanga*: Traditional and Contemporary Leadership." In: T. M. Ka'ai, J. C. Moorfield, M. P. J. Reilly and S. Mosley (eds.), *Ki Te Whaiao: Introduction to Māori Society.* Auckland: Pearson Education. 91–102.

Kachru, Braj B. 1995. "The Alchemy of English." In: Ashcroft, Bill; Griffiths, Gareth; Tiffin, Helen (eds.), *The Post-Colonial Studies Reader.* London, New York: Routledge. 291–5.

Kahukiwa, Robyn; Grace, Patricia. 1984. *Wahine Toa: Women of Maori Myth.* Auckland: Viking.

Katene, Paul. 1974. *"Tangi."* Te Ao Hou 75 (March). 60.

King, Michael. 1985. *Being Pakeha: An Encounter with New Zealand and the Maori Resistance.* Auckland: Hodder & Stoughton.

Kluckhohn, Clyde. 1966. "Myths and Rituals. A General Theory." In: Vickery, John B., ed. *Myth and Literature: Contemporary Theory and Practice.* Lincoln, NE: University of Nebraska Press: 33–44.

Kohere, Reweti T. 1951. *The Autobiography of a Maori.* Wellington: Reed.

Kolig, Erich. 2003 [1981]. *The Noonkanbah Story: Profile of an Aboriginal Community. (Te Whenua. Pacific People, Land and Literature)* Dunedin: University of Otago Press.

Korte, Barbara; Müller, Klaus Peter (eds.). 1998. "Unity in Diversity Revisited: Complex Paradoxes Beyond Post-/Modernism." *Unity and Diversity Revisited? British Literature and Culture in the 1990s.* Tübingen: Narr. 9–33.

Kramer, Jürgen. 1998. "A Note on 'Third Terms'." In: Korte; Müller (eds.). "Unity in Diversity Revisited: Complex Paradoxes Beyond Post-/Modernism." *Unity and Diversity Revisited? British Literature and Culture in the 1990s.* Tübingen: Narr. 263–4.

Kristeva, Julia. 1980. *Desire in Language: A Semiotic Approach to Literature and Art.* New York: Columbia University Press.

Lacan, J. 1968. *The Language of the Self: The Function of Language in Psychoanalysis.* Trans. with notes and commentary by Anthony Wilden. Baltimore, MD: John Hopkins University Press.

Lachmann, Renate. 1990. *Gedächtnis und Literatur: Intertextualität in der russischen Moderne.* Frankfurt a.M.: Suhrkamp.

Lang, Andrew. 1893 [1884]. *Custom and Myth.* 2nd ed. London: Longmans, Green and Co.

Lanser, Susan Sniader. 1992. *Fictions of Authority: Women Writers and Narrative Voice.* Ithaca, NY: Cornell Univ. Press.

Leeming, David. 2002. *Myth: A Biography of Belief.* Oxford: Oxford University Press.

Leggewie, Claus. 1993. "Vom deutschen Reich zur Bundesrepublik – und nicht zurück. Zur politischen Gestalt einer multikulturellen Gesellschaft." Bredella, Lothar; Christ, Herbert (eds.), Zugänge zum Fremden. (Gießener Diskurse 10) Gießen: Verlag der Ferberschen Universitätsbuchhandlung. 37–55.

Lévi-Strauss, Claude. 1979 [1964]. *The Raw and the Cooked: Introduction to a Science of Mythology.* Vol 1. New York: Octagon.

Lyotard, Jean-François. 1984 [1979]. *The Postmodern Condition: A Report on Knowledge.* Trans. Geoff Bennington and Brian Massumi. Minneapolis, MN: University of Minnesota Press.

Macmillan Brown, John. 1907. *Maori and Polynesian: Their Origin, History and Culture*. London: Hutchinson.

Mai, Hans-Peter. 1991. "Bypassing Intertextuality: Hermeneutics, Textual Practice, Hypertext." In: Plett, Heinrich F. (ed.), *Intertextuality*. Berlin, New York: Walter de Gruyter. 30–59.

Manhire, Bill. 1992. "Hone Tuwhare/Interviewed by Bill Manhire." In: Alley, Elizabeth (ed.), *In the Same Room. Conversations With New Zealand Writers*. Auckland: Auckland University Press. 175–96.

Martin, Murray S. 1983. "The Blending of Traditions: Witi Ihimaera's Contribution to New Zealand Literature." *The International Fiction Review* 10(1): 53–5.

McLintock, A. H. (ed.). 2006a [1966]. "History, Myths in New Zealand." *An Encyclopaedia of New Zealand. Te Ara – The Encyclopedia of New Zealand*. <http://www.TeAra.govt.nz/1966/H/HistoryMythsInNewZealand/en> accessed March 10, 2008.

——2006b [1966]. "Literature – Fiction." *An Encyclopaedia of New Zealand. Te Ara – The Encyclopedia of New Zealand*. <http://www.TeAra.govt.nz/1966/L/LiteratureFiction/en> accessed March 10, 2008.

——2006c [1966]. "Maori Language." *An Encyclopaedia of New Zealand. Te Ara – The Encyclopedia of New Zealand*. <http://www.TeAra.govt.nz/1966/M/MaoriLanguage/en> accessed March 10, 2008.

——2006d [1966]. "Place Names." *An Encyclopaedia of New Zealand. Te Ara – The Encyclopedia of New Zealand*. <http://www.TeAra.govt.nz/1966/P/PlaceNames/en> accessed March 10, 2008.

McRae, Jane. 1995. "Patricia Grace and Complete Communication." In: Williams, Mark; Leggott, Michelle (eds), *Opening the Book: New Essays on New Zealand Writing*. Auckland: Auckland University Press.

——1997. "From Maori Oral Traditions to Print." In: Maslen, Keith; Penny Griffith and Ross Harvey (eds.), *Book and Print in New Zealand: A Guide to Print Culture in New Zealand*. Wellington: Victoria University Press. 17–39. <http://www.nzetc.org/tm/scholarly/tei-GriBook-_div2-N1066D.html> accessed June 7, 2010.

Mead, Hirini Moko. 2003. *Tikanga Maori: Living by Maori Values*. Wellington: Huia.

Mergenthal, Silvia. 2002. "Die Zukunft der Vergangenheit: Indigene Traditionen in Keri Hulmes *the bone people* und Patricia Graces *Potiki*." In: Pordzik, Ralph; Seeber, Hans Ulrich (eds.), *Utopie und Dystopie in den neuen englischen Literaturen*. Heidelberg: Universitätsverlag Winter. 129–42.

Metge, Joan. 1976. *The Maoris of New Zealand*. London: Routledge & Kegan Paul.

Ministry for Culture and Heritage. *Treaty of Waitangi*.
    <http://www.nzhistory.net.nz/category/tid/133> accessed June 10, 2010.

Ministry of Justice. 2001. *He Hinatore ki te Ao Maori: A Glimpse into the Maori World (Maori Perspectives on Justice)*. Wellington: Ministry of Justice.

MoNZTPT, History Sector Exhibitions Concept Description. Te Papa Archives. October 1993, p. 6.

Morrissey, Michael (ed.). 1987. *The New Fiction*. Auckland: Lindon Publishing.

Mottesheard, Ryan. 2005, "Girl Power: New Zealand Writer/Director Niki Caro Talks About *Whale Rider*." *Indiewire*.
    <http://www.indiewire.com/people/people_030606caro.html> accessed March 10, 2008.

Myth. Oxford English Dictionary. 1999. J. A. Simpson and ESC Weiner, Vol. X. 2nd ed. Oxford: Clarendon Press. 177–8.

Neill, Michael. 1992. "Albert Wendt/Interviewed by Michael Neill." In: Alley, Elizabeth (ed.), *In the Same Room. Conversations With New Zealand Writers*. Auckland: Auckland University Press. 100–18.

Neumann, Birgit. 2003. "Literatur als Medium (der Inszenierung) kollektiver Erinnerungen und Identitäten." In: Erll, Gymnich, Nünning (eds.), *Literatur – Kultur – Identität: Theoriekonzeptionen und Fallstudien* (ELCH 11). Trier: WVT.

—— 2005. *Erinnerung – Identität – Narration. Gattungstypologie und Funktionen kanadischer "Fictions of Memory"*. (Media and Cultural Memory/Medien und kulturelle Erinnerung) Berlin, New York: de Gruyter.

Newton, John. 2003. "The Death Throes of Nationalism: John Newton Reviews *Kin of Place* by C. K. Stead." *Jacket* 22 (May).
    <http://jacketmagazine.com/22/newt-stead.html> accessed June 7, 2010.

The New Zealand Book Council: Te Kaunihera Pukapuka o Aotearoa. 1998. "New Zealand Writers: Grace, Patricia."
    <http://www.bookcouncil.org.nz/writers/gracep.html> accessed June 7, 2010.

New Zealand Examiner. March 19, 1861

Nora, Pierre (ed.). 1997 [1984–92]. *Les Lieux de Mémoire*. 3 vols. Paris: Gallimard.

—— 1998 [1990]. *Zwischen Geschichte und Gedächtnis*. Frankfurt a.M.: Fischer.

O'Brien, Gregory. 1995. "Towards Evening." In: Williams, Mark (ed.), *The Source of the Song. New Zealand Writers On Catholicism*. Wellington: Victoria University Press. 23–39.

Ojinmah, Umelo. 1993. *Witi Ihimaera: A Changing Vision*. Dunedin: University of Otago Press.

Okereke, Augustine. 1998. "The Performance and the Text: Parameters for Understanding Oral Literary Performance." In: Kloos, Wolfgang (ed.). *Across the Lines:
Intertextuality and Transcultural Communication in the New Literatures in English*. ASNEL Papers 3. Cross/Cultures 32. Collier, Gordon; Maes-Jelinek, Hena;
Davis, Geoffrey (eds.). Amsterdam, Atlanta: Rodopi. 39–47.

Ooi, Kathy. 2004. "A Righter Shade of Pale: Literary Portrayals of Passing in a Colonial World." *Graduate Journal of Asia-Pacific Studies* 2(1): 21–31.

Orbell, Margaret. 1970. "Introduction." In: Orbell, Margaret (ed.), *Contemporary
Maori Writing*. Wellington: Reed. 7–8.

—— 1985. *Hawaiki – A New Approach to Maori Tradition*. Christchurch: The University of Canterbury.

Oxley, Brian. 1990. "Orphans and Bastards in the New World Novel." In: Davis, Geoffrey; Maes-Jelinke, Hena (eds.), *Crisis and Creativity in the New Literatures in
English*. Amsterdam, Atlanta: Rodopi. 419–30.

Panny, Judith Dell. 1997. *Turning the Eye: Patricia Grace and the Short Story*. Wellington: Lincoln University Press and Daphne Brasell Associates.

—— 2006. "A Cultural-Historical Reading of Patricia Grace's Cousins." *Kōtare* 6.
Wellington: Victoria University of Wellington. The New Zealand Electronic
Text Centre.
<http://nzetc.org/scholarly/tei-Whi06Kota-t1-g1-t1.html#name-100009-1>
accessed March 10, 2008.

Parameswaran, Uma. 2003. "Dispelling the Spells of Memory: Another Approach
to Reading Our Yesterdays." In: Fludernik, Monika (ed.), *Diaspora and Multiculturalism: Common Traditions and New Developments*. Collier, Gordon; Maes-
Jelinek, Hena; Davis, Geoffrey (eds.). *Cross/Cultures* 66. Rodopi: Amsterdam,
New York. xxxviiii – lxvii.

Pearson, Bill. 1982. "Witi Ihimaera and Patricia Grace." In: Hankin, Cherry (ed.), *Critical Essays on the New Zealand Short Story*. Auckland: Heinemann. 166–84.

Phillips, Jock. 1996. "Search For the Kiwi Identity." *Sunday Star Times*, April 14.

—— 2001. "The Politics of Pakeha History in a Bicultural Museum: Te Papa, the
Museum of New Zealand, 1993–1998." In: McIntyre; Whener (eds.). *National
Museums – Negotiating Histories Conference Proceedings*. Canberra: National
Museum of Australia. 149.

—— 2003. *Kiwi Myths and New Identities*. Public Sector Senior Managers' Conference, November 6. Wellington.
<http://pssm.ssc.govt.nz/2003/paper/phillipsj.ppt> accessed June 7, 2010.

Polkinghorne, Donald E. 1988. *Narrative Knowing and the Human Sciences*. Albany,
NY: State University of New York Press.

Poltermann, Andreas (ed.). 1995. *Literaturkanon – Medienereignis – kultureller Text. Formen kultureller Kommunikation und Übersetzung.* Berlin: Erich Schmidt.

Potiki, Roma. 1993. "The Journey From Anxiety to Confidence." In: Ihimaera, Witi (ed.). *Te Ao Marama 2: He Whakaatanga o te Ao.* Auckland: Reed. 314–19.

Prießnitz, Horst. 1990. "The Dual Perspective of 'Anglo-Colonial' Literatures and the Future of English Studies: A Modest Proposal." In: Zach, Wolfgang (ed.), *Literature(s) in English: New Perspectives.* Frankfurt a.M.: Peter Lang. 31–46.

Puketapu, Ihakara Porutu. 2007 [2006]. "Maori Language: Teaching of the Maori Language." *An Encyclopaedia of New Zealand. Te Ara – The Encyclopedia of New Zealand.*
    <http://www.TeAra.govt.nz/1966/M/MaoriLanguage/en> accessed March 10, 2008.

Ranapiri, Tāmati. 1895. Letter to Elsdon Best, 14 January 1895. *MS Papers 1187–127.* Alexander Turnbull Library, Wellington. Translation by Te Ahukaramū Charles Royal.

Rao, Raja. 1978. "The Caste of English." In: Narasimhaia, D. C. (ed.), *Awakened Conscience: Studies in Commonwealth Literature.* New Delhi, Sterling, London: Heineman. Quoted in: Kachru, Braj B. "The Alchemy of English." In: Ashcroft, Bill; Griffiths, Gareth; Tiffin, Helen (eds.). 1995. *The Post-Colonial Studies Reader.* London, New York: Routledge. 291–5.

——1995. "Language and Spirit." Ashcroft, Bill; Griffiths, Gareth; Tiffin, Helen (eds.). *The Post-Colonial Studies Reader.* London, New York: Routledge. 296–7.

Reedy, Anaru (ed. and trans.). 1993. *Nga Korero a Mohi Ruatapu, Tohunga Rongonui o Ngati Porou: The Writings of Mohi Ruatapu.* Christchurch: Canterbury University Press.

Riach, Alan. 1992. "Vincent O'Sullivan/Interviewed by Alan Riach." In: Alley, Elizabeth (ed.), *In the Same Room. Conversations With New Zealand Writers.* Auckland: Auckland University Press. 199–216.

Ricoeur, Paul. 1987. "Myth and History." In: Eliade, Mircea (ed.), *The Encyclopedia of Religion.* Vol. 10. New York: Macmillan. 273–82.

Rigney, Anne. 2005. "Plenitude, Scarcity and the Circulation of Cultural Memory." *Journal of European Studies* 35(1) (March): 11–28.

Robinson, Roger and Nelson Wattie (eds.). 1998. "Patricia Grace." *The Oxford Companion to New Zealand Literature.* In: *New Zealand Writers: Grace, Patricia.*
    <http://www.bookcouncil.org.nz/writers/gracep.html> accessed June 7, 2010.

Romaine, Suzanne. 2004. "Contested Visions of History in Aotearoa New Zealand Literature: Witi Ihimaera's The Matriarch." *The Contemporary Pacific* 16(1) (Spring): 31–57.

Royal, Te Ahukaramū Charles. 2006. "Whenua – how the land was shaped." *Te Ara – the Encyclopedia of New Zealand.* <http://www.TeAra.govt.nz/EarthSeaAndSky/Geology/WhenuaHowThe-LandWasShaped/en> accessed March 10, 2008.

——2007. "Some Speculations on Maori Identity in the New Zealand of Tomorrow." Paper delivered to the symposium Concepts of Nationhood – Marking 100 Years Since the Proclamation of Dominion Status for New Zealand. September 26, 2007. Legislative Council Chamber, Parliament Buildings, Wellington.

Rushdie, Salman. 1992. *Imaginary Homelands: Essays and Criticism 1981–1991.* London: Penguin.

Said, Edward W. 2003. *Orientalism.* New York: Vintage Books.

Schacter, Daniel L. 1996. *Searching for Memory: The Brain, the Mind, and the Past.* New York: Basic Books.

Schulze-Engler, Frank. 1998. "Cross-Cultural Criticism and the Limits of Intertextuality." In: Kloos, Wolfgang (ed.), *Across the Lines: Intertextuality and Transcultural Communication in the New Literatures in English.* ASNEL Papers 3. *Cross/Cultures* 32. Collier, Gordon; Maes-Jelinek, Hena; Davis, Geoffrey (eds.). Amsterdam, Atlanta, GA: Rodopi. 3–19.

Sharad, P. (ed.). 1984. *Poetry of the Pacific Region.* Adelaide.

Sharpe, Jenny. 1989. "Figures of Colonial Resistance." *Modern Fiction Studies* 35(1) (Spring): 137–55.

Shirres, Michael P. 1997. *Te Tangata: The Human Person.* Auckland: Accent Publications.

Shortland, Edward. 1882. *Maori Religion and Mythology.* London: Longmans, Green and Co.

Skinner, John. 1998. *The Stepmother Tongue: An Introduction to new Anglophone Fiction.* London: Macmillan.

Smart, Peter (ed.). 1980. *Landfall 133,* 34 (1) (March).

Smith, Anna. 1995. "Keri Hulme and 'Love's Wounded Beings.'" In: Williams, Mark; Leggott, Michele (eds.), *Opening the Book. New Essays On New Zealand Writing.* Auckland: Auckland University Press. 140–61.

Somerville, Alice Te Punga. 2007. "'If I Close My Mouth I Will Die': Writing, Resisting, Centring." In: Bargh, Maria (ed.), *Resistance: An Indigenous Response to Neoliberalism.* Wellington: Huia. 85–111.

Sommer, Roy. 2001. *Fictions of Migration. Ein Beitrag zur Theorie und Gattungstypologie des zeitgenössischen interkulturellen Romans in Großbritannien.* (ELCH 1) Trier: Wissenschaftlicher Verlag Trier.

Sorensen, M. P. K. (ed.). 1986. *Na To Hao Aroha/From Your Dear Friend. The Correspondence Between Sir Apirana Ngata and Sir Peter Buck, 1925–50.* Auckland: Auckland University Press.

Spivak, Gayatri Chakravorty. 1990. *The Postcolonial Critic: Interviews, Strategies, Dialogues*. Oxford: Routledge.

Stead, C. K. 1985. "Keri Hulme's *The Bone People*, and the Pegasus Award for Maori Literature." *Ariel* 16: 101–8. Repr. in: Stead, C. K. 2002. *Kin of Place*. Auckland: Auckland University Press.

Swarbrick, Nancy. 2006. "Creative Life." *Te Ara – the Encyclopedia of New Zealand*. <http//:www.TeAra.govt.nz/NewZealandInBrief/CreativeLife/en> accessed March 10, 2008.

Talmor, Sascha. 1991. "A Kiwi Tale of Love and Violence." *The Durham University Journal*. 52(1): 93–8.

Taonui, Rāwiri. 2006. "Canoe Traditions." *Te Ara – the Encyclopedia of New Zealand*.
<http://www.TeAra.govt.nz/NewZealanders/MaoriNewZealanders/CanoeTraditions/en> accessed March 10, 2008.

Taylor, Charles (ed.). 1994. *Multiculturalism and the Politics of Recognition*. Princeton, NJ: Princeton University Press.

Museum of New Zealand Te Papa Tongarewa. *Statement of Intent 2006–2009*. 2. <http://www.tepapa.govt.nz/SiteCollectionDocuments/AboutTePapa/LegislationAccountability/SOI2006.pdf> accessed June 7, 2010.

Thornley, Davinia. 2004. "Breaking With English: The Nation as Ethnoscape." *National Identities* 6(1): 61–76.

Thornton, Agathe. 1985. "Two Features of Oral Style in Maori Narrative." *Journal of the Polynesian Society* 94: 149–76.

—— 1989. *Maori Oral Literature. As Seen By a Classicist*. (Te Whenua Series No. 2: Pacific People, Land and Literature) Dunedin: University of Otago Press.

Todd, Loreto. 1982. "The English Language in West Africa." In: Bailey, R. W.; Görlach, M. (eds.). *English as a World Language*. Ann Arbour, MI: University of Michigan Press. Quoted in: Zabus, Chantal. 1995. "Relexification." Ashcroft, Bill; Griffiths, Gareth; Tiffin, Helen (eds.). *The Post-Colonial Studies Reader*. London, New York: Routledge. 314–18.

Tregear, Edward. 1985. *The Aryan Maori*. Wellington.

Turia, Tariana. 2007. *Book launch speech: The Maori Party. Resistance: An Indigenous Response to Neoliberalism*. Archives New Zealand. Scoop Independent News. May 2, 2007.
<http://www.scoop.co.nz/stories/print.html?path=PA0705/S00061.htm> accessed June 7, 2010.

Veracini, Lorenzo; Muckle, Adrian. 2003. "Reflections of Indigenous History Inside the National Museum of Australia and Aotearoa New Zealand and Outside of New Caledonia's Centre Culturel Jean-Marie Tjibaou." *The Electronic Journal of Australian and New Zealand History and H-Net*.

<http://www.jcu.edu.au/aff/history/articles/veracini_muckle.htm> accessed June 7, 2010.

Warner, Marina. 1994. *Managing Monsters: Six Myths of Our Time.* London: Vintage.

Watego, Cliff. 1984. "Cultural Adaptation in the South Pacific Novel." *World Literature Written In English* 23(2): 488–96.

Webby, Elizabeth. 1985. "Keri Hulme: Spiralling to Success." *Meanjin* 44(3): 17–20.

Welsch, Wolfgang. 1997. "Transkulturalität. Zur veränderten Verfassung heutiger Kulturen." In: Schneider, Irmela; Thomsen, Christian (eds.), *Hybridkultur: Medien, Netze, Künste.* Köln: Wienand. 67–90.

Wilcox, Leonard. 1985a. "More Versions of the Pastoral: Postmodernism In the New Zealand Context." *Journal of Popular Culture* 12(2) (Autumn): 107–20.

—— 1985b. "Postmodernism or Anti-modernism?" *Landfall* 39: 344–64.

Wilkinson, Jane. 1985. "Interview with Witi Ihimaera." *Kunapipi* 7(1): 98–110.

Williams, Herbert W. 1957. *A Dictionary of the Maori Language.* Wellington: Government Printer.

Williams, Mark. 1992. "Witi Ihimaera/Interviewed by Mark Williams." In: Alley, Elizabeth (ed.), *In the Same Room. Conversations with New Zealand Writers.* Auckland: Auckland University Press. 219–36.

—— 1995a. "Introduction." In: Williams, Mark (ed.), *The Source of the Song. New Zealand Writers on Catholicism.* Wellington: Victoria University Press. 7–22.

—— 1995b. "Introduction." In: Williams, Mark; Leggott, Michele (eds.), *Opening the Book. New Essays on New Zealand Writing.* Auckland: Auckland University Press. 9–27.

Wilson, Ch. A. 1932. *Legends and Mysteries of the Maori.* London: Harrap.

Wilson, Janet. 1998. "Intertextual Strategies: Reinventing the Myths of Aotearoa in Contemporary New Zealand Fiction." In: Kloos, Wolfgang (ed.), *Across the Lines: Intertextuality and Transcultural Communication in the New Literatures in English.* ASNEL Papers 3. *Cross/Cultures* 32. Collier, Gordon; Maes-Jelinek, Hena; Davis, Geoffrey (eds.). Amsterdam, Atlanta, GA: Rodopi. 271–90.

Wilson, John. 2007. "History." *Te Ara – the Encyclopedia of New Zealand.* <http://www.TeAra.govt.nz/NewZealandInBrief/History/en> accessed March 10, 2008.

Young, Robert J. C. 1995. *Colonial Desire: Hybridity in Theory, Culture and Race.* London, New York: Routledge.

Zabus, Chantal. 1995. "Relexification." In: Ashcroft, Bill; Griffiths, Gareth; Tiffin, Helen (eds.), *The Post-Colonial Studies Reader.* London, New York: Routledge. 314–18.

Index